PENGUIN CLASSICS

THE RAMCHARITMANAS 1

TULSIDAS (c.1532–1632), the most important of the saint-poets of the medieval bhakti movement in northern India, is also Hindi's greatest poet. Though very little is known about Tulsi's personal life, he left behind a considerable body of work, including his epic, the *Ramcharitmanas*, a retelling of the story of Ram in Avadhi. Tulsi was an ardent devotee of Ram, and his works have come to occupy almost a canonical status in the Ram tradition in northern India. His other important works include the *Gitavali*, the *Vinay Patrika* and the *Kavitavali*. In addition, the *Hanuman Chalisa*, a short devotional poem of forty verses in praise of Hanuman, is popularly ascribed to Tulsidas, and is considered by many to be his most important work after the *Manas*. Tulsidas's works continue to remain popular even today, more than four hundred years after their composition.

ROHINI CHOWDHURY is an established literary translator. Her primary languages are pre-modern (Braj Bhasha and Avadhi) and modern (Khari Boli) Hindi, and English. Her translations include the seventeenth-century Braj Bhasha text *Ardhakathanak*, widely regarded as the first autobiography in an Indian language, into modern Hindi and into English. She also writes for children, and has more than twenty books and several short stories to her credit. Her published writing, in English and Hindi, covers a wide spectrum of literary genres including novels, short fiction and non-fiction. Her literary interests include mythology, folklore, mathematics and history. She runs a story website at www.longlongtimeago.com.

THE RAMCHARITMANAS

1

Tulsidas

Translated by Rohini Chowdhury

PENGUIN BOOKS

An imprint of Penguin Random House

PENGUIN BOOKS

USA | Canada | UK | Ireland | Australia
New Zealand | India | South Africa | China | Singapore

Penguin Books is part of the Penguin Random House group of companies
whose addresses can be found at global.penguinrandomhouse.com

Published by Penguin Random House India Pvt. Ltd
4th Floor, Capital Tower 1, MG Road,
Gurugram 122 002, Haryana, India

Penguin
Random House
India

First published in Penguin Books by Penguin Random House India 2019

10 9 8 7 6 5 4 3 2

ISBN 9780143425878

Typeset in Adobe Caslon Pro by Manipal Technologies Limited, Manipal
Printed at Repro India Limited

www.penguin.co.in

MIX
Paper from
responsible sources
FSC® C047271

This is a legitimate digitally printed version of the book and therefore might not
have certain extra finishing on the cover.

Contents

Introduction

Amongst the most important of the saint-poets of the medieval bhakti movement in northern India, Tulsidas is also Hindi's most renowned poet. In 1574, he commenced the composition of his *Ramcharitmanas*, a retelling of the story of Ram, the legendary prince of Avadh. Tulsi's epic poem is unanimously regarded as the greatest achievement of Hindi literature, and is a significant addition to the Ramayana corpus. Composed in the vernacular Avadhi—a literary dialect of eastern Hindi—and therefore accessible to everyone without the need for learned intervention by the Brahmin, it became, and remains, the dominant and accepted version of Ram's story in the Hindi-speaking north.

My own engagement with Tulsidas began one crisp autumn night fifty years ago in a small town by the banks of the Ganga, when I saw my first performance of the *Ram Lila*. The sky was sprinkled with stars but I had eyes only for the drama unfolding upon the crude wooden stage before me, where the story had reached a critical point: Hanuman's tail was to be set on fire. The sets were crude, the costumes garish, the acting unsophisticated—but the story transcended all such concerns, such was its magic and power. I did not know it then, but that was also my first intimate encounter with the *Ramcharitmanas*, upon which the *Ram Lila* is based. Growing up, Tulsi's poem was always around me—chanted in the homes of friends or neighbours, sung on the radio, or the theme of plays and dance dramas. So when the opportunity came to translate it into English for Penguin India, I accepted it with alacrity—and the last five years that I have spent walking behind Tulsi, one of the greatest literary minds of all time, have been a pleasure and a privilege. My translation does not do justice to Tulsi's extraordinary poetic genius. His use of wordplay, his rhymes and alliteration, and the sheer musicality of his poem I have found impossible to capture in English. I have therefore contented myself with being as clear and accurate as possible in my translation, and to convey, to the best of my ability, the scale and grandeur of his great poem.

The Ramayana tradition

For at least the last two and a half thousand years, poets, writers, folk performers, and religious and social reformers have drawn upon the story of Ram as a source of inspiration. It has been told again and again in countless forms and dozens of languages, making it one of the most popular and enduring stories in the world. More than any other hero, Ram has been upheld as dharma personified, the epitome of righteousness, and his actions as the guide for right conduct. In recent times, the story has provided inspiration for films, novels, and in the late 1980s, a weekly television series watched by more than eighty million viewers.

The oldest and most influential surviving literary telling of the story of Ram is the Sanskrit epic called the Ramayana. Composed sometime during the first millennium BCE, and consisting of some 50,000 lines in verse set in seven kands or books, it is attributed to the poet Valmiki, and is widely regarded as the 'original'.[1] The influence of Valmiki's Ramayana has been so profound that the title of his epic has come to denote the entire tradition, from oral and folk performances to literary texts and translations. Within this rich and varied tradition also lie the Ramayana songs from Telangana, the folk performances of the *Ram Lila* in northern India, the

eleventh-century Tamil *Iramavataram* ('The Incarnation of Ram')
by Kamban, and Tulsidas's *Ramcharitmanas*.

The rise of bhakti

Scholars of the Ramayana tradition hold the view that Ram was
originally a human hero and was only later raised to the status of
avatar of Vishnu. In the five central books of Valmiki's epic, Ram
is portrayed as an earthly prince: though endowed with godlike
courage, fortitude and compassion, his exploits are those of a human
being. It is only in the first and last books of the poem—which are
considered to be later additions to Valmiki's epic—that Ram is
explicitly declared to be an incarnation of Vishnu on earth.

Soon after the beginning of the Common Era, Ram began to be
increasingly regarded as an avatar of Vishnu. At about the same time,
a new attitude towards the divine began to replace austere monistic
meditation, sacrificial rites and polytheistic practices. This was bhakti,
or intense emotional attachment and love towards a chosen, personal
god and his avatars—particularly Vishnu and his earthly incarnations,
Ram and Krishna—and joyous and public worship of that god.
Bhakti assumed a dualistic relationship between the devotee and his
god, as opposed to the monistic ideal of the Advaita or non-dualistic
school of philosophy. Its proponents considered the way of bhakti
(bhakti-marg) superior to other means of achieving salvation such as
knowledge or good works or ascetic disciplining of the body; it was
also open to everyone, regardless of their caste, class or sex. With the
advent of bhakti, Ram's transition from godlike prince to God became
complete. This was a critical transformation of the Ram story—and
it is within this bhakti tradition that Tulsi wrote his *Ramcharitmanas*.

The bhakti movement was characterized by its emphasis on the
use of vernacular languages, making its teachings directly accessible
to the common people, regardless of class or caste. This was in stark
contrast to traditional practice, within which Sanskrit, regarded as
the sacred language, was used for all important literary and religious

texts. Sanskrit was thus the preserve of an elite few, typically high-caste Brahmins, who would study, interpret and explain the texts to the common people. The earliest bhakti texts to appear were in Tamil—these were devotional poems in praise of Shiv and Vishnu, composed by saint-musicians, the Nayanars and Alvars, of southern India between the seventh and the tenth centuries CE. Also written in Tamil was Kamban's *Iramavataram*. Composed in the eleventh century, it is amongst the earliest vernacular Ramayanas. It became, and still is, the definitive version of the Ram story in the Tamil-speaking areas of the subcontinent. The bhakti movement soon spread northwards, appearing in texts such as the *Bhagavata Purana*, composed in Sanskrit in the tenth century and celebrating devotion to Krishna. More vernacular Ramayanas were composed. Amongst the more noteworthy of these were the thirteenth-century Telugu Ramayana of Buddharaja and the fifteenth-century Bengali *Sriram Panchali* by Krittibas. In Hindi, the bhakti movement reached its zenith in the sixteenth century, with Tulsidas's *Ramcharitmanas*.

The *Ramcharitmanas*: spread and impact

From Tulsi's own writings we infer that his poem, written in the spoken tongue rather than in the sacred Sanskrit, was criticized and ridiculed by the religious establishment of his times. Despite this initial disapproval by the Brahmins (ironically complicated by the fact that the *Ramcharitmanas* itself is so pro-Brahmin), it became hugely popular amongst other groups, especially the merchant caste and lower orders of society, and soon acquired the status and religious authority usually enjoyed only by Sanskrit texts. Within a very short time, carried by wandering sadhus, recited and performed by travelling bards and musicians across towns and villages, it had spread across northern India, from Tulsi's native Banaras in the east to the Rajput kingdoms of Rajasthan in the west. It is worth noting that this initial circulation of Tulsi's poem took place before the advent of printing in India, in areas and times of exceedingly low literacy, its currency strongly dependent on the oral tradition and remarkable feats of memorization by its devotees. Such was the rapid spread and influence of Tulsi's poem that his contemporary, the poet Nabhadas, declares Tulsi to be Valmiki himself, born again to bring his epic once more to the world.[2]

In the late eighteenth century, the *Ramcharitmanas* found royal patronage in the courts of resurgent Hindu kingdoms in northern India who found it a convenient, authoritative and accessible text through which to assert their Hindu identity and legitimize their rule by invoking Ram as the ideal and perfect king. In the nineteenth century, the *Ramcharitmanas* gained even greater currency as north Indian mainstream Hinduism found within it not only an answer to the Christian Bible, but also a nationalistic response to British colonialism. The development of movable type in Indian scripts led to the growth of vernacular presses and the printing of popular books in Indian languages, including, in 1810 in Calcutta, Tulsidas's *Ramcharitmanas*. By the end of the century, printed versions of Tulsi's epic were available all across the north of India—from Calcutta, in Bengali translation, to Gurmukhi-script editions in Delhi and Lahore, and Gujarati and Marathi versions from Bombay.[3] Today, known to its audience as 'Tulsi's Ramayan', or simply the *Manas*, Tulsi's great poem is read, sung, recited and retold in almost every Hindu household in northern India as the accepted and dominant version of the story of Ram. It is also the basis of the *Ram Lila*, a tradition believed to have been started in Banaras almost 500 years ago by Tulsidas himself and still enthusiastically observed.

Tulsidas

We know very little about Tulsidas himself, except what can be pieced together from autobiographical references in his own writings and some contemporary and later, not entirely reliable, accounts of his life. His date and place of birth are uncertain—though it is now generally accepted that he was born in 1532, possibly in the town of

Sukarkhet in the present-day state of Uttar Pradesh. From some of his later works, we know Tulsidas was abandoned in childhood by his parents, and that he was rescued and looked after by sadhus who introduced him to the worship of Ram. Some scholars believe that Tulsidas then took up the life of a sadhu. It is probable, though, that Tulsidas did not become a sadhu at once, but went to Banaras and acquired the traditional Sanskrit education of a Brahmin. He then returned to the village of his birth, where he married. He began to live as a householder, but an altercation with his wife caused him to renounce home and family and take up the wandering life of a sadhu. He lived for a while in Ayodhya, where he composed the initial parts of his *Ramcharitmanas*. Tulsi later settled in Banaras where he wrote most of his other major works; there, he also instituted the *Ram Lila*. He died in Banaras, probably in 1632.[4]

A synopsis

In the beginning sections of his poem, Tulsidas tells us that he commenced this work in Ayodhya, on the ninth day of the Hindu month of Chaitra—the day of Ram's birth—in the year 1631 of the Vikram Era, i.e., 1574 CE.[5] This also makes the *Ramcharitmanas* the earliest of his major works. Consisting of approximately 12,900 lines of Avadhi verse set in seven kands or books, it is also Tulsi's longest work, and its composition probably took him several years. The fourth book of his poem opens with an invocation to the city of Banaras, suggesting that he completed the epic after moving there.

In the beginning of the *Ramcharitmanas*, Tulsi explains that he first heard the story of Ram from his guru in Sukarkhet when he was still a boy, and that this is the story that he now seeks to set down in the spoken tongue.[6] In outline, the story of the *Ramcharitmanas* is as follows:

King Dasharath of Koshal rules in splendour from his capital city, Avadh. The king has all that a man could desire, except a son.

So, upon the advice of his guru, the sage Vasishtha, he holds a great fire-sacrifice, as the result of which four sons are born to him: Ram, the eldest, to his chief queen, Kaushalya; Bharat to his favourite wife, Kaikeyi; and the twins Lakshman and Shatrughna to his third queen, Sumitra. Ram is no other than the great god Vishnu, who has become incarnate in human form in order to rid the world of Ravan, the powerful king of the Rakshasas, who cannot be killed except by a mortal man and who has overrun the earth and overwhelmed even the gods.

The four princes grow up to be brave and skilled warriors. One day, when the princes are still youths, the sage Vishvamitra arrives at Dasharath's court and requests that Ram and his brother Lakshman be sent with him to help protect his fire-sacrifices from the depredations of the Rakshasas. Dasharath protests that his sons are still too young, and offers the sage his whole army instead. But Vishvamitra insists that he wants only Ram and Lakshman to help him. Finally, Dasharath agrees.

The two young princes leave with Vishvamitra for the forest, where they successfully kill the Rakshasas disturbing his worship. Vishvamitra then takes the princes to the city of Mithila, to the court of King Janak. There, Ram sees and falls in love with the king's daughter, Sita, and wins her hand in marriage by breaking the great bow of Shiv. The wedding of Ram and Sita is celebrated with great splendour. Lakshman, too, is married to Sita's sister Urmila, and Bharat and Shatrughna to her cousins, the daughters of King Janak's brothers. The four princes and their brides return to Ayodhya, where they continue to live in harmony for several years.

The aging Dasharath then decides to appoint Ram his heir. As preparations for his investiture get under way, Kaikeyi's old nursemaid Manthara convinces her that Ram's investiture would mean the end of her position as the king's favourite, and would cause Bharat to languish in a prison cell while Ram ruled with the help of his favourite, Lakshman. Once, in return for saving his life on the battlefield, Dasharath had given Kaikeyi the gift of two boons: she could ask of him anything that her heart desired and he would fulfil it. Kaikeyi now demands that Bharat be made heir in place of Ram, and that Ram be banished to the forest for fourteen years. Bound by his word, the old king is unable to deny her requests. Realizing the situation, Ram cheerfully accepts his exile and leaves for the forest. Sita and Lakshman, who refuse to stay back, accompany him. Dasharath dies of a broken heart, and all of Avadh is plunged into mourning.

Bharat, who has been away all this while, is summoned back urgently by Vasishtha. He returns and is devastated to find his brother exiled and his father dead. He denounces his mother's actions, refuses the kingship and sets out in pursuit of Ram, determined to bring him back as the rightful king of Avadh. Ram, however, refuses to return, saying that he must honour their father's word, and requests Bharat to go back and rule as their father had desired. Bharat returns heartbroken to Avadh, and taking up an ascetic residence in the nearby village of Nandigram, rules as Ram's regent till the end of his period of exile.

Ram, Lakshman and Sita wander through the forest, encountering demons, ascetics and sages, including the sage Valmiki, who directs them to make their home amongst the hills and forests of Chitrakut. There, Supnakha, the sister of Ravan, sees and falls in love with Ram. Turning herself into a beautiful woman, she approaches Ram, who rejects her advances. Lakshman cuts off her ears and nose in order to teach her a lesson. Mutilated and humiliated, she appeals to her Rakshasa brothers, Khar and Dushan, who attack Ram with their entire army. While Lakshman protects Sita and hides her away in a mountain cave, Ram single-handedly kills the demons and destroys their army. Supnakha then runs in despair to Ravan, who is infuriated by her story, in particular the killing of Khar and Dushan. Ravan decides to kidnap Sita and enlists the help of Marichi, another Rakshasa. Marichi turns himself into a golden deer and manages to lure Ram and Lakshman into the forest. In their absence, Ravan carries Sita off to his island kingdom of Lanka, where he keeps her prisoner.

The vulture Jatayu sees Sita being carried off and tries to save her, but is fatally wounded by Ravan. Ram and Lakshman return to find the hermitage deserted and Sita missing; as they search for her, they find the wounded Jatayu, who lives just long enough to tell them of her abduction. Ram performs his last rites, and Jatayu receives liberation.

Ram and Lakshman search desperately for Sita, and reach the monkey kingdom of Kishkindha. There, Ram meets Hanuman, who becomes a staunch devotee. He also meets the displaced monkey prince Sugriv, who has also lost both wife and kingdom to his brother Baali. Ram kills Baali and installs Sugriv as king of the monkeys; in return, Sugriv agrees to help him and sends his warriors in every direction in search of Sita. They discover that she is being held prisoner in Lanka.

Hanuman leaps across the ocean, locates Sita and gives her Ram's ring. He lays waste the ashok grove in which Sita is being held, and allows himself to be captured. On Ravan's orders, his tail is set on fire, but Hanuman escapes and, after setting the city of Lanka ablaze, returns to Ram. Meanwhile, Ravan's brother, Vibhishan, who is a devotee of Vishnu and opposed to Ravan's abduction of Sita, also joins Ram's forces. The monkeys build a bridge across the ocean to Lanka, and after a long and bloody battle, Ram kills Ravan. Vibhishan is crowned king of Lanka, and Sita is rescued.

The kidnapped Sita proves to be a shadow replica of herself— Ram, as Vishnu, had foreseen her abduction, and at his behest, the real Sita had stepped into fire, leaving behind a shadow image of herself. It was this shadow Sita that Ravan had kidnapped, while the real Sita had remained hidden, safe from dishonour till Ravan had been killed and the purpose of the gods achieved. Ram now orders Lakshman to light a great fire, and demands that Sita step into it as a test of her chastity. The shadow Sita steps into the fire and is destroyed, and the real Sita steps out, unharmed.

The period of his exile almost over, Ram returns to Ayodhya with Sita and Lakshman. There, he is crowned king amidst much joy and celebration, and so begins his long reign, during which pain or unhappiness were unknown, and all beings lived in harmony and joy.

The influence of Valmiki's epic upon Tulsi cannot be denied: in the initial verses of the *Ramcharitmanas*, Tulsi salutes Valmiki as the author of the Ramayana,[7] thus acknowledging him as one of the important sources for his own poem. Tulsi's epic, however, differs from Valmiki's in one very important particular: Valmiki's Ramayana was a secular text, whilst Tulsi's *Ramcharitmanas* is, without question, a devotional text. Tulsi's Ram is unequivocally divine. He is also Tulsi's chosen god, in whose worship the poet is totally, completely and blissfully immersed—as he tells us in the invocatory verses of the first book, he composed this story of Ram for 'his own delight and satisfaction'.[8]

Tulsi's telling of the Ram story in the *Ramcharitmanas* is very close to the version contained in the Sanskrit text known as the *Adhyatma-ramayana* (or 'spiritual' Ramayana). Composed sometime between 1450 and 1550, the *Adhyatma-ramayana* identifies Ram not only as an incarnation of Vishnu, but also as the personification of *brahm*, the ultimate Absolute of the Upanishads and the Advaita school of philosophy. It also emphasizes bhakti rather than knowledge, and recommends meditation on Ram's name as a means to salvation. It is only through intense devotion to Ram, says the *Adhyatma-ramayana*, that knowledge of the non-dual Self can arise in the individual soul. This is reflected in Tulsi's own, more skilful, amalgamation of the dualism of Vaishnav bhakti with Advaita monism in the *Ramcharitmanas*, particularly in the sections where Tulsi explains the reasons for Ram's actions and their significance. Tulsi's Ram, as the avatar of Vishnu, also has the attributes of the Supreme God—he is all-knowing and all-seeing, so that his actions are predetermined by him to suit his purpose and all that he does or causes to happen in his incarnate form is merely his *lila*, his divine play or pastime.

Tulsi's replacement of the kidnapping of Sita by the abduction of a 'shadow' or illusory Sita whilst the real Sita remains concealed in the abode of Agni, the fire god, is a major deviation from Valmiki and in keeping with the demands of bhakti. The idea of an illusory Sita arose as early as the eighth century and was further developed in the *Adhyatma-ramayana* where it became an integral part of the plot. Along with Ram's transformation from earthly prince to avatar of Vishnu, Sita acquired the status and attributes of Shri, Vishnu's divine consort. As the incarnation of the goddess upon earth, it became unacceptable that she be kidnapped and imprisoned by Ravan and defiled by his touch. Tulsi's substitution of the real Sita with a shadow replica of herself solved this problem and kept safe the purity and chastity of the goddess. In addition to protecting the sacred person of the goddess, it also justified Ram's demand that Sita prove her chastity after her long imprisonment in Lanka by stepping into the sacred fire. Sita's trial by fire thus becomes a device for the return of the real Sita rather than an unwarranted and unjust test of her purity as in Valmiki's epic.[9] Tulsi's poem ends on a 'happily-ever-after' note, with Ram ruling gloriously in Ayodhya, his beloved Sita by his side. Valmiki's epic does not stop there, but continues in the last book to describe Ram and Sita's later years, in particular the aspersions cast on Sita's chastity by the people of Ayodhya, and her consequent banishment by Ram to the forest. Though Tulsi does refer to this in passing in the first book—Ram, he says, has great affection for the people of Ayodhya, 'for although they maligned Sita, he freed them from all their sins and sorrows'[10]—his device of the shadow Sita precludes the need for him to include this in his version of the story.

Tulsi pays homage to the great and eminent poets who preceded him, as well as to the vernacular poets who told of the deeds of Ram in the spoken tongue.[11] The influence upon him of texts other than Valmiki's is evident in passages such as his delightful descriptions of Ram's childhood, which were probably inspired by the *Bhagavata Purana* and contemporary bhakti poetry in praise of Krishna, both of which celebrate the child Krishna. Tulsi's charming description of Sita's first meeting with Ram[12]—in a garden, where Ram has gone with Lakshman to gather flowers for his morning worship and Sita with her handmaidens to offer worship at a temple of the goddess Parvati—was possibly inspired by the fourteenth-century Sanskrit drama, *Prasannaraghava*, by Jaidev.[13]

In the *Ramcharitmanas*, Tulsi successfully brings together the many contrasting ideologies of his time—joyous, unrestrained Vaishnav bhakti and austere Advaita meditation, the worship of Vishnu and the worship of Shiv, the worship of the abstract, nirgun ('without attributes') Absolute and the adoration of the sagun ('with attributes') Incarnate endowed with form and beauty. Tulsi's Ram is the Supreme Being personified, and Sita is his Shakti, or primal energy. From Ram and Sita spring all the other gods, including Shiv and Parvati (whom Tulsi elsewhere calls 'the father and mother of the Universe'), and even Lakshmi and Vishnu. For Tulsi, Ram is the Supreme God, yet throughout the poem, Tulsi's Ram declares that without the worship of Shiv, no one can attain to his bhakti. Yet, the name of Ram is the high mantra chanted by Shiv, who declares it necessary for salvation even in his own holy city of Banaras. Tulsi takes every opportunity to describe the beauty of Ram's incarnate form in loving detail—his body dark as a rain-laden cloud, his radiant face and lotus eyes, the tilak upon his forehead—but reminds us at once that he is the all-pervading Spirit of the Universe, unborn, uncreated, without flaw, without form. Tulsi prostrates himself at the lotus-feet of the incarnate Ram and adores the name of Ram as borne by his chosen god. This integration of different ideologies in the *Manas* is one of Tulsi's most significant achievements.

Tulsi has been criticized in modern times for his apparent support of the caste system, his reverence for Brahmins and his characterization of women as inherently inferior to men. However, here too he brings together opposing views. While paying homage to

Brahmins as 'gods upon earth', he upholds the tribal woman Shabari, who waited in the forest for Ram, as the epitome of devotion and virtue.[14] So, while the social order must be upheld, within bhakti, the boundaries of caste, class and gender disappear. Tulsi's institution of the *Ram Lila* may be seen as an attempt at a degree of social integration, albeit within the Hindu framework—for everyone, regardless of caste, class and religion, was invited to take part in these performances, whether as actors or audience. This inclusivity remains, by and large, a feature of the *Ram Lila* even today.

Structure

The titles and line counts of the seven books of the *Ramcharitmanas* are as follows:

1. *Balkand* (Childhood)   4200 lines
2. *Ayodhyakand* (Ayodhya)   3300 lines
3. *Aranyakand* (The Forest)   750 lines
4. *Kishkindhakand* (Kishkindha)   400 lines
5. *Sundarkand* (The Beautiful)   750 lines
6. *Lankakand* (Lanka)   1700 lines
7. *Uttarkand* (Epilogue)   1800 lines

Each book begins with a *mangalacharan*, the traditional worship or salutation at the commencement of a written work, in which Tulsi calls upon various gods to bless his endeavour. In order to underline the sacred nature of what was to come, Tulsi chose to write these invocatory passages in Sanskrit.

Tulsi presents his story through a series of interwoven conversations between four narrator–listener pairs, whom he introduces at the beginning of his poem:[15]

- Shiv, and his wife, the goddess Parvati—the story arose in Shiv's heart and he revealed it to Parvati

- Kak Bhushundi, a sage in a crow's body, and Garud, king of the birds and Vishnu's divine steed—Shiv gave the same story to Bhushundi, who related it to Garud
- The sages Jagbalik and Bharadvaj—Jagbalik obtained the tale from Bhushundi and recited it to Bharadvaj
- And finally, Tulsidas and his audience—Tulsi heard the story from his guru and set it down in common speech for his audience

The narrative moves deftly, often unexpectedly, from one narrator to another and back again. The conversation between Bhushundi and Garud is contained mainly in, and takes up most of, the seventh book. Tulsi indicates the narrator–listener pairs sometimes directly, explicitly naming either the speaker or the listener ('Then said Mahesh [Shiv] with a smile . . .'),[16] or by frequent interjections that identify the listener ('O king of the birds' or 'O muni') and so, by extension, the speaker (Bhushundi in the first instance, and Jagbalik in the second). A fifth narrator is implied—just as Tulsi is relating the story to his listeners, in the same way, they too may tell this story to others.

The title of Tulsi's work deserves some attention.[17] The name 'Ram' needs little explanation. Not only is it the name of the hero of the epic, but it is also the name of Tulsi's chosen god, who is none other than the personification of the Supreme Spirit of the Universe. The word *charit* (from the root *char*, 'to move') means 'going, moving' and becomes by extension, 'movement or deeds'. Thus *Ram+charit* means 'the movements or doings of Ram'. The word *manas* is derived from the root word *man*, usually translated into English as 'heart' or 'mind', and means 'belonging to, or born from, the heart or mind'. 'Manas' is also the name of a lake in the Himalayas; lying at the foot of Mount Kailash, the abode of Shiv, the Manas lake, or Manasarovar, is considered to be sacred by many faiths and is used as a metaphor for the mind in its highest state of pure bliss. In the early sections of the first book, Tulsi tells us that this work arose in the mind of Shiv, who kept it within his heart, till, finding an auspicious moment, he revealed it to his wife, the goddess Parvati. And that is why, having seen this sacred story of the doings of Ram within his mind, Shiv called it '*Ramcharitmanas*'. Inspiration, by the grace of Shiv, then gladdened his own mind, says Tulsi, and he composed his great work, making it as pleasing to the heart as his wit allowed.[18]

Tulsi also compares his epic, the *Manas*, to the holy Manas lake—it is the reservoir that contains within it the sacred story of the doings of Ram. Its four narrators are the four ghats that surround it, and the seven books seven staircases that lead down to the clear waters of Ram's fame.[19] He introduces the imagery of the lake in Stanza 36 of the first book and builds it up over the next seven stanzas. He describes the clusters of waterlilies and many-coloured lotuses that grow upon the lake—these are the poetic metres he has used in his poem, and their fragrance the elegant language. Swans of wisdom and detachment float upon the tranquil surface of the lake, while the fish that are wordplay and allusion shimmer beneath its clear waters. The songs in praise of Ram are rare and wonderful water birds, while lustful and evil men are storks and crows that dare not come near the lake. The pleasure derived from this tale, says Tulsi, is a garden watered by the heart with tears of love, and the bliss that wells up in his heart and pours out in a flood of love and joy is the Sarju, Ayodhya's sacred river. This stream of love flows into the glittering Ganga of devotion to Ram, and is joined by the majestic Sone, the great river that is the splendour of Ram and Lakshman in battle. Together, these three streams flow into the ocean that is Ram himself. Tulsi reaffirms the imagery of the Manas lake through his entire work. He calls each of the seven books a 'sopan' or 'descent' into the lake, and reintroduces the imagery of the lake in the seventh book, in the conversation between Bhushundi and Garud.[20]

Tulsi wrote for an audience which was familiar not only with the story of Ram, but also knew the dozens of 'backstories' that weave in and out of the main narrative, or to which Tulsi refers, either directly or obliquely. I am aware that many of those who read my translation will not have the same familiarity with these tales, and so I have attempted, in footnotes, endnotes and a glossary, to give as much background information as I could. Also, the Hindu gods all have more than one name, and Tulsi refers to them by these different names, with which, once again, his audience would have been familiar. Each distinct name or epithet for a god or goddess refers to a quality, characteristic or action of that deity. So, for instance the god of love, Kamdev, or 'lord of passion', may also be referred to as Hridayniket, 'one whose abode is the heart', Manmath, 'he who churns the heart', or Manobhav, 'mind-born'. Similarly, the god Shiv ('the auspicious, the fortunate'), the Destroyer, the great and powerful third deity in the Hindu triad, is, as the lord of all creation, also called Akhileshvar, and as the Destroyer, he is also called Har. While I am aware that these different names for the same deity may be confusing to modern readers, reducing the gods to a single name would, I felt, take away from the meaning and atmosphere of Tulsi's poem. So, for the most part I have kept the names as Tulsi has used them; to make it easier, I have given the most familiar name of the deity as a footnote at the first occurrence of another name for the same god or goddess (for instance, 'Hridayniket' has been footnoted as 'Kamdev'; 'Har' has been footnoted as 'Shiv'). I have also included the various names with their meanings under the glossary entry for the relevant god or goddess (so all of the names of Kamdev used in the text are given under the entry 'Kamdev' in the glossary).

Tulsi may have composed his poem in the 'common tongue', but his control of language, his mastery of rhythm and his deliberate and skilful use of literary devices throughout display a literary virtuosity that is nothing short of genius. He composed his poem mainly in two alternating metres, the *chaupai* and the *doha*. A chaupai is a quatrain consisting of four parts or 'feet'; each quarter verse is made up of sixteen *matras* or 'instants', which is the time required to pronounce a short vowel (a long vowel is twice the length of a short vowel, and thus is equal to two matras). A doha is a couplet, each line of which consists of two unequal parts, usually of thirteen and eleven matras respectively, separated by a caesura; the rhyme occurs at the end of the lines. Thus the doha, though a couplet, may also be thought of as consisting of four, even if unequal, parts. Sometimes Tulsi uses the *sortha* instead of, or along with, the doha. Also consisting of two lines, a sortha is a mirror image of the doha, with its half-lines transposed so its lines are divided into eleven- and thirteen-matra segments separated by a caesura; the rhyme falls at the caesura in the middle of the line. I have rendered each metre in four lines in English translation: each quarter part of a chaupai translates into a single line of verse in English as does each part of a doha or sortha; the lines of the doha and sortha are usually shorter than those of the chaupai.

Tulsi uses the measured and regular chaupai metre in which to tell his story and take it forward. Each series of four to eight chaupais is followed by a doha or dohas (or sometimes a sortha or doha/sortha mix). Many oral performances of the epic take the doha/sortha as a unit of closure. I have followed the same approach, and for the sake of easy reference, taken each chaupai set along with its concluding dohas/sorthas to represent a stanza—though the term 'stanza' has no equivalent in medieval Hindi poetry and Tulsi's text shows no such divisions. I have numbered only the concluding couplets, and matched this numbering to my source text, the popular and widely available Gita Press edition of the *Ramcharitmanas* with a commentary by Hanuman Prasad Poddar. A stanza could just as well be defined as beginning with a doha and some commentators prefer this approach.

A fourth metre that occurs with some frequency in the *Ramcharitmanas* is the *chhand*.

The most musical of the metres used by Tulsi, a chhand consists of four equal lines of twenty-six to thirty matras, with the rhyme at the end of each line. Tulsi uses the chhand to highlight moments of intense emotion, or to further describe and thus emphasize critical scenes or events. The chhand's flowing lyrical nature makes it particularly well suited for such use. Chhands are usually inserted between chaupais and their concluding dohas/sorthas, and so appear within 'stanzas' as defined above.

Other metres used by Tulsi include the hymns of praise or *stutis* spoken by various characters, and the invocatory Sanskrit shlokas of the mangalacharan at the beginning of each book.

It is impossible to reproduce the beat and rhyme schemes of these metres in English, and I have not attempted to do so. However, I have attempted to give the reader some idea, at least visually, of the structure of the poem. Therefore, the dohas/sorthas are indented; chhands, stutis and shlokas are in italics; and the chaupais form the main body of the text.

Other works

Tulsidas has left behind a considerable body of work. However, of the twenty-two works popularly attributed to him, only twelve, including the *Ramcharitmanas*, can be ascribed to him with certainty. The story of Ram is a recurring theme in Tulsi's writings and his works have come to occupy almost a canonical status in the Ram tradition in northern India. The *Gitavali* is his second-longest work; it presents incidents from the life of Ram in 328 songs. The *Vinay Patrika*, considered Tulsi's second-most important work after the *Ramcharitmanas*, consists of some 280 songs, in the form of a personal petition to Ram asking for deliverance from the age of Kali. Both these works are in the western-Hindi Brajbhasha, and were composed in the middle years of the poet's life. A major work of Tulsi's later years is the *Kavitavali*. Also in Braj, it tells the Ram story in some 325 verses. Other, lesser, works include two poems on mythological weddings: the *Parvati-mangal*, a description of the marriage of Shiv and Parvati, composed in 1586, and the *Janaki-mangal* on the marriage of Ram with Sita, which is undated; both these poems are in Avadhi. Another minor work is the *Barvai-ramayan*, an abridged rendition of the Ram story in sixty-nine stanzas in the barvai metre; this is also in Avadhi. A large collection of verses in the doha and sortha metres, called *Dohavali*, is also ascribed to Tulsidas.

In addition, the *Hanuman Chalisa*, a short devotional poem of forty verses in praise of Hanuman, is popularly ascribed to Tulsidas. Though the poem begins with a doha from the second book of the *Ramcharitmanas*[21] and contains several lines that seem to have been taken from the epic, it remains doubtful that it was composed by Tulsidas. However, it is considered by many to be his most important work after the *Manas*. It is recited daily by millions of Hindus and is one of the most popular devotional poems of all time.

Tulsidas was a man of deep spiritual insight and a poet of extraordinary talent. His bhakti is joyous and intense, and very soon, his audience too is drawn into exuberant devotion to the 'feet of Ram'. He charms and moves his audience with his delicate descriptions and enthrals them with the intellectual force and clarity of his discourses on points of doctrine. His achievements are significant: not only did he successfully recast the ancient story of Ram in the mould of bhakti, but by composing it in the vernacular he took away forever the need for its interpretation by the Brahminical elite. His synthesis of contrasting ideologies and points of view in the *Manas* made it acceptable to a wider audience and led to greater integration within the Hindu community. Nothing that can be said about the beauty of his great poem or the significance of its contribution to the religious and social landscape of northern India is enough. Thus, it is perhaps best that we now 'listen' to this great story in the manner that Tulsi asks—with our full attention. I hope, despite its many shortcomings, my translation will give my readers an appreciation of this great work.

Book I

BALKAND
(CHILDHOOD)

Mangalacharan

To Vani[i] and Vinayak,[ii]
The inventors of the alphabet, of letters, their names and their
    myriad meanings,
Of poetry, its sentiments, and the multitude of poetical metres,
And from whom originates all that is benevolent and good—
I make obeisance.   (1)

To Bhavani[iii] and Shankar,[iv]
The personifications of faith and belief,
Without which even the greatest saints and ascetics
Cannot perceive the Divine present within them—
I bow in reverence.   (2)

The eternal guru,
Learned and wise, the very image of Shankar
Because of whose protection even the curved and crooked crescent moon[1]
Is venerated everywhere—
I salute with deference.   (3)

---

[i]   Sarasvati
[ii]   Ganesh
[iii] Parvati
[iv] Shiv

To Valmiki, king of the poets,
And to Hanuman, lord of the monkeys,
Of true wisdom and discernment,
Who disport themselves in the bright lands and pleasing forests of Sita
    and Ram's glory—
I pay homage.   (4)

From whom springs life, who preserves and nurtures, and from whom
    arises dissolution,
She who destroys anguish, pain and torment
And from whom comes all good fortune—
I bow before her, Sita, Ram's beloved.   (5)

He whose maya has in thrall the whole universe, including Brahma,
    the gods and the demon Asurs,
The brilliant splendour of whose presence manifests truth in this
    illusory world
As when a serpent is revealed to be a rope,
Whose feet are the only raft in which the world-ocean of this existence
    may be crossed to reach the farther shore,
He, who is the cause of all causes, supreme over them, yet distant
    from them—
I praise and offer him worship, Hari, whose name is Ram.   (6)

In accordance with the various Puranas, Vedas and Shastras,
And based on what has been related in the Ramayana and elsewhere,
Tulsidas, for his own delight and satisfaction,
Has composed the story of Raghunath
In elegant verses in the common speech.   (7)

Remembering whom ensures success,
The leader of Shiv's retinue, with the countenance of a
    noble elephant—
May he bestow his grace,
He, the accumulation of wisdom, the repository of
    auspicious qualities.^v   (0A)

By whose mercy the mute starts chattering,
And the cripple scales the mightiest mountain—
May he be moved to compassion,
He,^{vi} whose fire burns away the filth of Kaliyug.^{vii}   (0B)

He, whose body is as dark as the blue lotus,
Whose eyes are as bright as the red lotus—
May he make my heart his home,
He, who ever rests upon the Ocean of Milk.^{viii}   (0C)

He whose body is radiant like the jasmine flower and the moon,
Uma's^{ix} beloved, the destroyer of Mayan,^x
In whom resides compassion, and who loves the lowly
    and the meek—
May he show his mercy.^{xi}   (0D)

I revere my guru's lotus feet—
He who is an ocean of mercy, Hari in human form,
Whose words are like sunlight
In the dense darkness of delusion   (0E)

---

^v Ganesh
^{vi} Vishnu
^{vii} The last of the four yugas or ages of the world
^{viii} Vishnu
^{ix} Parvati
^x Kamdev
^{xi} Shiv

I revere the pollen-dust of the guru's lotus feet—
Lustrous, fragrant and imbued with the flavour of love,
It is the pleasing powder of the life-giving Sanjivani root
That calms and heals the many categories of ills in this world.
It is as the pure ashes upon righteous Shambhu's[xii] body,
From it arises good fortune and sweet delight.
It clears the mirror of the human mind of dirt,
And worn upon the forehead as a tilak, it confers mastery over
    all virtues.
Recalling the lustre of the revered guru's jewel-bright nails,
Fills the heart with divine insight
That rips apart the darkness of delusion with its radiance—
Fortunate indeed is the one in whose heart this vision dawns.
With it comes clarity of vision,
Dispelled are the shades and sorrows of the night that is
    this existence,
And the gems and jewels of the exploits of Ram become
    perceptible,
Whether obscure or manifest, wherever and in whichever treasure
    trove or mine they lie,

    As when, by applying siddhanjan[2] to the eye,
    The aspirant, the wise and the learned
    Are able to perceive, in astonished joy
    The abundant treasures of Ram's exploits—on mountaintops,
        in forests, and everywhere upon the surface of this earth.   (1)

The dust of the guru's feet is a gentle and pleasing collyrium—
Like life-giving nectar for the eyes—that removes and remedies all
    defects of vision.
Having thus cleared my sight of impurities, with true discernment,
I relate the story of Ram, which gives deliverance from this existence.

---

xii   Shiv

First I bow in reverence at the feet of the Brahmans, gods of
    this earth,
Able to destroy the doubts born of ignorance—
In fair and loving words I salute,
The community of saints and sages, who hold within them
    all virtues.
The deeds of the pious are like the fruit of the cotton plant,
The product of which is dry, without blemish, and with
    manifold uses,
Which suffers hardship, but allows itself to be spun and woven and
    pierced by needles to cover the faults of others,
And because of which it has earned in this world renown that is
    worthy of being worshipped.
The community of saints and sages is glad and full of joy,
The animate form of Prayag, that most sacred of pilgrimage sites,
    the confluence of the three sacred rivers.
Here, devotion to Ram is the stream of the divine Ganga,
The habit of contemplation on the Absolute, the stream of
    the Sarasvati,
And discussions on rituals, prescribed and proscribed, and their
    performance
To wash away the filth of Kaliyug, the River Jamuna, daughter of
    the Sun.
The tales of Hari and Har are the glorious braided stream of the
    three rivers,
Giving joy and gladness to all who hear them.
Unwavering faith in one's own dharma is the imperishable banyan
    tree that grows in this place of pilgrimage,
And noble actions and good deeds the courtiers that attend upon
    this king of holy sites.
Easily accessible to everyone, every day and everywhere,
If resorted to with devotion and respect, it alleviates all sorrow—
This extraordinary and indescribable, most spiritual of sacred sites
Of manifest glory, and granting immediate reward.

Those who hear of the glory of this Prayag of holy men,
Understand it with joyful hearts,
And immerse themselves in it with deep devotion—
They receive the four rewards[3] of existence in this life itself.   (2)

The result of this immersion is instantly visible—
Crows turn into cuckoos and storks into swans.
Hearing this, let no one be astonished,
For the influence of good company is no secret.
The sages Valmiki, Narad, and Ghatjoni,[xiii]
Have each related its effect upon them;
Whatever moves in the water, upon the earth, or in the sky,
Whether animate or inanimate, every creature in this world
That has attained wisdom or glory or salvation or power or virtue,
Whenever, wherever and by whatever effort,
Has done so by keeping the company of the good—
There is no other way either in the world or in the Vedas.
Discernment is impossible without association with the good,
And the company of the virtuous is unattainable without the grace
    of Ram.
Keeping company with the good and virtuous is the root of joy
    and felicity,
It is the consummation of all effort and endeavour, the fruit of
    the flower that is all the spiritual practices and good works
    performed for its attainment.
By association with the virtuous, the wicked are reformed,
As by the touch of the philosopher's stone, base metal turns
    into gold.
If by mischance, or compelled by destiny, good men fall into
    bad company,
Like the jewel in the cobra's hood, they still retain their
    noble qualities.

––––––––––––––––
xiii The sage Agastya

Even the divine words of Vidhi, Hari and Har,[xiv] and the
    compositions of poets and pandits,
Hesitate to describe the glory of the good—
I am as unable to describe it
As a vegetable seller is unable to describe the qualities of
    precious gems.

I bow in reverence to the saints of equitable disposition,
Who look upon none as either friend or enemy, but regard
    all equally
Like the auspicious flowers held as offering in cupped hands,
That bestow their fragrance equally on both hands.   (3A)

The saints who are pure of heart, and seek the welfare of one
    and all—
I acknowledge their benevolence and good nature.
Hear my childlike prayer and bestow your grace upon me,
And grant me ardent love for the feet of Ram.   (3B)

And now I salute the malicious and the malevolent,
Who, without reason, cause chaos and confusion,
Who look upon another's loss as their gain,
Who rejoice in desolation and are sorrowful in prosperity,
Who, to the full moon of Hari and Har's glory are like
    the moon-devouring demon, Rahu,
Who, in undoing the accomplishments of others, are as valiant
    as the thousand-armed warrior, Sahasrabahu,
Who have a thousand eyes to detect the faults of others,
And whose hearts are like flies to the ghee of another's well-being.
As fierce as fire, in their wrath as unrelenting as Mahishesh, the
    god of death,

---

xiv   The Hindu triad of Brahma, Vishnu and Shiv

The wicked are as rich in evil deeds as Dhanesh, the lord of wealth,
     is in gold.
Their advent is as the rising of the comet Ketu, which bodes no
     good for anyone,
And as with the Rakshasa, Kumbhakaran, in their inaction lies
     everyone's well-being.
They are willing to sacrifice even themselves to undo the
     accomplishments of another,
Like the hailstones that destroy the rice fields of the farmer.
I salute these malevolent people as I would the wrathful
     serpent Shesh,
As, thousand-tongued, they relate the faults of others.
Once more I bow before them, they who are like Prithuraj
And listen to the faults of others with ten thousand ears.
Once again, humbly, I bow before them as to Sakr,[xv] king of
     the gods,
They, who Sakr-like, forever delight in strong drink,
Who always prefer the thunderbolt of harsh speech,
And who, with a thousand eyes, regard closely the faults of others.

     The natural disposition of the malicious is to burn with jealousy
     Upon hearing of the good fortune of another, whether stranger,
          friend or foe—
     Aware of their nature, I, with folded hands,
     Entreat them with affection.   (4)

I have, for my part, made my humble request;
They, too, will not fail to do their part—
Even if you rear a crow with the greatest affection
Does it ever stop feeding on meat?
I pay humble homage at the feet of the virtuous and the wicked.
They each give pain, but between them there is a difference—

[xv] Indra

Separation from one takes life, while
Union with the other gives intense suffering.
Both are born into this world together, but are
As different from each other as the lotus and the leech;
The virtuous and the wicked are like nectar and wine—
Opposites, though they have the same progenitor, the bottomless
    ocean that is this world.[4]
The virtuous and the wicked, by their own deeds,
Attain to glory or dishonour.
Consider the good—nectar, the moon, the divine River Ganga and
    the sage,
And think of the vile—poison, fire, the stream of the Karamnasa
    that carries upon it the filth of Kaliyug, and the hunter.[5]
Virtue and vice are known to all,
But that which is in accordance with a person's inclination is what
    pleases him.

    The good tend to goodness,
    The vile to wickedness;
    Nectar is praised for giving immortality,
    And poison for causing death.   (5)

The enumeration of the vices of the wicked and the virtues of the
    good is never ending,
For both are limitless, like the boundless and bottomless ocean;
Even so I have described a few of these virtues and vices—
For they cannot be embraced or discarded without being
    recognized and understood.
The virtuous and the worthless have both been born of Vidhi,
The Vedas have enumerated their merits and their faults and
    distinguished one from the other.
The scriptures, tradition and the Puranas all say,
That in Vidhi's creation, good and evil are kneaded together.
Sorrow and joy, wickedness and virtue, day and night,

Good men and bad, high caste and low,
Demons and gods, the great and the small,
Life-conferring nectar and death-inducing poison,
Illusion and the Absolute, the Soul and the Supreme Being,
Prosperity and poverty, the beggar and the king,
The divine River Ganga and the Karamnasa, both of which flow
    through Kashi,
The arid desert of Marwar and the lush greenery of Malwa, the
    Brahman and the butcher,
Heaven and hell, attachment and renunciation—
The Vedas and the Shastras have divided vice from virtue.

    The Creator has made up this universe
    With the inanimate and the animate, with virtue and vice.
    The saints extract the good and reject the bad,
    As the swans of the sacred lake, Manasarovar, separate milk
        from worthless water.   (6)

When the Supreme Being blesses us with this discernment,
The heart renounces vice and dwells in virtue;
But under the influence of time and the force of fate,
Even the good may deviate from goodness.
The devotees of Hari remedy their lapse from virtue,
And by destroying sorrow and evil, restore glory untarnished;
Similarly, though the wicked may deviate from vice in the company
    of good men,
The evil in them is never effaced and their inherent nature remains
    unchanged.
Impostors wearing the guise of good men and taken as such
    by the world,
Are worshipped for the luminescence of their appearance;
In the end their true nature stands revealed, their deception cannot
    be sustained
As in the case of Kalnemi, Ravan and Rahu.[6]

A good and righteous man is honoured even when he assumes a
    form that is not pleasing,
As it was in the world with the bear, Jamvant, and the monkey,
    Hanuman.
Bad company is detrimental, good company is a gain—
Everyone says it is so—the world, the Vedas, the learned and wise.
Dust, in company with the wind, rises into the sky,
But turns into mud in the company of low-lying water.
In the home of the virtuous, the parrot and the mynah repeat the
    name of Ram;
In the home of the wicked, they repeat foul and abusive
    words endlessly.
Smoke, in bad company, becomes soot;
In good company, it also makes fine ink that may be used in
    copying a Purana.
Salt seawater, in the company of fire and wind,
Turns into life-renewing rainclouds.

    The planets, medicine, water, the wind, clothes—
    Everything becomes bad or good, harmful or useful,
    Depending on the use to which it is put.
    Wise and virtuous people discern this.   (7A)

    The two lunar fortnights in a month are the same in light
        and darkness,
    But Brahma has made a distinction in their names;[7]
    As the moon wanes in one fortnight and waxes in the other,
    The world, observing this, holds one in low, the other
        in high esteem.   (7B)

    The inanimate and animate beings of this world,
    Knowing them all to be pervaded by Ram—
    I venerate their lotus feet
    With folded hands, forever.   (7C)

Gods, Danavas, men, Nagas, birds, evil spirits and the spirits of
    the departed,
Gandharvas, Kinnaras and demons that wander in the night—
I salute you all and entreat you,
Upon me now bestow your grace.   (7D)

There are eighty-four lakh forms of living beings generated by
    four modes,
That inhabit water, land and sky—
Knowing the whole world to be permeated with the spirit of Sita
    and Ram,
I salute them with hands folded in respectful obeisance.
You, who are storehouses of compassion, look upon me as your
    humble servant,
And together, dissembling no more, bestow upon me
    your affection;
I have no confidence in the strength of my own wisdom
And that is why I beseech you all for your blessings.
I want to relate the story of Raghupati's accomplishments,
But my understanding is limited and his exploits fathomless.
I cannot think of a solution or even a part of one to
    overcome this—
My mind and intellect are beggarly, my desire and ambition kingly,
My ability low, my aspirations high,
I yearn for amrit, when in this world even buttermilk is not
    available for me.
Good men will forgive my impudence,
And listen with affectionate indulgence to my childish,
    inadequate words,
As when a child speaks in his lisping manner,
And the father and mother listen to him with joyous hearts.
The cruel, harsh and malicious will laugh,
They, who wear the faults of others as ornaments.
Who does not like his own verses,

Whether they be flavourful or insipid?
Those who take delight in hearing another's composition—
There are not too many such men in this world.
There are many in this world akin to lakes and rivers
That rise and swell in a flood of their own upon receiving water;
But only a few good men are like the generous ocean,
That swells upon beholding the full moon.

My lot is humble, my ambitions grand,
Yet I have faith in one thing—
That good men will be happy to hear me,
And only the vile and vicious will ridicule and mock.   (8)

The derision of the malevolent will only serve to benefit me—
The crow calls the sweet-voiced kokil harsh,
The storks laugh at the swans, the frogs at the chatak,
And the mean-minded and malicious mock pure discourse.
Those who take no pleasure in poetry and who have no love
    for Ram,
To them, this work of mine will provide much pleasant
    amusement.
My composition is in the spoken tongue, and my wit
    unsophisticated,
So it is worthy of being laughed at, and laughing at it is no crime.
For those who have no devotion for the Lord and no
    understanding of it,
This story will be dull to hear.
To those who cherish the feet of Hari and Har and whose minds
    do not pick at faults,
I relate this sweet and pleasing story of Raghubar.
Knowing in their hearts that it is adorned with devotion to Ram,
Good men, upon hearing it, will praise it with fair words.
I am not a poet, nor am I an adept at composition—
I am destitute in every art and skill.

The many and diverse uses of letters and syllables and nuances of
    meaning, embellished with figures of speech,
The countless variations of metre and the innumerable styles of
    literary composition,
The infinite distinctions of sentiment and emotion,
The diverse shortcomings and merits of poesy—
Of all of these, I am ignorant.
Poetic sense I have none—
I speak the truth and give it in writing.

    My composition is devoid of all literary merit;
    It has only one virtue, known throughout the world—
    Taking this one quality into consideration,
    Wise and discerning men will listen to my verses.   (9)

In this is contained the noble and illustrious name of Raghupati,
The exceedingly pure and purifying essence of the Puranas and
    the Vedas,
Which brings about felicity, and destroys misfortune,
And which Purari,[xvi] together with Uma, chants repeatedly
    in prayer.
The most extraordinary composition by the most outstanding
    of poets
Does not please or appeal if it does not have the name of Ram
    within it—
The most beautiful woman, with a face as radiant as the moon and
    endowed with every grace,
Is neither charming nor attractive without clothes.
A work devoid of all merit and composed by the most indifferent
    of poets,
When stamped with the glory of Ram's name,
Is recited and heard with reverence by the wise,

[xvi] Shiv

Who extract from it that which is good, like bees that gather honey.
Even though my verses do not have a single virtue,
Ram's splendour is manifest in them.
This is the hope that arises in my heart—
For who has not achieved greatness by associating with the good?
Smoke gives up its natural acridity and spreads instead a sweet
    fragrance
When derived from the aromatic agarwood.
My composition is awkward, but its subject noble,
For it tells the story of Ram which spreads joy and good fortune in
    the world.

Bringing forth felicity, destroying the filth of Kaliyug,
Is the story of Raghunath, says Tulsi.
The course of this stream of poetry is winding and meandering,
As is the course of the purifying and sacred stream of the Ganga.
My composition, in company with the Lord's glory, will be ennobled
And held dear in the hearts of good men,
As the ashes of the cremation ground, when upon Bhav's[xvii] body,
Become pleasing to the eye, and, remembered, purify.

    My composition will be loved by everyone
    Because of its association with the glory of Ram,
    Just as all wood from the Malaya mountains is valued
        as sandalwood,
    And no one questions its worth.   (10A)

    Even though a cow be black, its milk is pure and white;
    It is full of virtue, and everyone drinks it,
    Just as the glory of Sita and Ram, even when related in
        rustic speech,
    Is recited and heard by the good and the wise.   (10B)

[xvii] Shiv

A diamond in a serpent's hood, a ruby on a mountaintop and a
  pearl in an elephant's forehead,
Do not shine with their full brilliance;
Set in a king's crown, or adorning a young woman's delicate form,
All three attain their true lustre and their splendour increases.
In the same manner, the wise men say, the verses of a gifted poet
Are born in one place but take on beauty in another.
Drawn by his devotion, the goddess Sharada,[xviii] when invoked,
Abandons the abode of Vidhi himself and comes rushing to the poet;
Yet, without bathing in the lake of Ram's exploits,
The fatigue of her journey is not alleviated, not even by a crore
  of contrivances—
Poets and wise men, realizing this in their hearts,
Sing only of Hari's glory, which removes the filth of Kaliyug,
For composing verses in praise of ordinary people
Makes Gira[xix] beat her head in despair and rue her hasty coming.
The wise declare that the heart is the ocean, the intellect a shell
  within it,
And the goddess Sharada, the Svati nakshatra,
For if, under her influence, should it rain good and excellent
  thoughts,
The poet's verses become precious pearls of lustrous beauty.[8]

> With skill and dexterity they are pierced and strung,
> One by one, upon the thread of the story of Ram's exploits;
> Good men wear them upon their noble breasts
> Where they shine with the radiance of deep devotion. (11)

Those who have been born in this dark and dreadful Kaliyug,
Whose actions are those of the crow but whose appearance that of
  the swan,

[xviii] Sarasvati
[xix] Sarasvati

Who, having abandoned the path of true knowledge, walk in
    evil ways,
Who are embodiments of deceit, receptacles of the vices
    of Kaliyug,
Who profess to be devotees of Ram
But are slaves to greed, anger and lust,
Who make the greatest noise whilst hypocritically upholding the
    flag of faith and trading in deceit—
Amongst them place me first in this world.
Were I to relate all my faults and failings,
The recital would become so long that I would not reach
    the end of it;
That is why I have described only a very few,
For even by knowing a little the wise and astute understand it all.
Taking into account my many prayers and entreaties,
Let no one, upon listening to this tale, find fault.
Those who will even after this express doubt—
They are more stupid and slow of wit than I am myself.
I am not a poet, nor am I regarded as clever;
I sing the glory of Ram according to my understanding and ability.
How boundless are Raghupati's deeds,
How limited my intellect, entangled as it is in this world!
The wind that can uproot Mount Meru—
Tell me, before such a wind, of what account is the wisp of cotton
    that is my writing?
Understanding the immeasurable majesty of Ram,
My mind shrinks away from telling his story.

Sharada, Sheshnag, Mahesh,[xx] Vidhi,
The Vedas, the Puranas and all scripture
Cry, 'He is not thus! He defies all description!'
Even as they sing unceasingly of his glory.   (12)

[xx] Shiv

All know that the Lord's majesty is thus indescribable,
Even so, no one has refrained from recounting it.
The Vedas have explained this phenomenon thus:
There are many ways, in many tongues, to adore the Lord,
He who is one, without attachment, without form, without name,
Unbegotten, uncreated, who is truth, consciousness, bliss supreme
     and the ultimate refuge,
The all-pervading, universal, omnipresent God, who exists in all forms,
And who, assuming mortal form, has performed diverse deeds.
These he has enacted only for the well-being of his devotees,
For he is the most merciful, and compassionate towards those who
     seek refuge.
He showers great affection upon his own,
And refrains from anger against those whom he has favoured with
     his compassion.
Restorer of what is lost, friend of the poor and the miserable,
Simple-hearted, ingenuous, yet all-powerful is the Lord, Raghuraj.
Knowing this, the wise sing Hari's glory,
As a result of which their song becomes pure and brings salvation.
It is on this strength that I sing of the glory of Raghunath,
And relate it as I bow my head at his feet.
Ancient sages first sang Hari's fame—
On that same path, my friend, it is easy for me to walk.

     If, over a river whose breadth is unbounded,
     A king has a bridge constructed,
     Then, clambering upon it, even the tiniest of ants
     Can cross to the other shore without effort.   (13)

Reassuring my heart in this manner,
I shall relate the pleasing story of Raghupati.
Vyas and the many other great and eminent poets
Who have, with deep reverence, recounted Hari's fame and glory—
Their lotus feet I adore.
May they fulfil all my wishes and desires.

I salute, too, those poets of this Kaliyug
Who have related the virtues of Raghupati,
Those vernacular poets, most sagacious and discerning,
Who have told of the deeds of Hari in the spoken tongue.
Those who have been, those who now are and those who will be—
I salute them all with sincerity, discarding all deceit.
Show me your favour, poets, and grant me this boon,
That in the assemblies of good men my song may be honoured.
Compositions that are not esteemed by the wise and intelligent
Are but the worthless labour of foolish poets.
The only kind of fame, poetry and affluence that is good,
Is that which, like the divine River Ganga, is of benefit to all.
Ram's glory is sublime, my poetry clumsy—
This disparity fills me with misgivings.
But by your grace this will become possible for me,
For fine silk embroidery makes even coarse cloth beautiful.

Poetry that is clear and simple, and that tells of fame that is
    pure and untarnished—
That is what the wise revere;
Critics forget their natural hostility
Upon hearing it, and praise and commend it. (14A)

Such verse cannot be composed without clear and immaculate
    understanding,
But my intellect and ability are limited.
So bestow your grace upon me that I may sing of the
    glory of Hari—
Thus I beseech you again and again. (14B)

Poets and learned men, graceful swans
On the sacred Manas lake of Raghubar's exploits,
Hearing my childlike prayer and recognizing my deep interest
    and intense desire,
Be compassionate to me. (14C)

I pay homage to the lotus feet of the Muni Valmiki
Who composed the Ramayana,
Which, though it tells of the Rakshasa Khar,[9] is not harsh and
    coarse like him, but sweet and pleasing,
And though containing within it the tale of the vile demon
    Dushan,[10] is without fault or blemish.   (14D)

I praise all the four Vedas
Which are like boats on the ocean of this existence,
And never tire, even in dream,
Of relating the manifest glory of Raghubar.   (14E)

I do obeisance to the dust of the feet of Vidhi the Creator,
He, who has made this ocean that is the world, from which
Have sprung the saints, nectar, the moon and the wish-
    granting cow, Kamdhenu,
As well as men who are wicked and vile, and poison and
    strong liquor.   (14F)

I do obeisance to the feet of gods, Brahmans, sages,
    and planets,
And say to them with folded hands,
Grant me your favour and fulfil
All the sweet longings of my heart.   (14G)

Once more I pay homage to the goddess Sharada and the divine
    stream of the River Ganga,
A pair pure and sacred, and of pleasing disposition—
Immersion in one or drinking of its waters, removes evil,
The other, her name uttered or heard, dispels darkness
    and ignorance.
To Mahesh and Bhavani, who are guru, father and mother,
I pay homage—friends of the poor, giving every day of
    their bounty,

Followers, protectors and friends of Sita's beloved,
True benefactors of Tulsi in every way.
Looking upon the age of Kali, for the good of the world,
    Har and Girija[xxi]
Made up mantras and incantations in the common tongue,[11]
Ill-assorted syllables without meaning that no one can recite,
But whose force is manifest because of the glory and splendour
    of Mahesh.
Uma's Lord, being well disposed towards me,
Will make this story the root of bliss and joy;
Meditating upon Shivaa[xxii] and Shiv and receiving their favour,
I relate the exploits of Ram with an eager heart.
My composition, by Shiv's grace, will shine
Like a night made luminous by the light of the moon and his
    congregation of stars.
Whoever recites or listens to this story
With love and devotion and intelligent attention
Shall become a devotee of Ram's feet
And partake of bliss uncontaminated by the filth of Kaliyug.

    If I receive, in dream or in truth,
    The grace of Har and Gauri,[xxiii]
    Then all that I say will come true
    Of the influence and importance of this poem of mine in the
        spoken tongue.   (15)

I salute the most sacred city of Avadh,[xxiv]
And the River Sarju that flows beside it and washes away the sins
    of Kaliyug.
I salute also the men and women of the city

[xxi] Parvati
[xxii] Parvati
[xxiii] Parvati
[xxiv] Ayodhya, the capital city of the kingdom of Koshal, and the city of Ram's
    birth

For whom the Lord has no little affection—
For although they maligned Sita,[12] he freed them from all their sins
    and sorrows
And let them dwell within his realm.
I pay homage to Kaushalya, whose glory is spread over the
    entire world—
She is the east
From whence rose the beautiful moon, Raghupati,
Who bestows happiness upon the world and is the frost that blights
    the lotus of evil.
To King Dasharath and all his queens,
Looking upon them as the image of perfection and bliss,
I do humble reverence in my heart, in word and in deed—
Be gracious to me, knowing me a devoted servant of your son,
By creating whom the Creator became great.
The very extreme of glory are Ram's father and mothers.[13]

    I venerate the king of Avadh,
    Who had true love for Ram—
    When separated from his Lord,
    He gave up his precious body as a worthless blade of grass.   (16)

I salute Videh with his household—King Janak,
Who had deep love and devotion for Ram,
Which he kept secret, hidden in propriety and pomp,
But which was revealed the instant he looked upon Ram.
Amongst Ram's brothers, I pay homage first at the feet of Bharat,
Whose principles and strict observance of the vow he took
    defy description,
Whose heart is ever at Ram's lotus feet—
Like a bee greedy for honey, it never leaves Ram's side.
I venerate the lotus feet of Lakshman,
Who is calm and handsome, and confers happiness upon
    his followers,

Whose fame is the staff upon which flies
The flag of Raghupati's untarnished glory,
Who is Sheshnag of the thousand heads, who upon this earth
Became incarnate to drive away the terrors of the world—
May he always remain gracious towards me,
He, ocean of mercy, repository of virtue, Saumitri, Sumitra's son.
I bow with reverence at the lotus feet of Ripusudan,[xxv]
Who is valiant, good-natured and devoted to Bharat.
I bow before the great hero, Hanuman,
Whose glory Ram himself has related.

    Yes, I prostrate myself before him, Hanuman, son of the Wind,
    Of profound intelligence, the purifying flame that destroys
        the forest of wickedness and vice,
    And in the home of whose heart,
    The bow-and-arrows-bearing Ram has come to live.   (17)

To Sugriv, lord of the monkeys; to Jamvant, chief of the bears; and
    to Vibhishan, king of the demons that wander in the night,
To Angad, and the others who make up the monkey host—
I offer homage at their gracious feet,
They, who though lowly and wretched in form, found Ram.
All those who are worshippers at Raghupati's feet,
All the birds, animals, gods, men and demons—
I do obeisance at their lotus feet,
They, who without desire for reward or return, serve Ram.
To the sage, Shukdev, to the four mind-born sons of Brahma,
    Sanak, Sanandan, Sanatan and Sanatkumar, to Muni Narad,
And to all the munis most excellent, celebrated for their wisdom
    and learning—
To them I offer homage as I prostrate myself before them,
    touching my head to the ground—

[xxv] Shatrughna

O great munis, grant me your favour, knowing me to be your servant.
Janaki, Janak's daughter, mother of the world,[xxvi]
Deeply beloved by him in whom resides all mercy—
Upon her two lotus feet I meditate,
That by her grace I may be granted immaculate understanding and
    clear intellect.
Again, in my heart, in word, and in deed, Raghunayak's
Lotus feet I adore—he, who is all-powerful,
Lotus-eyed, bearing a bow and arrows,
The source of joy to his followers and the destroyer of their sorrows.

    Words and their meaning, water and the ripples upon its
        surface, are the same—
    Though called by different names, they are not different.
    So also Sita and Ram, who hold the distressed most dear—
    I prostrate myself at their feet.   (18)

I praise and adore the name *Ram* as borne by Raghubar[14]—
From it comes all light—of Fire, of the Sun and the Moon.[15]
It is Vidhi, it is Hari, it is Har—Creator, Preserver, Destroyer,
It is the life breath of the Vedas,
And, indescribable, without form, without attributes,
    incomparable, it is the abode of virtue.
It is the high mantra chanted by Mahesh,
Who declares it necessary for salvation even at Kashi.[16]
Its potency is known full well by Ganesh,
Who is worshipped before all others because of the power of
    the name.[17]
The first poet, Valmiki, knew the power of the name—
He had been cleansed and freed of blame by chanting it backwards.[18]
Learning from Shiv that the name of Ram is equal to the thousand
    other names of the Lord,[19]

_____

[xxvi] Sita

Bhavani chants it with her beloved.
Seeing her joy in the name, Har rejoiced
And made her, that jewel amongst women, his own ornament.[20]
Shiv knows well the power of the name,
By which the deadly poison yielded nectar.[21]

> Devotion to Raghupati is the season of rains;
> Tulsi, his devoted servant, is the rice that grows in deep water,
> And the two most excellent syllables of Ram's name
> Are the months of Savan and Bhadon.[22]   (19)

The two syllables are sweet and enchanting,
They are the alphabet-eyes of those devoted to the Lord.
Easy to remember and meditate upon, easy for everyone to chant,
Bringing gain in this world, and making the next possible,
Extremely pleasing to say, to hear and to meditate upon,
As dear to Tulsi as Ram and Lakshman—
When the two letters are uttered separately, their bond of
    love is broken,[23]
Yet, like the Absolute and the Soul, they are natural companions.
Devoted brothers like Nar and Narayan,[24]
They are the preservers of the world, the protectors of the elect,
Jewels that adorn the ears of fair Devotion,
Shining for the good of the world, clear and bright like the moon
    and the sun.
In flavour and satisfaction like the nectar that confers salvation,
Supporting the earth like the tortoise and the serpent Shesh,[25]
Like bees to the beautiful lotus of the heart of the devout,
And upon the tongue, like Hari and Haldhar to Jasomati,[26]

> One is the royal umbrella, the other the jewel in the crown[27]—
> Above all the other letters of the alphabet,
> Says Tulsi, shine the two consonants
> Of Raghubar's name.   (20)

The name and the named may be understood to be the same,
But the love between them is that of a master and his follower,
    the latter attached to and consequent upon the first.
Name and form are both attributes of the Supreme Being,
Who is indescribable, uncreated and requires a clear mind and
    discernment to understand.
To conjecture and compare which of the two is greater and which
    smaller is wrong,
But upon hearing their attributes, the wise will understand the
    difference between them—
Form is clearly subservient to name,
For without name, form cannot be known.
Any particular form, without its name being known,
Cannot be recognized even if placed upon the palm of the hand;
But if the name be remembered and meditated upon even without
    the form being seen,
The form enters the heart with special tenderness.
The nature of form and name is a tale beyond expression—
When understood, it gives joy, but it cannot be related.
Between nirgun and sagun, the Immaterial Absolute and the
    Incarnate, the name bears glorious witness—
It is the sagacious and skilful intermediary, who speaks both tongues,
    explains both points of view, and enlightens both sides.

    Hold the jewelled lamp of Ram's name
    Upon the threshold of your tongue
    If you want light, says Tulsi,
    Within as well as without.   (21)

As their tongues chant his name, the yogis awake
In a state of detached separation from Viranchi's[xxvii] illusory
    creation that is this world,

[xxvii] Brahma

Experiencing the bliss of the Absolute, which is incomparable,
Indescribable, confers well-being and has neither name nor form.
Those who wish to know the hidden mysteries,
Can come to understand them by repeating the name.
Holy men who chant the name with absorption and passion
Become Siddhas and acquire miraculous powers.
Those who are in pain or deep distress, when they chant the name,
Their troubles disappear and they become light of heart and happy.
Thus there are in this world four kinds of Ram worshippers
And all four kinds are virtuous, without blame or guilt, and generous.
All the four are wise and clever, and rely upon his name,
But the enlightened devotee is especially beloved of the Lord.
In all the four ages of the world, in all the four Vedas, his name
      is mighty—
But it is especially so in the Kaliyug, where there is no
      other recourse.

      Those who are free from all kinds of desire and sensual
            passions,
      And immersed in the pleasure of devotion to Ram—
      Their hearts are the fish
      In the lake of nectar that is supreme love for his name.   (22)

Nirgun and sagun, the Immaterial and the Incarnate, are the two
      aspects of the Absolute,
Neither can be described, each is fathomless, uncreated, immortal
      and incomparable.
In my opinion, the name is greater than both forms,
For it has made both subservient to itself on its own merit.
Good men, knowing my devotion, should not regard this statement
      as bold or audacious
For I say this with conviction, understanding and heartfelt
      devotion—
Like the two aspects of fire are the two aspects of the Absolute:

One is latent within the wood, one is visible and can be seen.
Each aspect is in itself inaccessible, each becomes understandable
    and within reach by means of the name.
Therefore, I say that the name is bigger than both brahm[xxviii] and
    Ram himself.
The Absolute is all-pervading, one and indestructible,
The sum of all truth, consciousness and intense bliss.
Even though this constant, unchangeable, unchanging Lord dwells
    in our hearts
All living beings in this world are wretched and miserable—
But a true appraisal of the name followed by its utterance with
    diligence and perseverance
Makes the Absolute manifest in the same way that assaying a jewel
    reveals its worth.

    Thus the glory of the name
    Is greater immeasurably than the Absolute.
    I declare that in my opinion,
    The name is also greater than Ram.   (23)

For the sake of his followers, Ram took on the form of a man
And endured misery and sorrow to secure their happiness—
But, freely and easily repeating his name with love,
Devotees become abodes of joy and bliss.
Ram redeemed one ascetic's wife,[xxix]
But his name has remedied the base acts of millions of evildoers.
To please Rishi Vishvamitra, Ram decided the fate of Taraka,
    Suketu's daughter,[28]
Together with that of her army and her son—
But together with sin and sorrow, his name destroys a
    devotee's despair

[xxviii] The supreme Absolute
[xxix] Ahalya, the wife of the sage Gautam

In the same manner that the sun puts an end to night.
Ram himself broke Bhav's bow—
But the power of his name demolishes the fears of this existence.
The Lord restored the Dandak[29] forest and made it charming
    and pleasant,
But his name has made pure uncountable hearts.
Raghunandan destroyed many demon armies,
But his name has destroyed all the evil of Kaliyug.

Raghunath gave salvation to his faithful servants
Shabari and the vulture, Jatayu,
But his name has redeemed innumerable evildoers—
Its virtues are proclaimed and celebrated in the Vedas.   (24)

Ram, as all men know, extended his protection
To two, Sukanth[xxx] and Vibhishan,
But his name has given refuge to countless of the poor
    and humble—
Its virtues are acclaimed and shine forth in the world and in
    the Vedas.
Ram gathered an army of bears and monkeys
And made no little effort to build the bridge to Lanka,
But the mere calling of his name dries up the ocean of
    this existence—
Reflect upon this, good people, in your minds.
Ram killed Ravan and all his kin in battle,
And with Sita, he then departed for his own city;
Ram became king, and Avadh his capital,
And gods and sages recounted his virtues in glorious song.
But his servants meditate upon his name with affection,
And vanquish the strong and mighty armies of worldly illusion and
    delusion with no effort,

[xxx] The king of the monkeys, Sugriv

To walk, immersed in devotion, along the paths of their
    own happiness.
By the grace bestowed upon them by his name, they have no care
    or sorrow, even in dream.

    The name is bigger than brahm and Ram,
    It is the giver of boons to the givers of boons.
    Mahesh knew this when he selected it
    From the hundred crore verses of the story of Ram.[30]   (25)

By the grace conferred upon him by the name, Shambhu became
    immortal,
And though his attire[31] is unsightly, he is the sum of all bliss.
It is by the blessing conferred upon them by the name that
Shukdev, Sanak and his brothers, and the various sages, saints and
    ascetics partake of divine bliss
Narad knows the glory and power of the name,
And so is as beloved of Hari and Har as Hari is beloved of the world.
By chanting his name, he pleased the Lord who bestowed his
    favour upon him,
And Prahlad became the foremost of all devotees, the jewel in the crest.
Dhruv in sorrow repeated Hari's name,
And received a fixed, everlasting and unparalleled place in the skies.
Hanuman, son of the Wind, meditated upon his sacred name
And kept Ram's favour and affection.
The dissolute Ajamil, the elephant, and the prostitute,[32]
All obtained liberation by the might of Hari's name.
How much more can I extol his name?
Even Ram himself could not adequately describe its glory.

    The name of Ram is the wish-granting tree, Kalpataru,
    It is the abode of blessedness in the age of Kali,
    And by meditating upon it Tulsidas
    Was transformed from bhang into the sacred tulsi.[33]   (26)

In all the four ages, in all time, past, present or future, and in all
    the three worlds,
Living beings have been freed from sorrow by chanting his name.
In the opinion of the Vedas, the Puranas, and all the saints,
The love of Ram is the fruit of all virtue.
In the first age, it was through meditation; in the second, through
    sacrificial rites;
In the Dwapar age[xxxi] the Lord was propitiated through worship;
But in this age of Kali, which is the root of corruption, and where
    there is only filth,
Where the souls of men are fish in a reservoir of sin—
In these terrible times, the name is the wish-fulfilling Kalpataru
And by meditating upon it, all the deceptive illusions of this world
    that trap and entangle are destroyed.
In the Kaliyug, Ram's name is the giver of all that is wished for
    and desired,
It makes easy the afterworld, and in this world it protects like a
    father and mother.
In the Kaliyug neither good deeds, nor piety, nor enlightened
    understanding is of any use—
The name of Ram is the only support.
The Kaliyug is the demon Kalnemi, the repository of treachery and evil,
And Ram's name the wise and able Hanuman.

    The name of Ram is Narkeshari[xxxii],
    Kaliyug is Kanakakasipu,
    And those who chant the name are like Prahlad,
    Protected by he who destroyed the enemy of the gods.   (27)

Whether with feeling or without, whether in anger or indolence,
Chanting the name yields felicity in all ten directions.[34]

[xxxi] The third of the four ages of the world.
[xxxii] Vishnu's fourth avatar

Remembering the name of Ram and bowing my head to Raghunath,
I sing his virtues—
He will mend all my various faults,
He, whose grace in bestowing grace never decreases.
Ram, the superlative Lord, has a servant as unworthy as me;
Yet, in keeping with his merciful nature, he, in his compassion,
      looks after me.
The world and the Vedas know a good master's ways—
In humble words he recognizes devotion.
Rich or poor, villager or city-dweller,
Learned pandit or blockhead, vile and low or celebrated and famous,
Good poets or bad poets—according to their abilities,
All men and women praise their king.
And a virtuous, wise and benevolent king,
Who is a part of God himself, and in this world, the most
      compassionate,
Hears their sweet words of praise and respect,
And in their discourses, recognizes their devotion and humility.
This is the nature of even ordinary kings—
And know that the king of Koshal is their crown, the jewel upon
      the crest!
Ram is pleased by love unalloyed.
But who in the world is more dull and poor of intellect than I?

      Yet, even this foolish devotee's passionate love,
      Ram, the merciful, entertains—
      He, who made rocks and stones into seaworthy ships,
      And turned bears and monkeys into wise counsellors.   (28A)

      I have become a byword because of my devotion, and
            everyone says
      That Ram has to endure this joke—
      That a master like Sita's Lord has
      A servant like Tulsidas!   (28B)

Very great is my presumption, very great my error—
Hearing of my crime, even hell wrinkled its nose in disgust;
Knowing this, I am afraid of my own fear,
But Ram has given my presumption no thought even
    in dream.
The Lord listened, observed and examined it with a careful eye
And then praised my devotion and my thoughts—
Though they may be ruined in the telling, they are true within,
And Ram is pleased knowing what is in his servant's heart.
The Lord does not dwell upon the mistakes of his followers,
Instead, he considers a hundred times the intentions of
    their hearts.
The crime for which Ram, like a hunter, killed Baali—
Sukanth then committed the same offence,
As did Vibhishan the same misdeed;
But Ram did not hold this against them even in dream.[35]
Rather, he honoured them at his meeting with Bharat,
And praised and commended them in his royal court.

    The Lord sat under the tree, the monkeys in the boughs
        above him,
    And he made them equal to him.
    Tulsi says that nowhere is there
    A master as gracious as Ram.   (29A)

    O Ram, your goodness
    Is good for everyone,
    And, if this be forever true,
    It is good for Tulsi too.   (29B)

    In this manner, relating my virtues and faults,
    And once again bowing my head to all,
    I relate Raghubar's unblemished glory,
    Hearing which the filth of Kaliyug is destroyed.   (29C)

The charming story that the sage Jagbalik
Related to the great sage Bharadvaj—
I relate here that same story at length.
Now listen to it, all good people, and rejoice in it.
Shambhu composed this pleasant tale of Ram's deeds
And then graciously related it to Uma.
Shiv gave the very same tale to Kak Bhushundi,
Knowing him to be a devotee of Ram, and therefore worthy of
     hearing it.
From him Jagbalik received the tale,
And recited it to Bharadvaj.
These listeners and reciters are of equal virtue,
With equal insight and understanding of Hari's playful exploits.
Their wisdom comprehends all the three phases of Time, the past,
     the present and the future,
As plainly as an amla fruit placed on the palm of the hand;
Other wise and intelligent devotees of Hari too
Relate, hear and understand this story in diverse ways.

     I heard the story from my guru
     At Sukarkhet,
     But I did not understand it then because
     I was just a boy and quite stupid and unaware.   (30A)

     The listeners and reciters of the mysteries of Ram's story
     Are repositories of wisdom—
     So how could I, a blockhead and an ignorant fool entrapped
     In the iniquities of the age of Kali understand it?   (30B)

Even so, my guru repeated the story again and again,
Till at last I understood it to the extent of my ability;
The same story, I shall now tell in the spoken tongue
So that my heart be awakened to understanding.
With whatever little intelligence and understanding that I have,

I will relate it—with a heart inspired by Hari.

The story that I have to tell vanquishes my doubts, delusions and
    misconceptions,

And is the boat across the river of this existence.

The story of Ram brings peace to the wise, and delight to everyone,

And destroys the impurities of the age of Kali—

His story is the peacock that kills the serpent that is the Kaliyug,

And the fire stick that kindles the flames of discernment and
    understanding.

The story of Ram is the wish-yielding cow, Kamdhenu, of the age
    of Kali;

For the good, it is the life-giving Sanjivani root.

It is a veritable river of nectar upon Earth,

And, the destroyer of fear, it is like the hooded cobra to the toads
    and frogs of doubt and misapprehension.

It is a veritable Girinandini,[xxxiii] destroying hell as she annihilated

An army of demons for the benefit of the saints and the gods.

Conceived in the community of sages, it is like the goddess
    Ramaa[xxxiv] who was born of the ocean,

And, steady and immovable like the Earth, it carries the weight of
    the whole world, and forgives it.

Like the sacred river Jamuna, it blackens the faces of the
    messengers of Jam, the god of death,[36]

And like the holy city of Kashi, it gives liberation from this
    existence.

It is as dear to Ram as the sacred tulsi,

And for Tulsidas, it is like his own mother, Hulsi, who holds his
    well-being in her heart.[37]

It is as beloved of Shiv as Mount Mekal's daughter, the holy river
    Narmada,

The accumulation of all success, well-being and wealth,

[xxxiii] Parvati
[xxxiv] Lakshmi, as the consort of Ram

And to noble virtues, it is as nurturing as the mother goddess Aditi
    to the gods.
It is the culmination of love and devotion to Raghubar.

> The story of Ram is the River Mandakini,
> The mind is the beautiful Chitrakut, says Tulsi,
> And love is the pleasing forest
> Wherein disport Sita and Ram.   (31)

The legend of Ram is the beautiful wish-fulfilling jewel,
    Chintamani,
The auspicious ornament that adorns the woman that is the
    wisdom of the saints and sages.
The sum of Ram's virtues is the bliss of the world,
It is the giver of liberation, riches, virtue and ultimate salvation.
The best, most excellent teacher of wisdom, detachment and
    spiritual contemplation,
Like the Ashvin twins, the physicians of the gods, it heals the
    dreadful disease that is this existence.
From it is born devotion to Sita and Ram,
And it is the seed from which springs all faith and holy vows
    and practices.
It is the destroyer of sin, anguish, distress and sorrow,
Our beloved protector in the next world and this;
It is the learned and distinguished minister to the monarch that is
    good judgment
And as the rishi Kumbhaj[xxxv] to the boundless ocean of greed.
The exploits of Ram are the young lions in the forest of the
    people's minds,
That kill the herd of wild elephants of lust, anger and the filth
    of Kaliyug;
They are the honoured and beloved guests of Purari,

[xxxv] Agastya

And the wish-fulfilling, rain-bringing clouds that put out the forest
    fire of poverty and wretchedness.
They are like protective incantations and talismans against the
    venomous snake of worldly enjoyment;
They erase the deep and cruel lines of fate upon the forehead,
And destroy the darkness of ignorance like the rays of the sun;
They are the clouds that nourish and nurture the paddy fields that
    are his devotees.
Ram's deeds are like the Kalpataru in granting that which is
    wished for;
Easily accessible to all devotees and granting peace and bliss, they
    are like Hari and Har;
They are like the stars in the clear autumn sky of the poet's mind,
And for the devotees of Ram, they are like the riches of life itself.
They are like the abundant enjoyment of the rewards of all
    good actions,
And like holy men in their sincere and guileless benevolence
    towards the world.
They are like swans on the Manas lake of the devotee's heart,
And like the waves on the purifying stream of the River Ganga.

    The evil ways, wrong thinking and misdemeanours prevalent in
        the age of Kali,
    The deceit and deception, hypocrisy and false pride, blasphemy
        and false doctrine—
    The sum of Ram's virtues is a conflagration that destroys these
    As a great fire consumes dry wood and kindling.   (32A)

    The exploits of Ram are like the beams of the full moon
    Giving peace to all,
    But they are especially beneficial to good men who are like
        the water lily that blooms in the moonlight,
    And whose hearts are like the chakor that draws nourishment
        only from moonbeams.   (32B)

The questions that Bhavani asked him,
And the manner and detail in which Shankar answered her—
All of that I will now sing in verse
In a unique and pleasing composition.
Those who have not already heard this tale—
Let them not be astonished by it.
Wise men who hear this sublime and extraordinary story,
Are not surprised by it knowing that
There is no measure of the stories of Ram in this world.
They know with certainty
That Ram has descended to this earth in many forms,
And that the Ramayana, with its hundred crore verses,
    is boundless.
The deeds of Hari have charmed and entranced across different
    ages and in many ways,
And have been sung and recited in many forms by many munis
    and sages.
So hold no doubt or mistrust in your hearts,
But listen with reverence and love.

    Ram is infinite, infinite are his virtues,
    And immeasurable is the breadth of his story—
    So they, whose thoughts are pure and who are given
        to reflection,
    Will not be surprised by anything they hear.   (33)

Banishing all doubt in this manner,
And placing upon my head the dust of my guru's lotus feet,
I again salute everyone with folded hands
So that no blame may attach to the recitation of my tale.
With reverence now I bow my head to Shiv
And recount the glorious story of Ram's virtues.
In Samvat sixteen hundred and thirty one,[38]
I commence this tale, my head at Hari's feet.

On Tuesday, the ninth day of the sweet spring month of Chait,
In the city of Avadh this story shed its radiance—
The day, the Vedas say, of Ram's birth,
When the fruit of all pilgrimages is attained here,
When demons, Nagas, birds, men, munis and gods
All come here to adore Raghunayak,
When good people celebrate the great festival of Ram's birth
And sing in sweet tones of his fame and glory.

Great multitudes of the good and the pious bathe
In the purifying waters of the sacred Sarju river;
They repeat the name of Ram as they meditate upon him,
Holding the image of his dark and beautiful form in
    their hearts.   (34)

The mere sight and touch of this sacred river, or just bathing in it,
    or drinking its waters,
Destroys sin, say the Vedas and Puranas;
Its waters are pure and clean, and even Sharada, with her clear
    mind and shining intelligence,
Cannot describe its immeasurable glory.
This pleasing city of Avadh, which was Ram's home, grants
    ultimate salvation through him;
Celebrated in all the worlds, it is the most holy and purifying.
The living beings in this world, generated by four modes of birth,
    are countless in number—
Those who give up their bodies in Avadh, never again enter the
    cycle of rebirth.
Knowing this city to be pleasing to the heart in every way,
Bestowing all success, and a treasure-house of bliss,
I begin composing here this sacred story,
Which will destroy all lust, pride and deceit in those who hear it.
It is called *Ramcharitmanas*, 'The Sacred Manas Lake of
    Ram's Exploits',

And listening to it, the hearer finds peace and rest.
The mind is an elephant caught in a burning forest of sensuality
    and lust—
It finds rescue and relief by plunging into this lake.
Ramcharitmanas is the delight of the munis;
Composed by Shambhu, it is pleasing and purifying.
It subdues the three kinds of sin, sorrow and poverty,[39]
And destroys the misdemeanours, impurities and evil of the age
    of Kali.
Mahesh composed it and kept it within his heart,
Till, finding an auspicious moment, he told it to his wife, Shivaa—
That is why, having seen it within his own heart, and rejoicing
    in it,
Har gave it the excellent name of *Ramcharitmanas*.
It is that same delightful and pleasing story that I relate here—
Listen to it with reverence, good people, giving it all your attention.

    The *Manas*, what it is like, how it came to be,
    And how its fame spread across the world—
    I will now relate these circumstances,
    Remembering Uma and Brishketu.[xxxvi]   (35)

Inspiration, by Shambhu's grace, gladdened the mind
Of Tulsi, the poet of this *Ramcharitmanas*.
He has made his composition as pleasing to the heart as his
   wit allows—
Listen to it carefully, good people, improving and correcting it.
Wisdom and intellect are the land, and within it the heart a
    deep place,
The Vedas and Puranas are the ocean, and the sages the clouds
That rain down the pure water of Ram's fame and glory
In sweet, heart-delighting and bliss-yielding showers.

[xxxvi] Shiv

Their detailed narration of his wondrous acts when in
    embodied form
Is the purity of this rainwater, destroying dirt and filth,
While love and devotion that defy description,
Are its sweetness and refreshing coolness.
This rain is beneficial for the paddy fields of good actions,
And is life itself for Ram's devotees.
This purifying water falls upon the earth of intelligence and
    understanding,
And collecting, flows through the pleasing channels of the ears
To fill the beautiful lake of the heart and become still—
It remains there a long time, tranquil, cool, sweet and pleasing.

    The four exceedingly wondrous and excellent conversations,
    That have been contrived in wisdom and composed with
       reflection,
    Are the four heart-enchanting ghats
    Of this sacred, purifying and pleasing lake.   (36)

The seven books that make up this work are its charming flights
    of stairs
Which, when seen with the eyes of wisdom, delight the mind.
Raghupati's majesty is formless, unqualified, unbounded—
Which, when narrated, is the fathomless depth of its clear water.
The glory of Ram and Sita is its nectar-like water,
The similes are the heart-captivating playfulness of its waves,
The elegant chaupais are its densely-growing waterlilies,
And the poetic devices, lustrous shells bearing precious pearls.
The lyrical chhands, sorthas and elegant dohas[40]
Are pleasing clusters of many-coloured lotuses,
While incomparable meaning, pleasing emotions and elegant language
Are their pollen, honey and fragrance.
The multitude of good actions is the softly buzzing swarm of
    black bees,

Wisdom, detachment and thoughtful reflection are the swans,
While allusion, wordplay, and the various verse forms
Are the many kinds of enchanting fish.
The four ends of existence—wealth, virtue, pleasure and the
    freedom from rebirth,
The considered and thoughtful reflections on spiritual and worldly
    knowledge,
The nine poetic sentiments, the repetition of his name, and the
    many references to penance, spiritual contemplation and
    detachment from the world—
All these are the water creatures in this beautiful lake.
The songs in praise of the pious, the good, and Ram's name—
These are like rare and wonderful waterbirds.
The assembly of saints and holy men is the mango grove that
    surrounds this lake,
While their faith and belief may be compared to spring.
The many and diverse explanations of devotion,
Forgiveness, compassion and temperance are a canopy of vines
    and creepers;
Equanimity, self-restraint, and religious vows are flowers, wisdom
    their fruit,
And love for Hari's feet, the juice of these fruits—so it has been
    said in the Vedas.
And all the many other stories and anecdotes in this tale—
They are the parrots, the koels and birds of many hues.

    The pleasure and delight derived from this tale are as a garden,
        grove, or wood
    Where birds of happiness sport and play;
    The heart is the gardener who waters it with tears of love
    From his beautiful eyes.   (37)

Those who recite this account of his exploits with care
Are the alert and watchful guardians of this lake;

And the men and women who forever listen to it with reverence
Are noble gods, rightful masters of this Manas.
The base and evil, interested only in the sensual and the worldly,
    are like storks and crows,
Unfortunates who do not go near this lake,
For here there are no snails, frogs or water-scum
In the form of prurient stories or discourses on sensual pleasures to
    attract them.
That is the reason why they do not come here, but turn away
    disappointed,
These unfortunate, lustful crows and storks.
It is very difficult to reach this lake,
And no one can come here without Ram's grace.
Bad companions are bad roads, difficult and frightening,
And their words are the tigers, lions and snakes along the way;
Domestic affairs, the demands of house and hearth, and other such
    entanglements—
They are vast and impassable mountains.
Worldly attachment, lustful desire and arrogance are dense and
    impenetrable forests,
And sophistry, wrong reasoning and false doctrine are various
    raging rivers, frightening and formidable.

    Those who are without the provisions of faith required for
        the journey,
    Who do not travel in the company of saints and good people,
    And who do not love Raghunath—
    For them, I say, the Manas is inaccessible.   (38)

And even if someone, undertaking great hardship, does go to
    the lake,
Sleep and shivering fits overcome him as soon as he arrives.
An intense and disagreeable cold settles upon his heart, leaving him
    as a thing inanimate,

And the unfortunate wretch is unable to take a dip in the lake.
Not having bathed in the lake or drunk its water,
He returns, full of arrogance,
And then when someone comes to ask him about his experience,
He speaks disparagingly of the lake and abuses it.
But all these obstacles do not stop one
Whom Ram looks upon with loving favour;
Such a one bathes in the lake with reverence
And is not burnt by the triple fires and fierce flames of the three afflictions.
Men who hold dear Ram's feet
Never leave or abandon this lake.
They who wish to bathe in this lake, my friend,
Should with diligence keep the company of good men.
Having contemplated this Manas lake with the mind's eye,
The poet's intellect became clear and profound;
Bliss and gladness welled up in his heart
And poured out in a flood of love and joy.
This glittering stream of elegant poetry flows on,
Swollen with the waters of Ram's unblemished glory.
Sarju is its name, it is the root of all bliss,
And worldly wisdom and Vedic doctrine are its two pleasing banks.
This sacred river, daughter of the beautiful Manas lake,
Uproots and destroys along its course, the small blades of grass and
    the mighty trees that are the sins, small and big, of the age
    of Kali.

    Gatherings of the three kinds of listeners[41]
    Are the towns, villages and cities on the two banks,
    While the assembly of saints is the incomparable city of Avadh,
    The source of all well-being.   (39)

Into the divine River Ganga that is devotion to Ram
Flows the beautiful Sarju that is Ram's glory and mingles with it;
The sparkling stream of the great River Sone,

That is the splendour of Ram and Lakshman in battle, joins it.
Between the Sarju and the Sone shines the divine Ganga's stream
    of devotion,
Made splendid with detachment and contemplation.
The triple fires of affliction are frightened away by this
    triple stream,
As it flows towards the ocean that is Ram himself.
With its source in the Manas lake, and flowing into the
    divine Ganga,
The Sarju purifies the hearts of those good people who listen to
    Ram's story;
The extraordinary and remarkable tales scattered here and there in
    his story
Are like the groves and gardens on each bank of the river.
The guests at the wedding of Uma and Mahesh,
Are the countless and diverse creatures dwelling in its waters.
The joyful celebrations of Raghubar's birth,
Are the heart-enchanting beauty of its eddies and waves.

    The childhood exploits of the four brothers,
    Are the abundant and many-coloured lotuses,
    And the virtuous deeds of the king, his queens and his
        household,
    Are the bees and waterbirds.   (40)

The charming story of Sita's svayamvar, where she chose Ram to be
    her husband,
Is the all-pervasive brilliance of this bright and pleasing stream.
The boats on the river are the many astute and incisive questions
    asked,
And the appropriate and discerning answers, the skilful boatmen.
Upon listening to this story, the discussions that arise amongst
    the listeners
Are the companies of travellers along the banks of this graceful river.

Its strong and powerful current is the wrath of Bhrigunath,[xxxvii]
While Ram's soft and gentle words, its sturdy and well-constructed
    ghats.
The joy with which Ram's wedding and those of his younger
    brothers was celebrated
Is the swelling tide bringing good fortune to all.
Those who rejoice in the telling of Ram's story and are enraptured
    upon hearing it
Bathe with delight in its waters with virtuous hearts.
The festive preparations for Ram's anointment as Dasharath's heir
Are the crowds that assemble on auspicious, sacred days;
The scum and water-moss are Kaikeyi's wilful mind,
The fruit of which was great misfortune.

    The deeds of Bharat are the prayers and fire-sacrifices
    That destroy and burn away all the wrongs in this world,
    While the accounts of the sins, the evil and the vices of the age
        of Kali
    Are the filth in the water, and the storks and crows.   (41)

This river of Ram's renown is beautiful in all six seasons,
Pleasing and exceedingly pure at all times—
Winter is the wedding of Parvati, daughter of the snowy
    mountains, to Shiv;
The season of dew and mist, the glad celebrations at the Lord's birth;
The account of the gathering for Ram's wedding celebrations
Is the joyous spring, that king of the seasons;
The intolerable summer is Ram's departure for the forest,
And the cruel tale of his wanderings is the searing heat of the sun
    and the wind.
The season of rains is his terrible battle with the demons of
    the night,

[xxxvii] Parashuram

Which was as beneficial to the gods as rain is to the
     paddy fields,
And the prosperity and well-being during Ram's reign, his
     greatness and gentle bearing
Are the bright, clear and pleasant days of autumn.
The singing of the virtues of Sita, that crowning jewel of
     chaste womanhood,
Is the matchless purity and clarity of this river's water,
And Bharat's gentle disposition is its pleasing coolness,
Which is unvarying, unchanging and cannot be described.

     The affectionate manner in which the four brothers
     Look at each other, talk to each other and embrace each other,
     The love between them and the laughter, their happy
          camaraderie—
     These are the water's sweetness and fragrance.   (42)

My own adoration of him, my reverence and humility,
Is the lightness of this graceful stream.
This astonishing water is beneficial even when merely heard,
Quenching the thirst of longing and cleansing the impurities of
     the heart.
This water nourishes true love for Ram
And washes away all the sins and debilities of the age of Kali.
It drains away the fatigue of rebirth, makes content
     contentment itself,
And annihilates evil, sorrow, poverty and vice.
It destroys lust, anger, arrogance and delusion
And encourages clear thinking, true knowledge and detachment
     from this world.
All sin and sorrow are effaced from the hearts
Of those who bathe in it or drink this water with reverence—
Those who have not cleansed their hearts in this water
Are cowards deceived by the Kaliyug;

They are as miserable as the thirsty deer that, seeing the sun change
    land into water,
Rushes to drink, but finds no water and returns disappointed.

    Thus, enumerating to the best of his intellectual ability,
    The many virtues of this sweet water, immersing his heart in it,
    And meditating upon Bhavani and Shankar,
    This poet will tell his beautiful story.   (43A)

    Now, placing my heart at Raghupati's lotus feet
    And receiving his grace,
    I relate the meeting of the two great munis,
    And their auspicious conversation.   (43B)

The Muni Bharadvaj lived in Prayag,
And was greatly devoted to Ram.
An ascetic, he was the embodiment of self-restraint, contemplation
    and compassion
And the most knowledgeable about the path to the Supreme Truth.
In the month of Magh, when the sun enters Makar,
Everyone visits Prayag, the first amongst pilgrimage places;
Gods, Danavas, Kinnaras and multitudes of men,
All bathe with great reverence in the triveni, the triple stream of
    the Ganga, the Jamuna and the Sarasvati.
They worship the lotus feet of Madhav,[xxxviii]
And rejoice in the touch of the imperishable banyan tree.
Bharadvaj's hermitage is a place holy and pure,
And so exceedingly pleasant that it delights the hearts of even the
    greatest sages.
There gather the rishis and the munis
Who come to bathe at Prayag,
And having with gladness taken the ritual dip at break of day,
They discuss with each other the virtues of Hari.

[xxxviii]   Vishnu/Krishna, as the presiding deity of Prayag

They examine the attributes of the Absolute, and discuss the
　　duties and laws of dharma,
They describe the various systems of philosophy,
And declare that devotion to the Lord
Requires both knowledge and detachment.　　　　　　(44)

In this manner they bathe here for the full month of Magh,
And then return, each to their own ashrams.
Every year the same joyful gathering takes place,
And after the ritual Makar bathing, the crowd of sages departs.
Once, after the full one month of the ritual bathing,
When all the other munis had returned to their ashrams,
Bharadvaj clasped the feet of Jagbalik, the wisest muni of all,
And begged him to remain.
With great respect he washed his lotus feet,
And led him to a seat most pure and sacred;
With great reverence he related the muni's glorious fame,
And then addressed him in the most gentle and respectful
　　of tones—
'My master, I am greatly confused,
And you, in your hands, hold the essence of the Vedas;
To speak my question aloud makes me afraid and ashamed,
But if I do not say it, I will lose a great opportunity.

　　The saints give this counsel, my lord,
　　And the Vedas, the Puranas and the sages declare it as well—
　　That true knowledge will not dawn in the heart,
　　If one conceals anything from one's guru.　　　　　(45)

Keeping this in mind, I reveal my ignorance.
Dispel it, my master, taking pity on your servant.
The name of Ram has immeasurable power—
The saints, the Puranas and the Upanishads all say so.
Immortal Shambhu chants it continuously,
The divine Lord Shiv, repository of knowledge and virtue;

And when the four kinds of living beings in this world
Die in Kashi, they attain the highest state that is salvation,
That too, O greatest of the munis, is by the glory of Ram's name,
The use of which Shiv in his compassion exhorts.
So I ask you this, my lord—who is this Ram?
Explain it to me, O compassionate one, make me understand.
One Ram is the son of the king of Avadh,
Whose deeds are renowned in all the world;
Separated from his wife, he suffered boundless grief,
Then, growing angry, he killed Ravan in battle.

> My lord, is it this same Ram or another,
> Whose name Tripurari repeats?
> You are the repository of truth, all-wise, omniscient—
> So with your wisdom, reflect upon my question and tell me.   (46)

So that my great confusion may be dispelled,
Relate his story in full, my master.'
Jagbalik replied with a smile,
'Raghupati's great majesty is already known to you,
You are Ram's devotee in thought, deed and word.
But I have understood your clever ploy—
You want to hear the hidden mysteries of Ram's virtues,
Which is why you question me as if you are a complete blockhead.
So listen then, my son, with reverent attention,
As I relate Ram's charming story—
Extreme delusion is the enormous buffalo demon, Mahishasur,
And the story of Ram is the formidable goddess, Kalika;[xxxix]
Ram's story is like the moonbeams
Which the saints, like chakors, drink.
Bhavani once expressed a similar doubt,
Upon which Mahadev narrated the story in detail.

[xxxix] Parvati, in her fierce form

I will now relate, to the best of my ability,
That conversation between Uma and Shambhu,
And when and why it took place.
Listen well, O muni, and your sorrows will vanish.   (47)

Once, during the Tretayug,[xl]
Shambhu went to visit the Rishi Kumbhaj.
With him went his devoted wife, Sati, who is also Bhavani, mother
     of the world,
The rishi honoured him, knowing him to be Akhileshvar, Lord of
     all Creation.
The great muni related at length the story of Ram—
To which Mahesh listened with the greatest delight.
The rishi then asked him about true devotion to Hari,
And Shambhu, seeing him to be deserving, replied.
Reciting and listening to the story of Raghupati's virtues,
The lord of Kailash spent several days there.
Then, taking his leave of the muni,
He turned towards home with Sati, daughter of Daksh.
At that very time, Hari, the destroyer of the burdens of the world,
Had become incarnate in the family of Raghu;
At his father's word, he, the Eternal God, had renounced
     the throne,
And was wandering as an ascetic in the Dandak forest.

As he went, Har kept thinking,
'How might I look upon him?
The Lord has become incarnate in a form unknown
     to anyone—
If I visit him, everyone will come to know the form
     that he has taken.'   (48A)

[xl]   The second of the four ages of the world.

In Shankar's heart there was great disquiet,
Though Sati did not see this secret distress.
He yearned to see the Lord, says Tulsi,
His heart was afraid, though his eyes were
     greedy for the sight.   (48B)

'Ravan was granted the boon of death only at the hands of a man[42]
And the Lord wants to make Vidhi's promise come true—
But if I do not go, I will regret it forever.'
Thus, he pondered but found no solution.
In this manner, Ish[xli] became lost in thought.
At that very moment, the ten-headed Ravan
Took with him the base Marichi,
Who immediately assumed the false form of a kurang deer.
Through deceit and subterfuge the fool carried off Vaidehi—[xlii]
He did not know the Lord's great power.
After killing the deer, Hari returned with his brother—
Upon seeing his empty hermitage, his eyes filled with tears.
Raghurai was distracted with grief like a mortal man,
And the two brothers wandered through the forest, searching
     for her.
He, for whom there is no union and no parting,
Showed the grief of separation from his beloved.

     Very mysterious are Raghupati's deeds—
     Only the most enlightened understand them;
     Those who are dull of wit and in the grip of illusion,
     Take some other, quite different meaning in their hearts.   (49)

It was then that Shambhu saw Ram—
In his heart arose joy extraordinary,

[xli] Shiv
[xlii] Sita

And he gazed his fill upon that ocean of grace and beauty.

Knowing that it was an inappropriate moment, he did not make
    himself known,

Instead, saying only, 'Hail Supreme Spirit, Sachchidanand,[43]
    redeemer of the universe!'

The destroyer of the heartborn god of love passed by.

As Shiv with Sati continued on his way,

He, the abode of compassion, was again and again overcome
    with joy.

When Sati saw Shambhu in this state,

A great doubt arose in her heart—

'Shankar is adored by the whole world, he is Jagadish, lord of
    the universe,

Gods, men and munis, all bow their heads to him,

And yet he saluted this king's son,

Hailed him as the Supreme Spirit and the saviour of the world,

And upon beholding his beauty he has become so enraptured

That even now he cannot contain the love he feels within his heart.

The Supreme Spirit, all-pervading, passionless, uncreated,
Who is unitary, without desire, without duality,
Which even the Vedas cannot comprehend—
Can it take on bodily form as a man?   (50)

Vishnu, who for the benefit of the gods, takes on human form,

Is as omniscient as Tripurari—

Would he then search for a woman like one who does not know,

He who is Shri's[xliii] lord, the abode of wisdom, and the enemy
    of demons?

And then again, Shambhu's words are never false,

For, as everyone knows, Shiv is all-seeing.'

Her mind was beset with this boundless doubt,

_____

xliii Lakshmi

And neither understanding nor explanation arose in her heart.
Even though Bhavani did not say anything out loud,
Har, who can see into the heart, understood everything.
He said, 'Listen, Sati, your nature is that of a woman—
Never hold such doubt in your heart!
He whose story the Rishi Kumbhaj related,
And whose true worship I explained to the muni—
He is that very same, my beloved god, Raghubir,
Who is forever worshipped by steadfast munis.

He is that same Ram upon whom steadfast munis and yogis, Siddhis
    and sages
Meditate with pure and unwavering hearts;
Whose glory is sung by the Vedas, the Puranas, and Shastras
By crying, "He is not this, he is not this";
Who is the all-pervading spirit of the universe,
Lord of all the worlds, master of maya;
And who, for the benefit of his devotees, by his own free will
Took incarnate form as the jewel of the clan of Raghu.'

    Shiv's explanation did not convince Sati
    Even though he repeated it several times.
    Recognizing the strength of Hari's maya
    Mahesh, smiling, said—   (51)

'If there is such great doubt in your mind,
Why don't you go and test him?
I will sit here, in the shade of this banyan tree,
Till you come back to me.
Think, use your judgement, strive to do that which
May resolve your overwhelming perplexity and confusion.'
So off went Sati with Shiv's permission—
'Now, what shall I do?' she wondered.
Meanwhile, Shambhu, reflecting, came to the conclusion that,

'There is no hope for Daksh's daughter,
For her doubts have not been dispelled even by my words.
But there is nothing to be gained by going against destiny,
And whatever Ram has ordained will come to pass—
So why speculate or dispute it any further and prolong the argument?'
So saying, he began to chant the name of Hari,
While Sati proceeded towards the Lord, that abode of bliss.

> Again and again she thought and she pondered.
> Then, assuming Sita's form,
> She went ahead upon on the same path
> Along which the king of men, Ram, was coming. (52)

Lakshman, seeing Uma's disguise,
Was astonished and greatly perplexed.
He could say nothing but became very grave—
He of the steadfast mind knew well the glory of the Lord.
The Lord of the gods recognized Sati's deception—
All-seeing, pervading all hearts,
Meditating upon whom removes all ignorance,
He was the same all-knowing Ram, supreme God.
Sati tried to deceive even him—
See the power of the female disposition!
But Ram acknowledged to himself the strength of his own maya
And smiling, spoke in sweet tones.
Folding his hands, the Lord saluted her,
And gave his father's name as well as his own.
He then asked, 'Where is Brishketu?
And why are you wandering alone in the forest?'

> Hearing Ram's sweet but profoundly perceptive words,
> Sati was greatly abashed.
> Fearful and afraid, her heart full of apprehension,
> She made her way back to Mahesh. (53)

'I did not listen to Shankar,
And imposed my own ignorance upon Ram.
Now what answer will I give Shiv upon my return?'
Dreadful anguish filled her breast.
Ram saw that Sati was suffering,
And revealed some of his glory to her.
As Sati walked along the path, she saw a strange and marvellous
     spectacle—
Ahead of her was Ram himself, with Shri and his brother!
Turning, she looked back and saw again the Lord,
And with him were his brother and Sita, gloriously attired!
Wherever she looked, she saw the Lord enthroned,
And attending upon him wise and accomplished holy men and munis.
She saw innumerable Shivs, Vidhis and Vishnus,
Each more splendid than the others in their boundless glory
     and grandeur.
She saw the gods in many and various forms,
All paying homage at the Lord's feet.

She saw Satis, Vidhatris and Indiras too,[xliv]
Countless and incomparable.
Whatever the forms the gods assumed,
According to those were the forms of these goddesses,
     their consorts.   (54)

Wherever she looked, she saw Raghupati.
There, too, were all the gods and with them were their Shaktis,[xlv]
And all created things, animate and inanimate, that are in this world—
She saw them all, in many shapes and forms.
Assuming many guises, the gods worshipped the Lord,

[xliv] Sati, consort of Shiv; Vidhatri, the goddess Sarasvati, consort of Brahma;
     and Indira, the goddess Lakshmi, consort of Vishnu
[xlv] The energy or active power of a deity personified as his wife

But of Ram, she saw no other guise—
Though she saw Raghupati countless times with Sita,
He did not assume different forms.
It was always the same Raghubar, the same Lakshman and Sita—
Seeing their constant forms, Sati grew afraid.
Her heart trembled, and losing all perception,
She shut her eyes and sank down upon the path.
When she opened her eyes and looked around again,
Daksh's daughter saw no one there.
Bowing her head again and again at Ram's feet,
She returned to where waited her lord of the mountains.

> When she reached Mahesh,
> He smiled and asked if she were well.
> 'What was the manner in which you tested him?
> Come, truthfully tell me all,' he said.   (55)

Sati had now understood Raghubir's glory—
Afraid, she hid the truth from Shiv.
'I did not try to test him, lord
I merely paid him homage as you do.
What you said could not be false—
I am certain of that in my heart.'
Then Shankar, through meditation, saw and
Understood all that Sati had done.
Once more he bowed his head to the strength of Ram's maya
Which had caused even Sati to speak an untruth.
'The future ordained by Hari will prevail,'
Reflected all-wise Shambhu in his heart.
But Sati had assumed Sita's form,
And great desolation arose in Shiv's heart.
'If I were to love Sati now as I did before,
I will commit a great wrong, and the path of devotion will be mine
    no longer.

She is most chaste, she cannot be abandoned,
But to love her will be a grievous sin.'
Mahesh did not speak a word aloud,
But his heart burned with anguish.   (56)

Then Shankar bowed his head at the Lord's feet,
And as he meditated upon Ram, he realized,
'As long as Sati remains in this body, I cannot touch her!'
So Shiv resolved in his mind.
Reflecting thus, Shankar of the steadfast mind
Turned towards home, meditating upon Raghubir.
As he walked came a glorious cry from the heavens,
'Hail Mahesh, glory to you, who has shown such
      firm devotion!
Who but you could have taken this vow,
You, Ram's devotee, and mighty, all-powerful God!'
Hearing this voice from the sky, Sati's heart grew troubled.
Hesitantly, she asked Shiv,
'Tell me, O compassionate lord, what vow is this that you
      have taken,
You who are the abode of truth, and merciful to the distressed?'
But though Sati asked many times, in many ways,
The enemy of Tripur did not reply.

In her heart Sati supposed
That the all-seeing Shiv had understood all,
'I tried to deceive Shambhu!
Woman that I am, by nature foolish and ignorant!'   (57A)

Water, when mixed with milk, sells at a similar price—
See how this mixture is like the ways of love!
The moment the sourness of deceit is added
The lovers separate like curds and whey, and love loses its
      flavour and delight.   (57B)

Her heart full of regret, and realizing what she had done,
Her anxiety knew no bounds.
'Shiv is an infinite ocean of compassion,
So he does not mention my offence aloud!'
Bhavani looked at Shankar's countenance and understood—
'My lord has abandoned me!' She was distracted with grief.
She understood her mistake, but there was nothing she could say—
The anguish in her heart was as intense as the heat of a furnace.
When Brishketu saw Sati so full of sorrow,
He began to relate pleasant and pleasing tales.
Thus, telling stories and recounting various legends along the way,
The lord of the world, Vishvanath, reached Kailash.
There, remembering his vow, Shambhu
Sat down in the lotus pose under a banyan tree.
Shankar withdrew into his own true self,
And passed into samadhi, profound, endless, infinite.

> Sati dwelt on Kailash,
> Great sorrow in her heart;
> No one knew her secret grief,
> The days passed like aeons. (58)

A new and daily grief made Sati's heart heavy—
'When will I cross this ocean of sorrow,
I, who was disrespectful to the lord of the Raghus
And then believed my own lord's words to be untrue?
For these faults Fate has rewarded me,
And bestowed upon me that which I deserved.
But now, O Vidhi, with Shankar having turned his face away from me,
It does not befit you to keep me alive!'
The weariness of her heart cannot be told.
Wisely, Sati then meditated upon Ram himself—
'The Lord who is called the merciful one
Whom the Vedas celebrate as the destroyer of distress,

Him I beseech with folded hands
To free me quickly from this body of mine.
If I have any love for Shiv's feet,
And if that vow of love is true in thought, word and deed,

> Hear me, O all-seeing Lord,
> And quickly find a way
> By which I may effortlessly die,
> So that this intolerable agony may pass.'   (59)

Thus was the daughter of Prajesh afflicted
With sorrow so cruel and intense that it cannot be described.
Eighty-seven thousand years passed,
And immortal Shambhu broke his samadhi.
As Shiv began to chant the name of Ram,
Sati knew that the lord of the world had awakened.
She went to Shambhu and bowed in reverence at his feet—
Shankar gave her a seat facing him
And began relating Hari's stories, so filled with joy and delight.
It was at that very time, that Daksh became Prajesh—
Vidhi, considering him able and deserving in every way,
Made him the supreme lord of created beings.
When Daksh attained this high title
Great arrogance filled his heart—
Never has one been born in this world,
Who has acquired power and not become intoxicated by it.

> Daksh gathered all the munis together
> And ordered them to hold a great fire-sacrifice
> To which he respectfully invited all the gods
> Who receive a share of the sacrificial offerings.   (60)

Kinnaras, Nagas, Siddhas and Gandharvas set off,
And all the gods with their wives—

All except for Vishnu, Viranchi and Mahesh—
All the gods made ready their chariots and set forth.
Sati saw their chariots in the sky,
So many of them, gaily decorated, flying past,
As celestial nymphs sang songs so sweet
That, hearing them, even munis were distracted from their meditations.
When she asked, Shiv explained.
Hearing of her father's fire-sacrifice, she felt a little happier.
'If Mahesh gives me permission,
I will use this excuse to visit my father's house and stay there for
    a few days.'
Her heart was still heavy from her husband's renunciation of
    their love,
But she, poor woman, conscious of her transgression, had uttered
    not a word in protest;
Now, afraid, hesitant, steeped in love,
Sati spoke these sweet and gentle words—

'There's great rejoicing in my father's house.
If my lord permits,
I will go, O compassionate one,
To attend that celebration in duty and respect.'   (61)

'Your suggestion is good and it pleases me,' said Shiv,
'But it is not feasible since he has not sent you an invitation.
Daksh has invited all his daughters
But because of his enmity with me, he has left you out.
Once, in Brahma's assembly he was displeased with me,
And because of that he shows us disrespect today.
If you go without being invited, Bhavani,
Neither propriety nor any affection or regard will remain.
Even though there is no doubt that it is possible to go
To the house of a friend, a master, a father, or a guru
    without invitation,

Going where someone holds a grudge against you
Results in nothing good.'
Shambhu tried to explain this to her in many ways,
But Sati, in destiny's grip, did not understand.
The Lord said, 'In my opinion, it is not right
To go without being invited.'

> He made every effort to convince her but saw that despite all
>   his explanations,
> Daksh's daughter would not stay.
> So, assigning the best of his servants to accompany her,
> Tripurari bade her farewell.   (62)

When Bhavani reached her father's house,
Out of fear of Daksh, no one greeted her or paid her homage.
Only her mother met her with respect and affection
And her sisters with many smiles.
Daksh did not utter a word of welcome nor ask after Sati's well-being,
Rather, he burned with rage to see her;
Sati then went to look at the fire-sacrifice,
But nowhere did she see Shambhu's share of the offering.
She then understood what Shankar had been saying,
And her heart burned within her at this insult to her lord.
Her earlier sorrow did not overwhelm her heart
As much as the great grief that overtook her now,
For though there are many cruel sorrows in the world,
The most difficult to bear is an insult to one's own.
Thinking of this, Sati was overcome with fury;
Her mother tried in many ways to calm her.

> She could not bear this insult to Shiv,
> And her heart would not be pacified.
> Reproaching violently all those gathered there,
> She cried out in anger.   (63)

'Listen to me, all you gathered here, you great saints and holy men—
Those who have insulted Shankar or heard him being insulted,
They will get their reward at once.
My father too shall dearly rue it!
Whenever the saints, Shambhu, or Shri's lord are spoken ill of
     or maligned,
The prescribed and principled course of action is
To cut out, if you can, the tongue of the one who speaks ill,
Or close your ears and run away!
The Spirit of the Universe, Mahesh, Purari,
The father of the world, benefactor and friend to all—
It is him that my foolish and wicked father has insulted!
This body of mine was born of Daksh's seed—
For that reason I discard it at once,
Holding in my heart moon-crested Brishketu!'
As she said this, her body was consumed by yogic fire,
And loud lamentation arose from the gathering.

> Hearing of Sati's death, Shambhu's servants
> Began to lay waste the sacrificial feast.
> Seeing the destruction of the fire-sacrifice,
> The great sage Bhrigu protected the munis.   (64)

When Shankar heard the news
He, in his fury, created Virbhadra[44] and sent him there—
He laid waste the fire-sacrifice,
And gave all the gods their just reward.
As is known around the world, Daksh was reduced to the
     same plight
To which are reduced those who turn away from Shambhu.
The whole world knows this story—
Which is why I have related it only in brief.
Sati, dying, asked Hari for this boon
That she find love at Shiv's feet in every successive birth.

For that reason, in Himgiri's[xlvi] home,
She was reborn as Parvati.
From the moment that Uma was born in the mountain king's home,
Felicity and prosperity pervaded it.
Munis set up their hermitages all about
In suitable abodes upon the mountain that Himvat[xlvii] gave to them.

> There, young trees of different kinds appeared,
> Always in flower, always laden with fruit,
> And upon that beautiful mountain became manifest
> Mines of precious stones of many kinds.   (65)

The rivers all flowed with pure and clear water,
The birds, the deer and the bees all lived in happiness
      and harmony.
All creatures that dwelt upon that mountain gave up
Their natural enmity and regarded each other with affection.
With Girija's arrival in Himalaya's home, the mountain became a
      place of splendour
As a man finding devotion to Ram becomes suffused with light;
Every day new celebrations took place in his home,
As Brahma and the other gods sang his glory.
Upon hearing the news, Narad
Set off for Himalaya's home in great joy;
The king of the mountains greeted him with great respect,
And washing his feet, gave him a seat of high honour.
With his wife, he bowed his head before the muni,
And had his whole house sprinkled with the water he had used to
      wash the sage's feet.
The king declared in detail his own good fortune
And summoning his daughter, he placed her at the muni's feet.

[xlvi] Himalaya
[xlvii] Himalaya

'You are omniscient, and pervade all time, past, present
   and future,
Your reach is everywhere—
So consider carefully in your heart, great muni,
And tell me the virtues and faults of my daughter.'   (66)

The muni replied with a smile in sweet but enigmatical words,
'Your daughter has an abundance of every virtue,
She is beautiful, amiable, good-natured and intelligent,
And her names will be Uma, Ambika and Bhavani.
The maiden is endowed with every good quality.
She will always be her husband's beloved,
Who will be forever steady and firm by her side—
From this her father and mother will find fame and glory.
She will be worshipped throughout the whole world,
In her service, nothing will be impossible or difficult to attain.
Remembering her name, women in this world
Will walk the narrow, sword-sharp path of fidelity to their husbands.
O king of the mountain, your daughter is blessed with every good
   fortune and auspicious quality,
But hear now the two or three shortcomings—
Without virtue, without pride, without mother or father,
Indifferent to the world, without concern or care,

   A yogi with matted locks, and a heart without desire,
   Naked, in appearance disagreeable—
   Such a husband will your daughter find,
   For such are the lines on her palm.'   (67)

Hearing the muni's words, and realizing their truth,
The father and mother were sorrowful, but Uma was delighted.
Even Narad did not see this difference,
For their outward reaction was the same, though their
   understanding was different.

Girija and her companions, and Himvat and his wife, Maina,
All trembled with emotion, and their eyes filled with tears.
A divine rishi's utterance could not be wrong—
Knowing this, Uma held his words carefully in her heart.
Love for Shiv's lotus feet sprang up in her heart,
Though in her mind she was apprehensive that finding him would
        be difficult.
Knowing it was not the right moment to declare it, she hid
        her love,
And went again to sit with her friends.
A divine rishi's words are never untrue—
Thinking thus, her parents and her wiser companions
        grew anxious.
Steadying himself, the mountain king asked,
'Tell us, O lord, what can we do to remedy this?'

        Said the muni, 'Listen to me, Himvant—
        No god, no demon, no man, Naga, or muni
        Can erase
        That which Fate has written upon the forehead.   (68)

Even so, I will suggest a stratagem
Which may be successful if the gods help.
There is no doubt that Uma will get
A bridegroom such as I have described.
But each of the faults and shortcomings of the bridegroom that I
        have delineated,
May all be found in Shiv.
If she were to marry Shankar,
Everyone would declare these faults to be virtues.
Though Hari, reposing upon Sheshnag, uses a serpent as his bed,
The wise and learned do not hold it as a fault in him;
The sun and fire consume all moisture,
But no one calls them evil.

Clear as well as dirty water flows into her,
Yet no one calls the divine Ganga impure;
The mighty have no faults, O king,
Just as the sun, fire, or the divine river have none.

> If foolish men, arrogant in their intelligence,
> Try to emulate them,
> They fall for an aeon into the mouth of hell.
> Can any man be equal to the Supreme Lord?   (69)

Even if liquor was made with Ganga water,
Holy men would never drink it;
Yet, when poured into the Ganga, it becomes pure—
Such is the difference between God and man!
Shambhu is the inherently all-powerful Supreme Lord,
And in this marriage there is every kind of good.
Though it is certainly true that Mahesh is difficult to worship,
He is also quickly pleased by penance;
If your daughter practises penance,
Tripurari can erase what has been ordained.
Though there are many bridegrooms in the world,
For her there is Shiv and no other.
He is the giver of boons, the destroyer of the enemies of
    the humble;
An ocean of compassion, he delights the hearts of those who
    serve him.
No wish, no desire may be attained without propitiating Shiv,
Even if countless austerities and penances be practised
    or performed.'

> So saying, and remembering Hari, Narad
> Gave Girija his blessings, and said,
> 'This good fortune will come to pass,
> So now abandon all doubt, O lord of the mountain.'   (70)

Thus saying, the muni left for Brahma's abode.
Now listen to what happened next—
Finding her husband alone, Maina said,
'My lord, I did not understand the muni's words.
If there be a family, a bridegroom, and a lineage without equal
Worthy of our daughter, let the wedding be performed,
Otherwise, let the girl remain unwed.
Husband, Uma is as dear to me as life itself—
If we cannot find a husband worthy of Girija
Everyone will say, "That Himvant is a blockhead and a fool."
Bear that in mind, my husband, while arranging her wedding,
So that there be no grief or regret later on.'
Speaking thus, she fell at his feet and laid her head upon them.
The lord of the mountain lovingly replied,
'Flames may appear and fire become manifest in the moon,
But Narad's words can never be untrue.

    Beloved, cast aside all worry
    And meditate upon the Supreme God.
    He who has created Parvati
    Will also ensure her well-being.   (71)

Now, if you love your daughter,
Go to her and advise her that
She should practise those austerities by which she may find Mahesh—
There is no other way to get rid of this distress.
Narad's words are full of meaning and uttered for a reason—
Brishketu is endowed with every good quality.
Reflect upon this and abandon doubt—
Shankar is, in every way, without fault or blemish.'
Hearing her husband's words she rejoiced in her heart,
And, rising, went at once to Girija.
On seeing Uma, her eyes filled with tears,
And lovingly she took her on her lap.

Again and again she hugged her to her bosom,
Her throat full, choking with emotion, unable to speak.
Then all-knowing Bhavani, mother of the universe,
Spoke in sweet tones to reassure her mother.

>'Listen, Mother, I had a dream
>Which I will relate to you—
>A noble Brahman, handsome, fair-skinned,
>Instructed me thus: (72)

"Go, practise penance, O daughter of the mountain,
Regard as truth Narad's words;·
Your mother and your father have liked this idea too,
For penance gives happiness and destroys sorrow and sin.
It is through the power of penance that Brahma creates
     this universe,
It is through the power of penance that Vishnu protects the
     whole world,
It is through the power of penance that Shambhu destroys it,[45]
And it is through the power of penance that Sheshnag supports the
     weight of the earth.
Upon penance rests all creation, Bhavani—
Knowing this in your heart, go then and practise it.'"
Hearing these words, her mother was wonderstruck,
And calling out for her husband, related the dream to him.
Reassuring her mother and father in many ways,
Uma, in great joy, set off to practise penance.
Her beloved family, her father and her mother,
Grew distressed and sorrowful and no words came to their lips.

>Then came the great Muni Vedashira
>And reassured them.
>Hearing of Parvati's glory,
>They were comforted and consoled.   (73)

Uma, with devotion to her beloved lord's feet in her heart,
Went into the forest and began her penance.
Her youthful body and delicate frame were not suited for
      such austerities,
But meditating upon her lord's feet she gave up all comforts.
Each day, her love gained new strength,
She grew unmindful of her body, and fixed her mind only
      upon penance.
For a thousand years she ate only roots and fruits,
Then, eating only leaves and herbs, she passed another
      hundred years.
For some days, her food was air and water,
And for some days, she observed a strict and severe fast.
For three thousand years, she ate
The withered leaves of the bel tree[46] scattered upon the ground.
Then she gave up even those dry leaves.
Thus did Uma's name become 'Aparna', 'she who is deprived
      of leaves'.
Seeing Uma's body wasted by fasting,
Brahma's deep voice filled the sky—

      'Listen, O daughter of the mountain!
      Your heart's desire has been fulfilled.
      Abandon all these intolerable austerities,
      For now you will find Tripurari.   (74)

No one has performed such penance, Bhavani,
Though there have been many saints, steadfast and wise.
Now keep in your heart these words from heaven,
Knowing them to be always true and forever holy.
When your father comes to call you
Give up your austerities and go home with him.
And when you meet the Saptarishi, the seven sages,
You will understand the truth of these words.'

Hearing Vidhi's proclamation from the skies,
Girija, thrilled, rejoiced.
I have sung the enchanting story of Uma—
Now listen to the charming story of Shambhu.
From the moment that Sati had left, giving up her body,
Shiv's heart had lost all interest in this world.
He constantly chanted Raghunayak's name,
And wandered here and there, listening to the recitation of
     Ram's virtues.

Shiv, who is knowledge, joy, and bliss embodied,
Who transcends love, desire and passion,
Wanders the earth, holding Hari,
The delight of all the worlds, in his heart.   (75)

Here he discourses to the munis upon knowledge and true
     wisdom,
There he relates and describes the virtues of Ram.
Though he is forever detached and free from desire,
The all-wise Supreme Lord suffered the grief of separation from
     his devoted wife, Sati.
In this manner many ages passed,
And each day Shankar's love for Ram was renewed.
Seeing his great piety and love,
And the steadfast devotion he held in his heart,
Ram appeared before him.
Compassionate, ever mindful of former favours,
Full of beauty and grace, and radiant in his majesty,
He praised Shankar in many ways,
'Who but you could have sustained such a vow?'
Ram consoled Shiv in every way he could,
And told him the story of Parvati's birth.
The compassionate Lord related at length
Her exceptionally pure and virtuous actions, then said,

'Now listen to my plea, Shiv—
If you have love for me,
Go and marry the daughter of the mountain.
Grant me this request of mine.'   (76)

'Though this is not appropriate,' replied Shiv,
'The Lord's words, once spoken, cannot be denied.
Holding your wish in deepest reverence, I will do as you desire,
For this, Lord, is my greatest duty.
The words of one's mother, one's father, one's teacher and
    the Lord
Must be regarded as right and obeyed without thought or question.
You are in every way my greatest benefactor—
Your command, Lord, I honour.'
The Lord heard Shankar's words with satisfaction,
Imbued as they were with devotion, wisdom and righteousness.
Said the Lord, 'Har, your vow has been fulfilled.
Now keep in mind what I have said.'
So saying, he disappeared,
But Shankar kept his image in his heart.
At that very moment the Saptarishi came to Shiv,
And the god addressed them in pleasant tones.

'Go to Parvati, all of you,
And test her love;
Then send the mountain king to her and have her brought
    home,
And remove her anxiety and uncertainty.'   (77)

When the rishis saw Gauri there,
She looked like penance personified.
Said the munis, 'Tell us, daughter of the mountain,
Why do you practise such harsh penance?
Whom do you worship and what do you desire?

Why don't you tell us the truth hidden in the recesses of your heart?'
'I shrink from telling you my secret,
For you will laugh to hear of my foolishness.
My heart is obstinate and heeds no counsel—
It would raise a wall on water!
Taking Narad's words as truth,
Without wings I want to fly.
Look at my foolishness, O munis—
I long constantly for Shiv as my husband.'

> Hearing her words, the rishis laughed and said,
> 'You have truly been begotten of the mountain!
> Tell us, who has ever attained home and hearth
> Listening to Narad's words?   (78)

He had instructed the sons of Daksh
Because of which they never saw their home again,[47]
He ruined Chitraketu's home,[48]
And reduced Kanakakasipu to the same state.[49]
The men and women who listen to Narad's advice
Most certainly lose their homes and become beggars.
Though outwardly he bears all the signs of a good man, his heart
     is deceitful—
He would make everyone like himself!
It is his words you have believed, and trusting them,
You want a husband who is inherently disinterested in everything,
Who is without attributes, cares nothing for the world, and has
     neither lineage nor a home;
With only the sky for a robe, skulls around his neck and serpents
     wound upon him, his attire is most inauspicious.
Tell us, what happiness will you get with such a husband?
It best that you forget the ravings of that thug Narad!
Shiv married Sati because the elders said he should,
And then he abandoned her and caused her to die.

Now he has no care and sleeps in peace,
And lives on the alms that he begs.
Can a woman ever stay and be happy
In the home of one so inherently solitary?   (79)

Even now, listen to what we say:
We have thought of a very good husband for you,
Exceedingly handsome, honest, courteous, who will make
        you happy,
The glory of whose deeds even the Vedas sing,
Without fault or blemish and the sum of every virtue—
He is Shri's lord, who resides in the celestial city of Vaikunth.
We will bring that bridegroom to meet you.'
Hearing this, Bhavani laughed and said,
'You are right that this body of mine has been begotten from
        the mountain—
I will die, but I will not give up my resolve!
Gold, too, is born of rock,
And does not give up its essential nature even if thrown into fire.
I will not disregard Narad's words—
Whether my home will flourish or be ruined, I am not afraid.
The one who has no faith in his guru's words
Does not attain to happiness even in dreams.

Mahadev may be the home of all vices,
And Vishnu the abode of all virtues—
But he in whom the heart delights,
Is the one with whom the heart concerns itself.   (80)

Had I met you earlier, great munis,
I would have listened to your advice and followed it most willingly.
But now I have spent my life on Shambhu,
So to what purpose should I consider his virtues or faults?
If your hearts are resolved upon this

And you cannot refrain from matchmaking—
Well, those given to making mischief are not lazy,
And there are many other bridegrooms and maidens in
      the world!
Even if my struggle takes countless lifetimes,
My husband will be Shambhu, or I shall remain unwed.
I will not abandon Narad's counsel,
Not even if Mahesh himself tells me to a hundred times.
I fall at your feet and beseech you—return home, it is too late.'
So said Jagadamba, mother of the world.
Seeing her love, the wise munis cried,
'Praise be to Jagadambika Bhavani!

>   You are Maya, Shiv is God Supreme
>   Mother and father of the universe!'
>   Bowing their heads at her feet the munis left,
>   Ecstatic with delight.   (81)

The munis sent Himvant to her;
Entreating her repeatedly, he brought his daughter back home.
The Saptarishi returned to Shiv,
And related to him all that had occurred with Uma.
Shiv, absorbed and enchanted, listened to the account of her love
      for him.
Rejoicing, the seven sages returned home.
Then, steadying his heart, all-wise Shambhu
Began to meditate upon Raghunayak.
It was during that time that the demon Tarak appeared.
The strength of his arm was formidable, his valour immense and
      his splendour great,
He had won all the worlds and conquered their rulers,
And the gods were left without peace or riches.
Exempt from decrepitude and death, he could not be defeated—
The gods fought many battles, but lost them all.

At last they went to Viranchi and told him of their woes.
The Creator saw that the gods were deeply distressed.

> Reassuring them all, Viranchi explained,
> 'This Danuj will die
> When a son shall be begotten of Shambhu's seed,
> For he alone will conquer him in battle.   (82)

Listen to what I say and devise a plan
By which such a god may be born to help you.
Sati, who gave up her body at Daksh's sacrifice,
Has been born again in the home of Himachal.
She has practised penance in the hope of making Shambhu her husband,
Who, meanwhile, has given up everything and sits in profound
      meditation.
Even though it may seem devoid of sense and greatly inappropriate,
Listen to a suggestion of mine—
Send Kam, the god of love, to Shiv,
And let him break his meditation.
Then I will go to Shiv with bowed head
And persuade him to marry her.
This is the only way to help the gods and ensure their well-being.'
'It is a good suggestion,' agreed everyone.
With great devotion, they then invoked the god of love,
And he, who bears five arrows and a fish on his banner, appeared.

> The gods related to him their woes—
> He heard their story, and reflected for a while.
> 'Conflict with Shambhu will bring me no good,'
> He then replied with a laugh.   (83)

'Even so, I shall do as you ask,
For the Vedas say that the highest duty is to help others,
And the saints forever praise the one

Who gives up even his body for the good of others.'
So saying, he bowed his head to everyone, and set out
His bow of flowers in his hand, his helpers, Spring and soft
    breezes, with him
And as he went, Mar[xlviii] reflected in his heart,
'Opposing Shiv means my death is certain.'
Then he unleashed his power and let it spread,
And brought the whole world under his sway.
When he who bears a fish upon his banner is aroused,
All the bounds imposed by the Vedas are destroyed in an instant.
Continence, austerity, and every kind of abstinence
    and restraint,
Fortitude, duty, knowledge and learning,
Virtuous conduct, prayer, penance and detachment—
The legions of discernment all fled, terrified.

Discernment with his helpers fled,
His great warriors upon the battlefield turned,
And, like fleeing soldiers who take refuge in mountain caves,
Hid themselves in holy books.
The world was in turmoil and cried to the Creator,
'What is to happen? Who will protect us?
Who is this foolhardy being with two heads against whom Rati's lord
Has unleashed his power and taken up his bow and arrows?'

Whatever creatures there were in the world, moving
    or unmoving,
Whether called female or whether called male—
Each and every one of them threw away restraint, abandoned
    all decorum,
And became subject to Love's desire.   (84)

[xlviii] Kamdev

Every heart was overcome with lust and a longing for the
    exhilaration of love.
Beholding the vines, the trees bent down their boughs
    towards them,
The rivers swelled, and exulting, rushed towards the ocean,
And ponds and lakes joined with each other.
When the inert were in such a state,
Who can describe the doings of sentient beings?
The beasts and the birds, which move in the sky, in water or on land,
All came under the sway of Love, forgetting time and season.
All the worlds were bewildered and blinded by passion,
Even the kok birds did not consider night or day.
Gods, demons, men, Kinnaras and serpents,
Spirits of the dead, demons, ghosts and goblins—
Their condition I shall not describe in detail,
Knowing them to be forever slaves to lust.
But Siddhas, hermits, yogis and great munis—
Even they fell under the sway of lust and suffered the pain
    of separation.

When even yogis and ascetics came under the sway of passion,
What can one say of lesser men?
Those who once looked upon all creation as imbued with the
    Absolute Spirit,
Now perceived it as consisting of women.
Women saw the world filled with men,
And men saw it filled with women!
For two measures of time, the whole universe
Was filled with the spectacle produced by Kam.

No one remained unmoved,
For the heart-born god had stolen every heart.
Only those whom Raghubir protected,
Remained unaffected during that time.   (85)

For two measures of time this spectacle continued,
The time it took Kam to reach Shambhu;
Looking upon Shiv, Mar grew apprehensive,
And the world returned to what it used to be.
All creatures at once grew peaceful and content,
As when the effect of wine passes off the intoxicated.
Looking upon Rudra,[xlix] the god of love grew afraid—
Rudra, Supreme Lord, so difficult to worship and so hard to attain.
To go back meant disgrace, but neither was Madan[1] able to do anything,
So, deciding to die, he made a plan.
He at once made glorious spring appear—
Row upon row of young trees burst into flower,
Forests, groves, wells and ponds
Became beautiful and exceedingly pleasant, as did every part of
    each direction.
Love bloomed and exulted everywhere
So that passion awoke even in the hearts of the dead.

Love awoke even in the hearts of the dead,
The loveliness of the forest then cannot be described.
Cool, fragrant, and gentle breezes began to blow,
True friends of passion, fanning Love's fire.
Upon the lake many lotuses bloomed,
And swarms of honeybees softly hummed;
Swans, cuckoos and parrots sweetly called,
As apsaras sang and danced.

   He tried all his innumerable tricks,
   But Love and his army were defeated—
   Shiv's steadfast samadhi did not break.
   Now he grew angry, he whose abode is the heart.   (86)

[xlix] Shiv
[1]   Kamdev

Madan climbed the beautiful branch
Of a spreading mango tree, his heart vexed.
On his flowery bow he fitted his arrows,
And in his great passion, took aim, drew the string to his ear,
And let fly the five arrows which pierced Shiv's heart.
His samadhi broken, Shambhu awoke.
In the heart of the Lord arose great turmoil,
Opening his eyes he looked all around,
And when he saw Madan amongst the leaves of the mango tree,
His wrath made the three worlds tremble.
Then Shiv opened his third eye
And turned it upon Kam, who was burnt to ashes.
A great tumult arose in the world—
The gods were afraid, their enemies glad,
Those devoted to sensual pleasures remembered the joys of love
        and grew anxious,
While saints and yogis became free of the thorn of desire.

The yogis became free of the thorn of desire,
But hearing of her husband's fate, Rati fell into a faint.
Weeping and lamenting, and grieving in many ways,
She went to Shankar.
With great love, and beseeching him in diverse ways,
She stood in from of him, her hands folded.
The Lord, compassionate Shiv, who is so easy to please,
Saw the weak and helpless woman and said gently,

        'From now on, Rati, your lord's name
        Will be "Anang", "the bodiless one",
        Even without a body, he will pervade all.
        Now listen to the circumstances in which you will
                meet him again.   (87)

'When Krishna shall take birth in the family of Jadu,
A big burden will be destroyed from the earth.

Your husband will be his son—[50]
My words are never untrue.'
Hearing Shankar's words, Rati returned.
I will now relate the remaining story:
When the gods received news of these happenings,
They—Brahma and the others—went first to Vaikunth.
Then, with Vishnu and Brahma,
The gods went to Shiv, the abode of mercy.
Each of them sang his praises in diverse ways,
And the moon-crested one was pleased.
Said Brishketu, ocean of compassion,
'Tell me, immortals, why have you come?'
Replied Brahma, 'Lord, you pervade our very hearts and know
     what lies within—
Even so, bound by devotion, I place before you this respectful
     petition:

     In the hearts of all the gods,
     There is joyous anticipation, Shankar.
     They wish to see, with their own eyes, Lord,
     Your wedding.   (88)

'That we may gaze upon this celebration and fill our eyes with it—
Towards this end take action, you who have set us free from
     Love's frenzy.
Granting Rati a boon after destroying Kamdev—
This was well done, compassionate one.
The great punish, but then show their mercy—
Such is the grace inherent in masters and gods.
But Parvati has practised endless penance,
So now accept her.'
Hearing Vidhi's request and recalling Ram's words,
Shiv joyfully declared, 'So be it!'
Then the gods beat on their drums,
And showered him with flowers, crying, 'Hail to the lord of the gods!'

Knowing it to be the right moment, the Saptarishi arrived,
And Vidhi sent them at once to Himachal's home.
They went first to Bhavani,
And spoke sweet words that were filled with guile—

    'You would not listen to us then
    But took Narad's counsel,
    And now your penance has been in vain
    For Mahesh has burnt Kam to ashes.'   (89)

At their words, Bhavani smiled and said,
'You speak fittingly, O great and learned munis,
For in your understanding, it is only now that he has
        destroyed Kam,
And that up until now Shambhu was subject to desire.
But I know that Shiv has always been a yogi,
Eternal, faultless, free from lust and without desire.
And if, knowing him to be thus, I have served Shiv
With love, and in deed, thought and word,
Then—listen, great munis—that compassionate Lord
Will make true my penance.
When you said that Har burnt Mar—
That showed a great lack of discernment in you.
Respected fathers, it is the inherent nature of fire
That ice never dares go near it,
For it will be most certainly destroyed.
It is the same with Manmath[li] and Mahesh.'

    The munis were delighted to hear her words,
    And to see her love and belief.
    Bowing their heads to Bhavani, they left
    And went to Himachal.   (90)

[li] Kamdev

They related all the circumstances to the lord of the mountains.
Hearing of Madan's annihilation, he was greatly grieved;
Then they told him of the boon given to Rati,
And hearing about this, Himvant was greatly gladdened.
He reflected upon Shambhu's divine majesty,
And respectfully summoned wise men and sages.
Bidding them determine an auspicious day, star and hour,
He had them quickly set the wedding date in the manner
    prescribed in the Vedas.
Himachal gave the letter with this information to the Saptarishi,
And humbly clasped their feet.
The Saptarishi took the letter to Vidhi,
Who, reading it, could not contain his delight.
Reading the time and date of the wedding, he announced it
    to everyone,
And the munis and the entire gathering of gods rejoiced.
Flowers rained down, while in the heavens, music played,
And in all ten directions, sacred pitchers of good omen
    were placed.

The gods all began preparing and making ready
Their vehicles and diverse chariots.
Auspicious omens of felicity and joy were seen,
As the apsaras sang.   (91)

As for Shiv himself, his host of attendants began to adorn him—
They arranged his crown of matted locks and set upon it a crest
    of serpents.
Wearing snakes for earrings and bracelets,
His body smeared with ashes, and a lion skin around his waist,
The moon upon his handsome brow, and Ganga upon his head,
With his three eyes, and a serpent for his sacred thread,
Poison in his throat, and a garland of human heads upon
    his chest—

In such awful attire was the great god Shiv, the abode of felicity
    and compassion!
The trident and the damru resplendent in his hands,
He set off, mounted upon a bull, as music played.
Seeing Shiv, the wives of the gods smiled,
'No bride in the world is worthy of this groom!'
Vishnu, Viranchi and the other gods
Climbed into their chariots, and joined the wedding
    procession.
'The assembly of gods is in every way incomparable,
But the wedding procession is still not worthy of the groom!'

    Said Vishnu thus with a smile.
    Then, summoning the guardians of all the quarters of the
        world, he said,
    'Proceed separately, all of you,
    Each with his own retinue.   (92)

The wedding procession does not equal the bridegroom—
Do you want to be laughed at when we reach that foreign city?'
The gods smiled at Vishnu's words
And each followed separately with his own legions.
Mahesh smiled to himself—
'Hari's playfulness will not stop!'
Hearing these dear words of his own most dear friend,
He sent Bhringi to fetch all his attendants.
Hearing Shiv's command, they all came
And bowed their heads at the lotus feet of the Lord.
They came riding in diverse vehicles, in diverse garb and guise—
Shiv laughed, seeing his own company.
Some were headless, some many-headed,
Some had no hands or feet, some had several,
Some were many-eyed, some without eyes,
Some were fat and well-fed, some thin and emaciated.

Some were very thin, some very stout,
Some in pure and pious guise, some in wicked and foul.
With frightful ornaments, and skulls in their hands,
Their bodies all drenched in fresh blood,
With the faces of donkeys and dogs, pigs and jackals—
Who can enumerate the uncountable forms of his attendants?
Ghosts and goblins and troops of witches—
It is impossible to describe them all.

> The ghouls and goblins dance and sing,
> Weaving to and fro,
> Most fantastical, repulsive to behold,
> Uttering strange and peculiar cries.   (93)

As was the groom, now was his wedding procession—
It continued on its way with song and dance and spectacle.
Meanwhile, Himachal had had a canopy erected,
So extraordinary and wonderful that it defied description.
All the hills and mountains, wherever they were in the world,
Whether small or tall, more than can be counted or described,
The forests, the seas, and all the rivers and lakes—
Himgiri had invited them all.
They, who could take any shape at will, assumed handsome and
      pleasing forms,
And with their attendants, and accompanied by beautiful women,
They went, all of them, to the home of the lord of the snowy mountains,
Singing with love, songs of celebration and good fortune.
Himachal had readied many houses,
In which the guests were lodged most appropriately.
Looking at the beauty of the city,
Viranchi's skill seemed trivial.

Vidhi's skill seemed trifling,
Upon looking at the splendour of the city

With forests, gardens, wells, ponds and rivers,
All so lovely that none can describe their beauty.
Gateways were festooned with festive flowers, while innumerable flags,
Pennants and bunting adorned each and every home,
And the men and women of the city were so handsome and accomplished
That even munis were enraptured by them.

> How can one describe
> The city where Jagadamba had descended to earth?
> Prosperity, affluence, wealth and happiness
> Increased each and every day there.   (94)

As the wedding procession neared the city,
There was a happy bustle in the town that increased its glory.
Ornamenting and decorating their various chariots,
A welcoming party set off to receive the wedding procession and
    usher it in with due honour.
They rejoiced to see the assembly of gods,
And looking upon Hari they rejoiced even more.
But when they saw Shiv's retinue,
Their steeds took fright and bolted.
Holding fast their courage, the men remained,
But the children all ran for their lives.
When they reached home, their parents questioned them,
And trembling with fear, they replied—
'What can we say? We can't explain
Is this a wedding procession or Death's[51] army?
The bridegroom is a madman and is mounted upon a bull,
And snakes, skulls and ashes are his ornaments!

Ash-smeared body, snakes and skulls for ornaments,
Naked, with matted hair, he is terrifying to behold!
With him are ghouls and ghosts, goblins and witches,
And crooked-faced demons that wander in the night!

He who remains alive after seeing this wedding procession
Is a man of great good fortune indeed—
Let him watch Uma's wedding!'
So the boys cried from house to house.

    Knowing that this was Mahesh's entourage,
    Their mothers and fathers smiled,
    And explained to their children in various ways,
    'Be brave, do not be afraid!'   (95)

Those who had gone to receive the wedding procession escorted
    them into the city
And led them to the gracious dwellings arranged for them.
Maina prepared the auspicious arti
As the women sang songs of felicity and joy.
A golden platter gracing her lovely hands,
She set off joyfully to welcome Har.
But when the women saw Rudra's odd and frightening attire,
Great fear arose in their hearts.
They ran into the house, terrified,
While Mahesh continued to the lodgings prepared for him.
A great sorrow arose in Maina's heart.
She sent for the daughter of the mountain king,
And with deep love, took her upon her lap.
The dark lotuses of her eyes filled with tears,
'The Creator has given you such beauty and grace
So how could the fool make your bridegroom a madman?

How could Vidhi make your bridegroom a madman,
He who has given you such beauty?
The fruit that should grow on the tree of the gods
Is being forced to grow on a thorn bush!
Taking you with me, I will throw myself from a mountain top,
Leap into a fire, or jump into the sea.

Even if my home is ruined, and disgrace and infamy be our lot in
      the world,
As long as I live, I will not allow this wedding!

      The women grew troubled
      Seeing the wife of the mountain so sad—
      Calling upon her love for her daughter,
      She lamented and wept.   (96)

'What harm have I ever done Narad,
That he should have so destroyed my happy family,
And given Uma the advice that he did
To do penance for a lunatic husband?
In truth, he feels neither love nor compassion.
Indifferent to this world, he has neither friend nor foe, nor any
      possessions, nor a home, nor a wife,
He knows only to destroy the homes of others, and has neither
      shame nor fear.
After all, how can a barren woman know the pain of labour?'
Bhavani, seeing her mother distraught,
Said to her words both wise and sweet,
'Do not be troubled, Mother, by such thoughts,
That which destiny has ordained cannot be avoided.
If a lunatic husband is written in my fate
Why blame anyone?
Can you erase the writing of destiny?
Mother, do not uselessly open yourself to shame.

Do not take shame upon yourself, mother,
This is not the time for tears or blame.
I will find the grief or joy written upon my forehead
Wherever I go.'
Listening to Uma's soft and gentle words
The women all began to muse and reflect;

In diverse ways they blamed the Creator,
As tears flowed from their eyes.

> At that very moment, accompanied by Narad
> And the Saptarishi,
> Hearing what had happened, Tuhingiri[lii]
> Quickly entered the house.   (97)

Then Narad reassured them all
By relating to them the stories and circumstances of previous lives.
'Maina, listen to my words, they are the truth,
Your daughter is Bhavani, the mother of the world, Jagadamba
      herself.
She is Shakti, the unbegotten, uncreated, indestructible energy of
      the Universe,
Who resides always in half of Shambhu's body,
Makes this world possible, nurtures it and dissolves it,
And takes bodily form of her own will and volition.
She was born first in Daksh's house—
Her name was Sati, and she was beautiful.
In that birth too, Sati married Shankar—
The story is famous throughout the world.
Once, as she was walking along with Shiv,
She saw the sun of the lotus clan of Raghu.
Perplexed at the sight, she did not do as Shiv said,
And swayed by doubt, assumed the form of Sita.

Sati, who took on Sita's form,
Was abandoned by Shankar for that offence.
In her grief at being parted from Har, she went to her father's
      fire-sacrifice,
And there, in yogic fire, she immolated herself.

[lii] Himalaya

Now she has been reborn in your house,
And, for her husband's sake, has done great penance.
Abandon all doubt, knowing that
Girija is forever Shankar's beloved.'

    Upon hearing Narad's words,
    Everyone's grief melted away.
    In a moment this news spread,
    From house to house across the town.   (98)

Then Maina and Himvant rejoiced,
And did homage again and again at Parvati's feet.
Men, women, children, the old and the youthful—
All the townspeople were overjoyed.
All across the city, songs of happiness began to be sung
And festive pitchers of gold were put out.
Many kinds of food were prepared
In accordance with the rules of cooking.
Beyond description was the feast
Served in the palace of Bhavani, the mother of the universe.
All the guests in the bridegroom's wedding party—Vishnu,
    Viranchi and all the many gods—
Were invited with respect and courtesy.
They sat down in several rows to eat,
And the accomplished cooks began to serve them.
The women, learning that the gods had sat down to feast,
Began to mock and tease in sweet tones.[52]

In sweet voices, the lovely women teased and taunted,
And sang charming songs full of mocking satire.
The gods, delighted with the entertaining chatter,
Took a long time over their meal.
Even ten million tongues cannot describe
The joy and merriment during the feast.

The meal done, the gods rinsed their mouths and were served paan;
They then made their way to where they had been lodged.

Soon the munis came to Himvant,
And proclaimed the hour of the wedding;
Seeing that it was time,
He sent for the gods. (99)

He summoned the gods with great respect,
And seated them with honour on seats appropriate to
   their station.
The vedi was made ready as prescribed in the Vedas
The women sang songs of blessing and joy.
Upon a throne of divine splendour,
Of indescribable magnificence, wrought by Viranchi himself,
Shiv seated himself, bowing his head to the Brahmans,
And remembering his own Lord Raghurai in his heart.
The munis then sent for Uma—
Her friends led her in, adorned as a bride.
Gazing upon her beauty, all the gods were enraptured—
What poet in the world could describe such loveliness?
Knowing her to be Jagadambika and the Lord's beloved,
The gods silently paid her homage.
The culmination of beauty, Bhavani
Cannot be described even by ten million tongues.

Ten million tongues cannot describe
The great beauty of the mother of the universe.
Even the Vedas, Shesh and Sharada hesitate to describe her,
So how can the dimwitted Tulsi even presume to do so?
A mine of beauty, goddess Bhavani
Walked to the centre of the wedding pavilion where sat Shiv—
In shyness she could not look at her husband,
But the bee that was her heart flew to his lotus feet.

Directed by the munis
Shambhu and Bhavani worshipped Ganpati.[liii]
If anyone, hearing this, wonders at it,
Know that the gods are uncreated, unborn and
    exist without beginning.   (100)

The priests performed all
The wedding rites as laid down in the Vedas.
Holding the kush grass, Girish took his daughter's hand
And knowing her to be Bhavani, entrusted her to Bhav.
When Mahesh took her hand,
The gods all rejoiced in their hearts.
The priests chanted the mantras from the Vedas,
And 'Hail be to Shankar!' cried the gods.
Musical instruments of diverse kinds began to play,
Flowers of all hues rained down from the sky.
The wedding of Har and Girija was accomplished,
The universe was filled with joy.
Attendants and handmaidens, horses, chariots and elephants,
Cows, costly garments, precious gems and various other articles,
And wagons filled with grain and golden vessels
Were given as her wedding portion, which could not be described.

A magnificent dowry was given.
Himbhudhar,[liv] folding his hands, said,
'What can I give you, Shankar, you who have no need or any desire?'
And he clasped his lotus feet.
Shiv, ocean of compassion, reassured his father-in-law
In many ways.
Then Maina, filled with love,
Clasped his lotus feet and said,

[liii] Ganesh
[liv] Himalaya

'Lord, Uma is my life breath.
Take her to be your bondswoman
And forgive her all her faults—
Grant me your favour and give me this boon.'   (101)

Shambhu comforted his mother-in-law in diverse ways,
And she bowed her head at his feet and returned home.
She then called Uma,
And taking her upon her lap, offered her sage advice:
'Always worship Shankar's feet—
This is a woman's dharma, for her there is no other god but her
      husband.'
Her eyes filled with tears as she spoke
And once more she clasped her daughter to her breast.
'Why did Vidhi create woman in this world?
Always dependent, she cannot even dream of happiness.'
The mother was distraught with love,
But held herself in check, knowing it was not an appropriate
      moment for tears.
Again and again she took her in her arms, or fell at
      her feet—
With love so deep that it cannot be described.
Together the women all embraced Bhavani,
Who clung once more to her mother.

She embraced her mother once more and left,
As the women showered her with blessings.
She turned back again and again to look at her mother
Till at last, her friends led her to Shiv.
Shankar fulfilled every petitioner's plea,
Then set off for his abode with Uma.
The immortals all rejoiced and rained down flowers upon the
      newly-weds,
While the beat of joyous drums filled the air.

Himvant accompanied them
With great love to see them on their way—
Till, reassuring him in many ways,
Brishketu bade him farewell.   (102)

The mountain king returned home at once,
And summoned all the mountains and lakes.
With great respect and courtesy, and honouring them with gifts,
Himvant bid them all farewell.
When Shambhu reached Kailash,
The gods all left for their various realms.
Shambhu and Bhavani are the father and mother of the universe,
Therefore, I will not describe their passionate love.
But they indulged in all kinds of amorous pleasures,
And along with their attendants, settled down in Kailash.
Har and Girija engaged in some new dalliance every day,
And in this way, many ages passed.
Then was born the six-bodied Kumar,
The one who killed the asur Tarak in battle.
The story of Shanmukh's[lv] birth is in the Vedas, the Shastras and
     the Puranas,
It is famous and the whole world knows it.

The world knows of Shanmukh's birth,
His deeds, his glory and his great valour—
For that reason I have only briefly related
The story of Brishketu's son.
The men and women who will sing or relate
This tale of Uma and Shambhu's wedding,
Will always find success and happiness,
In any auspicious undertaking or marriage.

[lv] Skand

The deeds of Girija's beloved are an ocean
Of which even the Vedas cannot find the shore;
Then how can Tulsidas describe them,
Slow-witted bumpkin that he is?   (103)

Hearing this charming and delightful narrative of
    Shambhu's exploits,
Muni Bharadvaj was filled with great joy.
His longing to hear Ram's story increased enormously,
His eyes filled with tears and his body trembled with rapture.
Overcome with love, he could find no words.
Seeing his state, the wise Muni Jagbalik rejoiced,
'Thy birth is blest, O muni,
That dear to you as life itself is Gauri's lord.
Even in his dreams Ram does not like
Those who have no love for the lotus feet of Shiv.
Sincere love for the feet of Vishvanath, lord of the universe,
Is the indication of true devotion to Ram.
Who but Shiv is as devoted to Raghupati
That he could give up a sinless woman like Sati,
And fulfilling his promise, showed his devotion to Raghupati?
Who, my friend, is as beloved of Ram as Shiv?

By relating first the story of Shiv's exploits,
    I have understood your heart—
You are a true servant of Ram,
Steadfast and free of all sins.   (104)

I have understood your character and your disposition
So now listen as I relate the story of Raghupati.
And listen, muni, I cannot express the happiness in my heart,
At this meeting with you today.
The deeds of Ram are immeasurable, great muni,
So that even a hundred crore serpent-kings cannot relate them all.

Yet I will relate his story as I have heard it,
Invoking Ram armed with a bow, who is also the master of the
    goddess of speech.
Sharada is like a wooden puppet, while Ram,
Who knows the inner hearts of all, is the puppet-master holding
    her strings.
The poet to whom he shows his grace, knowing him to be his devotee—
In the courtyard of that poet's heart he makes Vani dance.
I do obeisance to him, the compassionate and merciful Lord,
    Raghunath,
And relate the story of his pure virtues.
The most agreeable and best of all mountains is Kailash
Where forever dwell Shiv and Uma.

> Siddhas, ascetics and yogis
> Gods, Kinnaras, numerous munis—
> All fortunate souls—live there,
> Serving Shiv, the root of all joy.   (105)

Those who avert their faces from Hari and Har, and have no love
    for dharma,
Cannot go there even in their dreams.
On that mountain top grows a vast and spreading banyan tree,
Which is always young and fresh, and beautiful in all seasons.
Its shade is cool and refreshing, and there, cool, soft and fragrant
    breezes blow.
That is the tree under which Shiv rests, and which has been sung
    of in the Vedas.
Once, the Lord went to the tree,
And looking upon it, his heart filled with great joy.
Spreading a lion-skin with his own hands,
Shambhu, the compassionate one, sat there at his ease.
His body fair of hue, like the jasmine, the moon and the conch-shell,
His arms long, an ascetic's garment made of bark around his loins,

His feet like freshly blooming red lotus flowers,
The brilliance of his toenails dispelling the darkness from the
      hearts of the devoted—
Serpents and ashes were Tripurari's ornaments,
While the radiance of his face stole even the brilliance of the full
      moon in autumn.

    His matted locks his crown, upon his head the divine Ganga,
    His eyes like great lotuses,
    His throat blue with poison, the crescent moon upon his brow—
    He was a treasure house of beauty.   (106)

As he sat there, the annihilator of Kamdev looked so serene,
That it seemed that tranquillity itself had taken bodily form.
Parvati, mother of the world, recognizing it as a good opportunity,
Went up to Shambhu.
Seeing his beloved, Har welcomed her with great courtesy,
And gave her the left half of his seat.
She sat down happily near Shiv,
And into her mind came the events of her earlier birth.
Knowing that in her husband's heart there was greater love for her now,
Uma, smiling, spoke in loving tones.
(The daughter of the mountain wanted him to tell her
The story that is the benefactor of all the worlds.)
'Vishvanath, lord of the world, and my lord Purari,
Your majesty is renowned through the three worlds;
All creatures, moving and unmoving, Nagas, men and gods—
All worship your lotus feet.

    My lord, you are all-powerful, all-knowing and bliss itself,
    You are the repository of all arts and all virtue,
    A treasure house of meditation, wisdom and detachment,
    And your name is the wish-granting Kalpataru
        for humble devotees.   (107)

If you are pleased with me, you who are the sum of all bliss,
And know me in truth to be your devoted slave,
Then, my lord, dispel my ignorance
By relating to me the many stories of Raghunath.
One whose house is beneath the divine Kalpataru,
Should such a one suffer the sorrow born of poverty?
Lord, you who wear the moon as an ornament upon your brow,
    reflect on this
And dispel the grave doubt in my mind.
Lord, munis who discourse on the Supreme Truth
Say that Ram is the uncreated brahm with no beginning,
And Shesh, Sharada, the Vedas and the Puranas,
All sing the glory of Raghupati.
You, too, all day and all night, chant "Ram, Ram"
With reverence, you who reduced the god of love to ashes.
Is this Ram the same as the son of the king of Avadh,
Or is he some other unborn, attributeless, invisible one?

    If he is only a king's son, who lost his mind upon separation
        from a woman,
      How can he be brahm, the all-pervading Spirit of the Universe?
      Looking at his actions and then hearing of his majesty,
      My mind is utterly confused and bewildered.   (108)

If there be another who is passionless, all-pervading and
    all-powerful,
Lord, explain it to me.
Knowing me to be ignorant, do not be angry with me,
But do what you can to remove my delusion.
I saw Ram's divine greatness in the forest—
Distracted with fear, I did not tell you—
Even so, my mind was so dull and obscured, that I did
    not understand,
And the fruit of that I received in full measure.

Even today, there is some confusion in my mind,
And with folded hands I beseech you, show me your compassion.
Lord, you had explained it to me then in many ways, but I had
    not understood—
Thinking on that, my husband, do not be angry with me.
My confusion now is no longer as it was then
And there is now an intense desire in my heart to listen to the story
    of Ram.
Please tell me the pure and lustrous story of Ram's virtues,
O lord of all the gods, you who wear the serpent king as
    your ornament!

    I do humble obeisance at your feet, my head upon the ground,
    And beseech you with folded hands—
    Relate the story of Raghubar's pure glory,
    Extracting from it the essence and truth of the Vedas.   (109)

Though as a woman, I am not entitled to hear it,
I am your slave in thought, deed and word.
What's more, the sages do not hide even the deepest secret
When they find someone privileged by distress to receive it.
And it is in great distress that I ask you, O lord of all the gods,
Show me your favour and tell me the story of Raghupati.
First explain to me, after reflecting upon it, the reason why
The formless, unqualified nirgun brahm assumes a sagun body.
Then, my lord, tell me about Ram's descent upon earth,
And after that, about his gentle and delightful deeds as a child.
Tell me, too, how he wed Janaki,
For what fault he left his father's kingdom,
And of his innumerable noble deeds whilst he lived in the forest.
Tell me, my husband, how he slew Ravan,
And how he disported himself once he assumed the throne.
Tell me everything, Shankar, you who are of such an amiable and
    pleasant disposition.

Next tell me, my gentle lord,
Of the miraculous and marvellous acts Ram performed,
And how, with all his people, the jewel of the line of Raghu
Went to his final abode.   (110)

Then, my lord, explain that essence
In the understanding of which learned sages remain absorbed.
Bhakti, gyan, vigyan, vairagya—[53]
Explain to me all these ideas with all their parts and
    interpretations.
The many other mysteries of Ram—
Tell me about those, too, my husband, you who have such
    clear discernment.
And, my lord, whatever I may have forgotten to ask,
Those matters, too, in your mercy, do not keep hidden.
The Vedas declare you the guru of the three worlds.
Other, foolish beings—what do they know?'
Hearing Uma's simple, gentle questions,
Devoid of guile or deceit, pleased Shiv greatly.
Into Har's heart came all of Ram's deeds,
And he trembled with joy and his eyes filled with tears.
Lord Raghunath's image entered his heart,
And he, who is himself Supreme Bliss, found immeasurable joy.

For two measures of time, Mahesh remained immersed in
    contemplation of this pleasure—
He then pulled his mind outwards
And joyfully began
To relate the deeds of Raghupati.   (111)

'Without knowledge of whom falsehood becomes truth
In the way that without recognition a rope becomes a serpent,
And by knowing whom the illusion that is this world disappears
In the way that upon waking the delusion that is a dream disappears—

I do obeisance to the child-form of that Ram,
The abode of bliss and the destroyer of misfortune,
Chanting whose name makes accessible all accomplishment—
May he who plays in Dasharath's courtyard be merciful.'
Thus Tripurari paid homage to Ram,
And filled with joy, he spoke in a voice like nectar,
'Blessings, blessings on you, daughter of the mountain king,
There is no such benefactor as you!
You have asked me to tell you Raghupati's story,
The Ganga that purifies all the worlds.
You are full of love for Ram's feet,
And it is for the good of this world that you have asked
    these questions.

    With Ram's mercy upon you, Parvati,
    In your heart
    There can be no grief, delusion, apprehension or doubt even
        in dream—
    That is what I believe.   (112)

Despite that, you have expressed the same old doubts
So that the story may be told once more and benefit all those who
    relate or hear it.
Those who have not listened to Hari's story with their ears—
Their earholes are like the holes in which snakes and
    serpents dwell.
Those who have not gazed upon the saints with their eyes—
Their eyes are like the false eyes upon a peacock's feathers.
Those heads that do not bow at Hari's feet
Or at the feet of their guru are like bitter pumpkins.
And those beings in whose hearts devotion to Hari has not entered
Live like corpses though alive.
The tongue that does not sing the virtues of Ram,
Is like the tongue of a frog,

And as cruel and pitiless as the thunderbolt is the heart
That is not gladdened upon hearing the deeds of Hari.
Listen then, Girija, to the wondrous and playful exploits of Ram,
Which delight the gods and confound the demons.

    Ram's story is like the divine cow of the gods
    That confers every blessing upon those who serve it,
    And the company of the good is like the abode of all the gods.
    Who, knowing this, will not listen to it?   (113)

Ram's story is like the pleasant clapping of hands
That causes the birds of doubt to fly away.
It is the axe that cuts down the spreading tree of the age of Kali,
So listen with reverence, daughter of the mountain king.
Ram's names, his noble qualities, charming stories,
His births, and his deeds are innumerable—as the Vedas declare.
Just as Ram, the Supreme God, is infinite,
So also are his story, his renown and his virtues without end.
Even so, as I have heard it, and according to my ability,
I will relate it, seeing your deep love.
Uma, your questions are artless and charming,
Approved of by the saints, and pleasing to me.
But there was one thing that I did not like,
Even though you said it swayed by delusion, Bhavani—
That there may be another Ram
Whose praise the Vedas sing and upon whom the munis meditate.

    Only those seized by the demon of delusion
    Utter and hear such impiety.
    Hypocrites who have turned away from Hari's feet,
    And do not know truth from falsehood.   (114)

Ignorant, foolish and blind unfortunates,
The mirrors of their minds coated with the scum of lust,

Dissolute, deceitful and utterly depraved,
Who have not experienced the company of good men even in
    their dreams—
Only they utter words that contradict the Vedas,
Who have no understanding of good or bad, gain or loss.
With the mirrors of their minds so clouded, and lacking eyes,
How can such poor wretches see Ram's beauty?
Those who have no discernment of the divine, whether as nirgun
    or sagun, Immaterial Absolute or Incarnate god,
Who babble false and fabricated nonsense of all kinds,
And who wander the world in the grip of Hari's maya—
For them, no utterance is impossible.
The mad, those possessed by malignant spirits, and
    the intoxicated—
They speak without thought or reflection.
Those who have drunk the liquor of extreme delusion—
One should never lend an ear to what they say.

    Reflecting upon this in your heart,
    Abandon doubt and worship Ram's feet.
    Listen well, daughter of the mountain king—my words
    Are the sunbeams that destroy the darkness of doubt.   (115)

There is no difference between sagun and nirgun,
Say the munis, the Puranas, the Vedas and the learned.
That One without attributes, without form, invisible
    and uncreated,
Acquires attributes by the power of a devotee's love.
How can one who has no qualities also be one with qualities?
In the same way that rain and icy hail are not substantially different
    from each other.
The one whose name is the sun that destroys the darkness
    of delusion,
How can he be spoken of in connection with attachment and desire?

Ram is the sun, the aggregation of truth, consciousness, and bliss—
In him there is not the smallest trace of the night of delusion.
He is light itself, Supreme Lord,
In whom neither knowledge nor wisdom need dawn.[lvi]
Joy and sorrow, wisdom and ignorance,
Arrogance and pride—these are customary for finite beings.
But Ram is the absolute, all-pervading Spirit of the Universe,
He is Bliss Supreme, God transcendental and primeval being—all
    the world knows this.

    He who is celebrated as the primordial being, the source of
       all light,
    The manifest Supreme God, master and protector of all—
    That jewel of the dynasty of Raghu is my Lord.'
    So saying Shiv bowed his head.   (116)

'The ignorant do not perceive their own confusions,
Instead, these foolish people blame the Lord for the darkness of
    their minds,
Just as, when seeing a canopy of dark clouds in the sky,
Those without discernment say that the sun is hiding itself,
Or one who looks at the moon with a finger in his eye
And believes that two moons have appeared.
Uma, attributing such darkness and delusion to Ram
Is the same as attributing darkness, smoke and dust to the sky.
The objects of sense, the senses, the gods of the senses and the
    soul together
All derive consciousness successively, one from the other,
But the Supreme Illuminator who reveals them all,
Is the eternal Ram, that same king of Avadh.
The Illuminator who lights this world, Ram
Is the lord of delusion and the abode of wisdom and virtue,

[lvi] For only where there is darkness is dawn possible or even required

Through whose reality inert, inanimate maya,
Helped by ignorance, appears to be real.

> Though the apparent gleam of silver in a shell or the shine
> of water
> In a mirage created by the rays of the sun
> Be false in all time, past, present and future,
> No one can dispel such illusions.   (117)

In this manner the world remains subject to Hari.
Though it is an illusion, it still causes pain
As when, if someone is beheaded in a dream,
Without waking, his pain does not disappear.
He by whose grace such perplexity is removed,
Girija, is none other than the merciful Raghurai.
No one has ever discovered his beginning or his end;
Based on inference and speculation, the Vedas have sung of
    him thus:
"Without feet he walks, and hears without ears,
Without hands he performs many kinds of deeds,
Without mouth or tongue, he enjoys all flavours,
Without speech or voice, he is the most eloquent speaker,
Without body, he touches, without eyes he sees,
And without a nose, he smells every scent."
In all these ways his deeds are miraculous—
He, whose majesty cannot be described.

> He of whom the Vedas and the wise thus sing
> And upon whom the munis meditate—
> He is the very one, Dasharath's son, benevolent to the faithful,
> King of Koshal, and Lord Supreme.   (118)

Gazing upon those who die in Kashi,
It is by the power of his name I free them from sorrow.

He is my Lord, master of all creation, moving or unmoving,
Raghubar, the one who pervades all hearts.
His name, when taken by men in despair,
Burns away the sins of many previous births;
If men remember him with reverence,
They cross the ocean of this existence as easily as if it were a puddle
    made by the hoofprint of a cow.
Ram is that Supreme Spirit, Bhavani,
And your words, that in him appears delusion, were inappropriate.
The instant such doubt enters the heart,
Wisdom, detachment and all virtues disappear.'
Listening to Shiv's delusion-destroying words,
The whole fallacious argument she had built up broke down.
Love and belief for Raghupati's feet grew strong
And her agonizing uncertainty vanished.

    Again and again she clasped her lord's lotus feet;
    Folding her delicate lotus-like hands,
    Her heart steeped in love,
    Girija sweetly spoke.   (119)

'Listening to your words that were as cool and soothing
    as moonbeams,
My deep perplexity, that was like the sultry heat of autumn,
    has vanished.
O merciful one, you have removed all doubt,
And I have understood the true nature of Ram.
My husband, by your grace my distress has disappeared,
And by your favour, I am now happy.
Now look upon me as your bondswoman,
And even though I am an ignorant woman, by nature stupid
    and dull,
Answer the question that I had asked before,
If you are pleased with me, my lord.

Ram is the Supreme Absolute, he is pure consciousness,
    indestructible
He is removed from all, yet dwells in every heart—
Why, then, did he assume the body of a man, lord?
Explain it to me, Brishketu.'
Hearing Uma's gentle and demure words
And perceiving her pure love for Ram's story,

    The conqueror of Kamdev rejoiced in his heart,
    Shankar, all-wise and easily pleased.
    After praising Uma in many ways
    The all-merciful Lord spoke.   (120A)

    'Now listen to this auspicious story, Bhavani,
    The clear and pure *Ramcharitmanas*,
    Which Bhushundi related at length
    And which the king of the birds, Garud, heard.   (120B)

    How that great conversation took place
    I will tell you later.
    Listen now to Ram's descent upon earth and his deeds
    Most beautiful and sinless.   (120C)

    Hari's attributes and names are infinite
    His stories and forms, incalculable and immeasurable.
    I will relate these according to my understanding—
    Listen, Uma, with reverence.   (120D)

Hear then, Girija—Hari's charming deeds,
Profound and pure, have been sung by the Vedas and the Shastras,
And it cannot ever be precisely said
That the cause of Hari's descent to earth was 'this' or 'only this'.
Ram is beyond discussion or speculation through intellect, mind
    and speech—

Such, wise one, is my opinion.
Yet as the saints and the munis, the Vedas and the Puranas
Explain according to their respective understanding,
In the same way, O lovely woman, I will now explain to you
The cause as I have understood it.
Whenever dharma is diminished,
And vile and arrogant demons increase in number
Committing such injustices as cannot be described,
And Brahmans, cows and gods become distressed, and the earth
    itself is troubled,
At such times the all-merciful Lord assumes diverse forms
And removes the pain of the good and the virtuous.

    He destroys the demons, reinstates the gods,
    Protects the bridge of sacred knowledge that he
        himself revealed,
    And spreads his pure glory across the world—
    This is the reason for Ram's incarnation.   (121)

Singing his glory, the devout cross this ocean of existence,
And it is for their sake that the ocean of compassion assumes a body.
The causes of Ram's incarnation are many,
Each more extraordinary and marvellous than the other.
I will relate one or two of his earlier incarnations—
Listen carefully, wise Bhavani.
Hari had two beloved doorkeepers,
Jay and Vijay, as everybody knows.
By a Brahman's curse, both brothers
Were reborn in the bodies of the dark and malignant Asurs,
Kanakakasipu and Hataklochan.
They became renowned in the world as the destroyers of
    Indra's pride,
And, victorious in battle, were celebrated warriors.
Taking on the form of a boar, the Lord got rid of one;

Becoming Narhari, he slew the other,
And spread the glory of his devotee Prahlad.

These same two brothers were born again as night-wandering
   demons,
Most valiant and very strong,
The great warriors, Kumbhakaran and Ravan,
Who defeated even the gods, as all the world knows.   (122)

They did not attain liberation from rebirth even though they had
   been slain by the Lord,
For the Brahman's curse prevailed for three births.
So, once more for their sake,
The Lord, who loves his devotees, assumed bodily form.
In that birth, Kashyap and Aditi were his father and mother,
Renowned as Dasharath and Kaushalya.
This was how, in one particular cosmic cycle of creation, the Lord
   descended to earth
And through his deeds, purified the world.
In another kalpa, seeing the gods unhappy and distressed
Having lost all battles against the demon Jalandhar,
Shambhu waged a fierce and unending war against him,
But the Danuj was extremely strong and could not be killed.
The wife of the demon prince was supremely chaste,
And it was because of the strength of her virtue that Purari could
   not win against him.

Through deceit and trickery, the Lord broke her vow
And so helped the gods;
When she discovered the secret,
She was furious and in her anger cursed him.[54]   (123)

Her curse Hari acknowledged and made true,
He, the playful and compassionate god.

So Jalandhar was born as Ravan,
And Ram killed him in battle and gave him the supreme state that
    is salvation.
So this was the purpose of one birth
For which Ram took on a man's body.
The story of each of the Lord's descents upon earth,
Has been sung by poets in many ways—listen to it, O muni.
Once, Narad cursed him,
Because of which, in that particular kalpa, he descended to earth.'
Girija was astounded to hear this—
'Narad is a devotee of Vishnu and very wise and learned.
Why did the muni curse him?
What offence had Ramaa's lord committed?
Tell me this story, Purari,
It is astonishing that a muni's mind should be thus subject to
    illusion and folly.'

Then said Mahesh with a smile,
'There is no one wise or foolish—
Whatever Raghupati makes anyone at any point in time
That is what, at that instant, one becomes.'   (124A)

'I will now relate the story of Ram's virtues,
Listen with reverence, Bharadvaj!'
Worship Raghunath, the destroyer of the perpetual cycle of
    birth and rebirth
Says Tulsi, abandoning pride and arrogance.   (124B)

In the Himalaya mountains, there was a cave most sacred,
Near it flowed the graceful stream of the divine River Ganga.
Seeing this abode most pleasant and holy,
The divine rishi Narad was greatly pleased.
Gazing upon the mountain, the river and the forest groves,
Great love for Ramaa's lord arose in his heart.

As he remembered Hari, Daksh's curse upon him was broken,
And his inherently pure mind became absorbed in intense
     meditation.
Seeing the muni absorbed in such deep meditation, the king of the
     gods became afraid.
He summoned Kamdev to him and doing him every honour, said,
'For my sake, go with your helpers to where Narad sits in samadhi
     and break his meditation!'
He who bears a fish upon his banner, set off gladly to do
     Indra's bidding.
In Indra's heart was the fear
'The divine rishi wants to rule over my kingdom!'
The greedy and grasping in this world
Are, like the dishonest crow, afraid of everyone.

     Just as a foolish dog, seeing the king of the beasts
     Runs away with a dry bone
     For fear that it will be snatched from him—
     In the same way, the king of the gods was shameless in his
          suspicion of Narad.   (125)

When Madan reached that hermitage where Narad sat in meditation,
Through his own maya, he created spring.
Trees burst into flowers of many colours,
The kokil began to call and the bees to hum.
Pleasing breezes, cool, soft and fragrant, blew
Fanning the flames of desire.
Rambha and other celestial courtesans, ever youthful
And skilled in all the arts of love,
Sang all kinds of songs and melodies
And, ball in hand, amused themselves with games and sport.
Madan, delighted by his helpers,
Employed once more his many tricks and illusions.
But Kamdev's skill had no effect on the muni,

And the mind-born god, guilty as he was, began to fear for himself—
Can anyone trespass within the boundaries
Of one whose protector is Ramaa's lord himself?

> Afraid and apprehensive, together with his helpers,
> Kamdev acknowledged defeat,
> Then went and clasped the muni's feet,
> And spoke to him in abject, humble tones.   (126)

In Narad's heart there arose no anger,
And he reassured Kam with affectionate words.
Bowing his head at the muni's feet and receiving his permission,
Madan, with his companions, left.
The muni's good-natured forgiveness and his own doings—
He related it all in Indra's court.
Hearing this, the gathering was astonished—
They praised the muni and bowed their heads to Hari.
Then Narad went to Shiv,
His heart full of pride at his victory over Kam.
He related to Shankar the doings of Mar,
And Mahesh, holding him in deep affection, advised him,
'Again and again I entreat you, muni,
Never, on any account, repeat to Hari
This tale that you have related to me!
Should it come up in conversation, even then keep it secret.'

> The advice that Sambhu gave for his own good
> Did not please Narad.
> Bharadvaj, now listen to the amusing and curious events that
>   took place—
> Hari's will is truly mighty!   (127)

Whatever Ram wishes to do, that alone happens,
And no one can make it otherwise.

Shambhu's words did not please the muni,
And he departed for Viranchi's heaven.
Once, with his cymbals and his divine vina,
And, with great skill and proficiency, singing the virtues of Hari,
The great muni went to the Ocean of Milk
Where Shrinivas,[lvii] the pinnacle and summation of the Vedas,
    lives.
Ramaa's lord met him with joy,
And seated the rishi by his side;
Smiling, the Lord of all creation, moving and unmoving, said,
'You have graced us with your presence after many days, muni!'
Narad related all the doings of Kam,
Even though Shiv had earlier forbidden him.
Most mighty is Raghupati's maya—
Who, born in this world, can resist it?

    With a stern face, the Lord
    Spoke sweet words.
    'Reflecting upon you, Narad,
    Illusion, lust, pride and arrogance disappear.   (128)

Listen, muni, delusion arises only in the minds of those
Whose hearts are bereft of wisdom and detachment.
You are of steadfast mind and resolute in your vow of celibacy,
So how can the mind-born god cause you distress?'
Narad replied, but with conceit,
'It is all your grace, Lord.'
But he in whom resides compassion reflected deeply and discerned
The first shoots of the enormous tree of pride in Narad's heart.
'I must quickly pull it out by the roots and throw it away,
For it is my vow to help my devotees.
For the good of the muni and for my entertainment,

[lvii] Vishnu

I will for sure contrive a scheme.'
Then Narad bowed his head at Hari's feet,
And took his leave, his heart filled with conceit.
Then Vishnu, Shri's lord, pressed his own maya into action—
Now listen to the ruthless deeds it performed.

> His maya created on the road a city
> A hundred yojans wide,
> Wondrously built and more splendid
> Than even Vishnu's city, Vaikunth.   (129)

Within the city dwelt men so handsome and women so beautiful
That they appeared to be incarnations of the heart-born Kamdev
    and his consort, Rati.
Over that city reigned King Shilnidhi, endowed with every virtue.
He had horses, elephants and soldiers beyond number,
His pomp and splendour were equal to that of a hundred Indras,
And he himself was the abode of beauty, magnificence, strength
    and statesmanship.
His daughter was Vishvamohini.[55]
Even Shri herself was captivated gazing upon her beauty,
For she was Hari's maya, the accumulation of all virtues—
How can her radiance be described?
The king's daughter was to choose a husband,
And to her svayamvar had come innumerable kings and princes.
The muni, always fond of a spectacle, also went to that city
And inquired of its residents the details of all that was going on.
Having heard what was happening, he went to the royal palace—
The king paid him homage and seated him with great respect.

> Summoning his daughter, the king
> Showed her to Narad and said,
> 'Lord, after due reflection, tell me
> All her virtues and faults.'   (130)

Seeing her great beauty, the muni forgot his vow of celibacy
And remained staring at her for a long time.
Perceiving her auspicious attributes, the muni was lost
     in thought—
He rejoiced in his heart, silently thinking to himself,
'He who weds this girl will become immortal,
No one will be able to defeat him on the battlefield.
All creation, animate and inanimate, will worship the one
Shilnidhi's daughter marries.'
Though he had interpreted her attributes and their indications, he
     kept his thoughts to himself,
And made up something to say to the king.
After telling the king that his daughter was blessed with auspicious
     attributes presaging good fortune,
Narad left, his heart full of anxious worry.
'I must devise some way
To make the princess marry me.
In such a situation, prayer and penance are of no use.
O Lord, arranger of destiny, how can I get this girl?

     On this occasion I need
     Extreme majesty and exceeding good looks
     At the sight of which the princess will become enraptured
     And bestow the garland[56] upon me, thus choosing me
          for her bridegroom.   (131)

I could ask Hari for the gift of beauty—
But going to him will cause much delay.
Still, I have no other benefactor like Hari,
So, on this occasion, let him be the one to help me.'
Narad at once petitioned and prayed to Hari in many ways,
And the compassionate Lord, who delights in playful deeds, appeared.
Upon seeing the Lord, the muni was reassured—
'Now my work will be done,' he thought, delighted.

With great humility he related his story.
'Grant me your favour, and in your mercy help me—
Your own beauty, Lord, give to me,
For in no other way can I win her.
Whatever will benefit me, Lord,
Make haste to accomplish that, for I am your servant!'
Seeing the great strength of his own maya,
The Lord, ever merciful to the humble, laughed to himself and said,

'Listen, Narad,
Whatever will your greatest good achieve,
I will do that and nothing else—
My promise is never untrue.   (132)

When a sick man, distracted by illness, asks for food that is not
     good for him,
The doctor does not give it to him, devoted muni.
In the same way I have resolved to do what is best for you.'
So saying, the Lord disappeared.
Under the spell of the Lord's maya, the muni had become so dull
     and stupid
That he did not understand the hidden significance of
     Hari's words.
Instead, that foremost of all rishis hurried at once to the place
Which had been made ready for the svayamvar.
There, upon their respective thrones, sat the royal suitors,
Dressed in all their finery, and with their attendants and servants.
The muni, rejoicing, thought, 'My form is so handsome
That she will not, even by mistake, reject me and choose
     another bridegroom.'
For the muni's good, the abode of mercy
Had given him such a hideous form as cannot be described,
Though looking at him, no could discern the change—
Everybody just saw him as Narad and bowed their heads to him.

But two of Rudra's attendants were there,
And they had guessed the whole secret.
Disguised as Brahmans, they roamed about, observing
     and watching—
They, too, were great tricksters.   (133)

The crowd in which the muni seated himself,
His heart full of conceit over his beauty,
There the two servants of Mahesh also sat down—
In their Brahman disguise, no one paid them any attention.
They made disparaging and sarcastic jokes, speaking so that Narad
     might hear—
'Hari has truly given him such good looks!
Gazing upon his beauty, the princess will be delighted
And will choose him to be her husband, thinking him to be "hari"
     in truth!'[57]
The muni was infatuated, his heart in the hands of another,[58]
And Shambhu's attendants laughed with delight at the sight.
Even though the muni heard their nonsensical chatter,
He did not understand it, his mind steeped in delusion.
No one could see the change in him,
Except the king's daughter, who saw his hideous form—
Perceiving his monkey face and ugly body,
Her heart filled with revulsion.

With her friends and handmaidens, the princess
Walked away, as graceful as a swan,
Observing and surveying the assembled kings—
In her lotus hands she held the garland with which she would
     signal her choice.   (134)

She refused to glance again, even inadvertently,
At Narad swelling with conceit.
Again and again the muni would jump up, anxious and agitated,

And seeing his condition, Har's attendants laughed.
Then, assuming a kingly body, the compassionate Lord, too,
    went there—
The princess rejoiced and placed the garland round his neck.
Thus Lakshmi's lord carried off the bride,
And the assembled kings were left, despairing and disappointed.
The muni, his reason overcome by his infatuation, was distraught,
Like one who has lost a precious jewel he had securely tied in a
    knot at the end of his robe.
Then Har's attendants, grinning, said,
'Go look at your face in a mirror!'
So saying, the two fled away in fear.
The muni looked at his reflection in the water—
Seeing his transformed appearance, he was furious
And immediately pronounced a most dreadful curse:

    'Go, be reborn as night-wandering demons,
    You wicked and deceitful pair of sinners—
    You laughed at me, so reap the fruit of that.
    Dare you laugh again at a muni!'   (135)

He looked again into the water and saw that he had regained his
    own form,
Even so, his heart was not content—
His lips trembling with fury, his mind filled with rage,
He set off at once in pursuit of Kamla's lord.[lviii]
'I will either curse him or I will die,
For he has made me an object of derision in the world!'
On the way he met that enemy of the Danavs, the Lord himself—
With him were the goddess Ramaa and the same princess.
The Lord of gods spoke in sweet tones,
'Muni, where are you off to in such distress?'

[lviii] Vishnu

Hearing these words, Narad was overcome by fury—
For his mind, completely in maya's grip, had become bereft
    of reason.
'You have never been able to stomach another's prosperity,
Your jealousy and deceit are extraordinary!
Upon the churning of the ocean, you made a fool of Rudra,
And induced the gods to make him drink poison.

> You gave liquor to the demons, poison to Shankar,
> And took Ramaa and the beautiful Kaustubh jewel
>   for yourself!
> You are crooked and wily, and look only to accomplish
>   your own interest,
> You behaviour is always deceitful!   (136)

You are supremely self-willed, there is no one above you to whom
    you are accountable,
You do whatever comes into your mind,
You debase the good and make good the base
And hold neither regret nor joy in your heart.
Constantly cheating and duping everyone, you have become used
    to such tricks.
You are completely unafraid, and your heart is full of enthusiasm
    for your pranks,
Neither good nor bad deeds impede your actions,
And till now no one has set you straight.
This time you have sent your gift of deceit to a worthy adversary,
And you will receive the fruit of your doings!
The body that you took on to cheat me—
I curse you—go assume that same form of a man!
You made me look like a monkey,
So monkeys will be your helpers.
You did me great mischief,
And for that you will suffer the grief of separation from a woman.'

Gladly accepting the curse,
The Lord apologized profusely to Narad.
The compassionate one then withdrew
The force of his own maya.   (137)

When Hari withdrew his maya,
Neither Ramaa nor the princess were to be seen.
Then the muni, greatly afraid, fell at Hari's feet,
'Save me, you who removes the suffering of the humble!
Let not my curse come true, compassionate one!'
'It is my will,' replied the merciful Lord.
'I uttered many vile and evil words—
For those,' asked the muni, 'how will my sin be wiped off?'
'Go and chant the hundred names of Shankar,
And your heart will at once find peace.
There is no one as dear to me as Shiv—
Do not abandon this belief even by mistake.
One on whom Purari does not bestow his grace,
Muni, never finds faith in me.
Hold this firmly in your heart, and go wander the earth—
My maya will now never overwhelm you again.'

Thus reassuring the muni in many ways
The Lord disappeared.
Narad set off for Brahma's abode,
Singing the praises of Ram.   (138)

Now, Har's attendants saw the muni passing by on the road,
His mind free of delusion, and joyful and happy.
In great fear, they came up to Narad,
And clasping his feet, they spoke in piteous tones, words of
    deep distress:
'We are Har's attendants, not Brahmans, great muni!
We committed a grave offence and received our just reward—

But now, compassionate one, we beg you, free us of your curse.'
Narad, ever merciful to the humble, replied,
'Go, both of you, become night-wandering demons!
Great power, majesty and splendour will be yours!
When, by the strength of your arms, you will have conquered
    the world,
Vishnu will take on the body of a man.
Your deaths will be in battle at the hands of Hari,
So you will attain liberation and never have to be born in this
    world again.'
The pair bowed their heads to the muni and left,
And in due course were reborn as demons of the night.

    In one kalpa, it was for this reason
    That all-powerful Hari became incarnate as a man—
    To gladden the gods, comfort the virtuous
    And lighten the earth's burden.   (139)

Thus Hari's births and deeds are many,
All pleasing, beneficent and wonderful.
In every cycle of creation, the Lord descends to earth,
And performs beautiful deeds in many ways.
And at each descent, the munis sing his story
Composing narratives most pure and perfect,
With diverse events and incidents incomparably described,
Which the wise hear without wonder.
Hari is without end, without end is Hari's story,
Told and heard in many ways by all the saints.
Ramchandra's deeds are pleasing and charming
And cannot be sung even in countless kalpas.
I have related this incident, Bhavani,
To show that Hari's maya can delude even enlightened munis.
The Lord is playful, but benevolent towards the humble,
Easily accessible to his servants, and the destroyer of all sorrow.

God or man or muni, there is none
Whom the Lord's powerful maya cannot beguile—
Reflect upon this in your mind
And worship the master of this mighty maya.   (140)

Now listen, daughter of the mountain, to another reason for
    his descent—
I will relate this extraordinary tale at length,
Explaining why the uncreated, unqualified and formless
All-pervading Spirit of the Universe became the king of Koshal,
The Lord whom you saw wandering in the forest
With his brother, both in the garb of ascetics,
And seeing whose deeds, Bhavani,
You, in Sati's body, became so bewildered that
Even today the shadow of that madness has not left you.
Listen to his story, which cures the malady of doubt,
And the playful and wondrous acts that he performed in
    that incarnation—
I will relate them all according to my understanding.
Bharadvaj, when she heard Shankar's words,
Uma smiled, abashed but full of love.
Brishketu then began to relate
The reason for that particular incarnation.

All of that I will now tell you,
Listen attentively, greatest of munis—
Ram's story removes the impurities of the age of Kali,
Brings bliss and felicity, and is most pleasing.   (141)

Svayambhuva Manu and Satarupa,[59]
From whom was born the human race,
Were a couple whose conduct and behaviour were virtuous
    and good,
And of whose righteous nature, the Vedas sing even now.

The king Uttanapad was their son,
Whose son, Dhruv, became Hari's devotee;
Their younger son was called Priyavrat,
Whom the Vedas and the Puranas praise.
Then they had a daughter, Devahuti,
Who was the beloved wife of Muni Kardam.
She bore in her womb the first god,
The compassionate and merciful Kapil,
The divine sage skilled in the analysis of essential truths,
Who made manifest and expounded the Sankhya Shastra.[60]
That Manu ruled for many ages,
Observing, in every way, every directive of the Lord.

'The fourth stage of life has come upon me while I am still
    living in my palace,
I have not yet attained detachment from the senses.'
And his heart was filled with grief when he considered that
His birth had passed without true devotion to Hari.   (142)

Thus compelled, he gave his kingdom to his son
And left for the forest with his wife.
Amongst places of pilgrimage, the forest of Naimish is
    renowned—
Especially sacred, it grants success to all those who seek
    spiritual achievement.
A community of munis and siddhas lives there,
And there King Manu went, great gladness in his heart.
As they passed along the path, the royal couple of steadfast minds
    were so full of grace and beauty,
It seemed as though wisdom and devotion had assumed
    bodily form.
They reached the bank of the river Dhenumati,[lix]

[lix] The River Gomati

And bathed joyfully in its pure water.
Siddhas, munis and learned men came to meet them,
Recognizing the royal sage as a strong and mighty upholder
    of dharma.
The munis took them with reverence
To all the sacred and beautiful places of pilgrimage.
Their spare bodies clad in bark, like hermits,
They listened every day to the Puranas in the company of the sages.

    Then, repeatedly chanting with great love
    The twelve-lettered mantra,
    The couple's hearts became deeply devoted
    To the lotus feet of Vaasudev.[61]   (143)

They ate leaves, fruits and roots
And meditated upon the Supreme Spirit, who is existence, thought
    and bliss in one.
Then, in the hope of attaining Hari, they began to practice
    penance,
Living on water as their only nourishment, and giving up roots
    and fruits.
In their hearts was the endless desire
To see with their own eyes the Supreme Lord,
Without attributes, indivisible, infinite, without beginning or end,
Upon whom meditate those who seek the highest truth,
Whom the Vedas describe as 'Not this, not this',
Who is without form, without name, bliss inherent, incomparable,
And from a particle of whose being were born,
In a multitude of forms, the gods Shambhu, Viranchi and Vishnu.
'Even such a Lord is subject to his servants
And for the benefit of his devotees, assumes a body his playful
    wonders to perform—
If this is true, as the Vedas declare,
Our yearning will be fulfilled.'

In this way, six thousand years went by,
While they consumed only water;
And for seven thousand years more,
They subsisted only on air.   (144)

Then, for ten thousand years, they gave up even that,
And stood still, each on one leg.
Seeing their endless penance, Vidhi, Hari and Har
Came again and again to Manu.
'Ask us for a boon,' they said, tempting him in many ways.
Despite their attempts, the royal couple, supremely steadfast,
    remained unmoved.
Though their bodies were reduced to skeletons,
In their hearts and minds there was no distress.
The all-wise omniscient Lord now knew them to be his servants,
The ascetic king and queen, who sought no other refuge but him—
A voice, deep and profound, and steeped in the nectar
    of compassion,
Was heard in the sky. 'Ask, ask for a boon!' it cried.
This voice was so pleasing that it could infuse the dead with life.
When, through their ears, it entered their hearts,
Their bodies grew so strong and beautiful,
It seemed as though they had just come from their palace.

Hearing the voice that was as nectar to the ears,
Their bodies thrilled with joy.
Prostrating himself upon the ground,
His heart overflowing with love, Manu spoke.   (145)

'You are the wish-fulfilling tree and the wish-granting cow to
    your servants,
Vidhi, Hari and Har pay homage to the dust of your feet,
Easily attained by those who serve you, you grant all happiness
And are the protector of your devotees, Lord of all beings.

Protector of the unprotected, if you have any love for us,
Grant us your favour and give us this boon:
The form in which you dwell in Shiv's heart,
That munis strive to attain,
Which is the swan upon the Manas lake of Bhushundi's heart,
And which the Vedas praise as both with attributes and without—
Grant us your grace and let us behold that form with our own eyes,
You who deliver all suppliants from distress.'
Greatly pleased by the royal couple's words,
So sweet and humble, and steeped in love,
The compassionate Lord, devoted to his devotees,
God himself, who pervades the whole universe, manifested himself.

His form was dark, as a blue lotus, a blue sapphire,
And a rain-bearing black cloud.
Seeing the splendour of his body,
Countless Kamdevs blushed.   (146)

His face, as radiant as the full moon in autumn, was the very
    epitome of beauty,
With lovely cheeks and chin, and conch-like neck with three fine
    lines behind,
With lips as red as the dawn, and lovely teeth, and shapely nose,
And a smile that put the moonbeams to shame;
His eyes were as lustrous as newly blooming lotuses,
And his glance charmed and enchanted the heart;
His brows stole the beauty of Kamdev's bow,
And upon his forehead glittered a sandalwood tilak.
Makar-shaped ornaments hung in his ears, a shining crown
    adorned his head,
His curly hair was like a swarm of bees,
Upon his breast was the Shrivatsa,[62] a beautiful garland of wild,
    forest flowers,
And necklaces interwoven with gems and precious stones.

Upon his shoulders, as strong as a lion's, gleamed a sacred thread,
The ornaments that encircled his arms were fine and elegant,
While his shapely and muscular arms resembled an elephant's trunk;
At his waist hung a quiver and in his hands he held a bow
    and arrows.

His gold-hued garments put the lightning to shame,
Upon his stomach were three auspicious folds,
And his navel was so heart-enchanting that
It robbed the whirlpools in the River Jamuna of
    their splendour.   (147)

His lotus feet, upon which the minds of munis
Dwell like so many bees, cannot be described.
Upon his left side, shining with a radiance that matches his own,
Is primal energy personified, the accumulation of all splendour, and
    from whom originates the world,
From a particle of whom spring forth the receptacles of virtue,
Lakshmi, Uma and Brahmani[ix] in countless forms,
And from the play of whose eyebrows the world is created—
It is her, Sita, on Ram's left side.
Beholding the ocean of splendour that is Hari's beauty,
They remained staring wide-eyed, unblinking.
Reverently they gazed upon his incomparable form,
But no matter how long they gazed, Manu and Satarupa were
    not satisfied.
In the grip of intense delight, they forgot their own bodies,
Falling prostrate upon the ground, they clasped his feet in
    their hands.
The compassionate Lord, touching their heads with his own
    lotus hands,
Immediately raised them up.

[ix] Sarasvati, as Brahma's consort

Then he, the abode of mercy, spoke—
'Know that I am exceedingly pleased,
And considering me to be the most bountiful,
Ask of me any boon that you desire.'   (148)

Upon hearing the Lord's words, Manu folded his hands
And taking courage, spoke in gentle tones,
'Lord, having seen your lotus feet,
All our desires are now fulfilled.
Yet, one longing remains in our heart—
I know not how to describe it, for it is both easy to accomplish and
      difficult to attain.
It is very easy for you to give it, Lord,
But to me, because of my need, it seems unattainable.
Just as a poor man, finding the divine wish-granting Kalpataru,
Shrinks from asking for great wealth
Because he does not know its power—
In the same way, my heart hesitates.
But you pervade all hearts and already know my desire—
Fulfil our wish, Lord.'
'Abandon hesitation, king, and ask of me—
There is nothing that I would not give you.'

      'O most bountiful and merciful Lord,
      I speak my heart's true desire—
      I want a son like you—
      How can one conceal anything from the Lord?'   (149)

Seeing his love and hearing his words beyond compare,
'So shall it be,' the compassionate Lord declared.
'But where will I search for another like myself?
King, I myself will come and be your son.'
Seeing Satarupa with folded hands, the Lord said,
'Devi, ask whatever boon you desire.'

'Lord, the boon that the wise and sagacious king has asked,
I, too, desire the very same one, merciful Lord.
But, Lord, it is exceedingly presumptuous of us—
Though you are pleased by it, for the sake of your devotees.
You are the progenitor of Brahma and the other gods, and the
    master of the universe,
You are brahm, Supreme Spirit, knowing all hearts.
And so, my heart is apprehensive and full of doubt,
Yet whatever the Lord has said must be fulfilled.
Lord, those who are your own devotees—
The bliss they find, and the final state of salvation that
    they attain—

That same bliss, that state,
That same devotion, that same love for your feet,
That same discernment, that same way of living—
Lord, by your grace, give to us.'   (150)

Hearing her sweet and gentle speech, most pleasing and
    profound,
The ocean of compassion gently replied,
'All the desires of your heart—
I grant them all, have no doubt.
By my grace, Mother, you will never lose
Your extraordinary wisdom and discernment.'
Then Manu, paying homage to his feet, spoke again and said,
'Lord, I have one more plea—
Let me have the same love for your feet as I would for a son,
No matter how big a fool anyone calls me,
Just as a cobra cannot live without the jewel in its hood, or a fish
    without water,
So let my life be dependent upon you.'
Having sought this boon, he remained clasping the Lord's feet.
'So shall it be,' said the compassionate Lord.

'Now obey my command—
Go and make your home in Indra's city.

> There, enjoy all its great delights, Father,
> And after some ages have passed,
> You will be born as the king of Avadh—
> Then I will become your son.   (151)

Assuming the form of a man according to my wish,
I will manifest myself in your home.
I will take on a body and become incarnate with all my parts, Father,
And will perform deeds that will bring bliss and joy to my devotees.
Fortunate men, hearing about my exploits with reverence,
Will cross the ocean of existence, abandoning attachment,
        self and pride.
The primal energy, of whom the world has been born,
This maya of mine—she too will descend upon earth.
I will fulfil your desire,
True is my promise, true, true.'
Repeating this again and again, the compassionate Lord,
Supreme God, disappeared from sight.
The royal couple, holding the merciful one in their hearts,
Stayed on for a while in that hermitage.
When it was time, they gave up their bodies without pain or effort
And went and made their home in Amaravati.

> This sacred history
> Brishketu related to Uma.
> Bharadvaj, now listen to another
> Reason for Ram's birth.   (152)

Listen, muni, to this old and sacred story
Which Shambhu related to Girija—
There was a country called Kaikeya, renowned in all the world,

And Satyaketu was its king.
A staunch upholder of dharma and knowledgeable in good
    government,
Great in glory and majesty, virtuous and strong,
To him were born two valiant sons,
Who were steadfast in battle and endowed with every virtue.
The older son, the heir to the throne,
Was called Pratapbhanu, sun of glory.
The other son was named Arimardan, destroyer of foes,
Of unparalleled strength and in battle as immovable as a mountain.
The two brothers were the best of friends,
And their love for each other was free of all deceit or guile.
The king bequeathed his kingdom to the older son,
And retired to the forest, devoting himself to Hari.

> When Pratapbhanu became king,
> It was proclaimed in all the land.
> He ruled his subjects in accordance with the ways set down in
>   the Vedas
> So that nowhere was there even the slightest trace of sin.   (153)

The prime minister, shrewd and wise, was devoted to the king;
A veritable Shukra,[lxi] his name was Dharmaruchi.[lxii]
Thus Pratapbhanu had a wise minister and a strong and
    valiant brother,
And was himself a mighty warrior, glorious and steadfast in battle.
He also had an unrivalled army complete with elephants, chariots,
    cavalry and infantry,
Its countless soldiers all fearless in war—
Looking upon his army, the king rejoiced,
As drums beat and thundered.

[lxi]   Priest and advisor to Indra
[lxii] Literally, 'one whose passion is dharma'

Preparing his army for conquest,
And choosing an auspicious day, the king marched forth to the
      beat of drums.
Fighting countless battles in every direction,
He conquered and humbled all the other kings of the earth.
With the strength of his arm, he brought all the seven continents
      under his sway.
Exacting tribute from the kings, he let them go—
And so, at that time, the whole world
Had one undisputed king: Pratapbhanu.

      Having brought the whole world under his sway by the might
            of his arm,
      He re-entered his own city.
      Here, in accordance with what was appropriate at a
            particular time,
      The king of men devoted himself to business, duty, the
            pleasures of love and so on.   (154)

The beautiful earth, infused with King Pratapbhanu's strength,
Became a veritable Kamdhenu.
His subjects, blissful and freed of all sorrow,
Were handsome and virtuous men and women.
The minister, Dharmaruchi, was devoted to Hari's feet—
With the good of the king always in mind, he instructed him daily
      in policy and statesmanship.
To his guru, gods, saints, forefathers and Brahmans,
The king rendered constant service.
The duties of a ruler as laid down in the Vedas,
The king gladly and with reverence fulfilled them all.
Every day he gave away alms and gifts of various kinds,
And listened to the sacred Shastras, the Vedas and the Puranas.
With countless baths, wells and ponds,
Flower gardens and pleasing orchards,

And beautiful residences for Brahmans and temples for the gods,
He adorned and made extraordinarily beautiful, all the places
    of pilgrimage.

    Each and every sacrifice that the Puranas and
        the Vedas enjoined—
    The king performed them all,
    Not once, but a thousand, thousand times,
    With love and deep devotion.   (155)

The king had no desire in his heart for reward,
For he was discerning and most wise.
Whatever duties he performed, whether in deed, thought
    and word,
The wise king offered to Lord Vaasudev.
One day, the king mounted one of his excellent horses,
And making all the necessary preparations, set off to hunt.
He went into the dense jungles of Vindhyachal,
Where he killed many pure and beautiful deer.
Wandering through the forest, the king saw a boar.
It was as though Rahu, having swallowed the moon, was hiding in
    the forest—
The moon was too big and didn't fit into his mouth,
But in his rage, he would not spit it out.
Such, as I have described it, was the splendour of the boar's
    formidable tusks.
His body, too, was huge and very heavy.
Hearing the tread of the horse's hooves, he grunted and snorted,
And stared in alarm, his ears pricked.

    Catching sight of that enormous boar,
    Like the summit of a dark mountain,
    The king whipped his horse into a gallop
    And shouted loudly, 'You cannot escape!'   (156)

Seeing the horse thundering towards him,
The boar took fright and fled as fast the wind.
At once the king fitted an arrow to his bow—
The boar, seeing the arrow, merged with the ground.
The king, taking swift aim, shot arrow after arrow,
But the boar craftily eluded them, and saving himself,
Ran away, sometimes coming into view, sometimes disappearing
    from sight—
The king, gripped by the passion of the hunt, followed in pursuit.
After some distance, the boar entered a dense thicket,
Where elephants and horses could not penetrate;
Even though he was completely alone in the great forest and the
    way was difficult,
The king did not give up his pursuit of the animal.
The boar, seeing the king so determined,
Ran into a deep mountain cave.
Seeing that the cave was inaccessible, the king was greatly disappointed;
But roaming in that great forest, he had lost his way.

    Weary, disheartened, hungry and thirsty,
    The king with his horse
    Searched desperately for a stream or pond—
    He was close to fainting for want of water.   (157)

Wandering through the forest, he saw a hermitage
Where, in secret and disguised as a muni, lived a king
Whose kingdom Pratapbhanu had wrested,
And who, abandoning his army, had fled the battle
Knowing that the times were favourable to Pratapbhanu
And considering them to be extremely unlucky for himself.
Greatly disheartened, he had not returned home,
But, being too proud, nor had he reconciled with the king.
Suppressing the anger in his heart, that king
Lived in the forest like a pauper, wearing the guise of an ascetic.

It was him the king approached—
He immediately recognized him as Pratapbhanu.
The king was tired and thirsty and did not recognize him,
And seeing his holy garb, took him to be a great sage.
Dismounting from his horse, the king saluted him respectfully,
But shrewdly did not disclose his own name.

> Perceiving that the king was thirsty,
> The ascetic led him to a large pond.
> The king, together with his horse,
> Gladly bathed in it and drank its water.　　　　　(158)

All his tiredness left him, and the king was happy again.
Knowing that the sun was about to set,
The ascetic took him back to his own hermitage and offered
　　him a seat.
Then said the ascetic in gentle tones,
'Who are you, and why do you wander in this forest alone?
You are young and handsome, why do you play with your life?
You bear all the marks of an emperor,
And looking upon you, I feel great compassion.'
'There is a king by the name of Pratapbhanu—
Listen, great muni, I am his minister.
I lost my way while hunting,
And it is by great good fortune that I have been led here to your feet.
It was not easy to come by your presence—
I believe this is a sign that something good will happen.'
Said the muni, 'Son, it is growing dark,
And your city is seventy yojans away.

> Listen, wise one, the night is very dark,
> The forest deep and there is no path through it.
> So, stay here tonight,
> And leave as soon as it is daybreak.'　　　　　(159A)

What has to happen will happen—
Circumstances will arise to make it so, says Tulsi.
Either they will bring the inevitable to you,
Or they will help to take you there.   (159B)

The king humbly accepted the hermit's suggestion. 'As you say,
     lord,' he said,
And tying his horse to a tree, sat down.
The king praised the ascetic in many ways,
And paying him homage, praised his own good fortune.
Then he said to him in soft and reverend tones,
'Regarding you as my father, lord, I will be bold and ask you—
Look upon me, great sage, as your son and servant,
And tell me, master, your name and about yourself in detail.'
The king had not recognized him, but he had recognized the king,
The king had a heart that was clean and pure, but he was deceitful
     and sly.
He was, first, the king's enemy, and then also a Kshatriya and of
     royal birth—
So he sought to achieve his purpose through deceit and the
     strength of his cunning.
Recalling the royal luxuries he too had once enjoyed, the king's
     enemy was deeply unhappy
And his heart burnt within him like flames in a furnace.
Hearing the king's ingenuous and sincere words,
He recalled the grudge he bore him, and rejoiced in his heart.

     He replied with sweet but deceitful words
     Steeped in cunning and guile,
     'My name is now simply "pauper"
     For now I am without money or home.'   (160)

Said the king, 'Those who are wise and discerning
Like you, and who have overcome all pride and self-conceit—

They forever keep their true selves concealed.
They are in all manner blessed, and rejoice in their
    wretched disguise.
It is because of this that sages and the Vedas proclaim
That it is the most destitute that Hari holds most dear.
Moneyless and homeless mendicants such as you,
Make even Viranchi and Shiv uncertain.
Whoever you are, I pay homage at your feet—
Now grant me your grace, lord.'
Seeing the king's simple and sincere affection,
The hermit grew more confident.
In every way he charmed the king and won him over,
And with a show of great affection, he said,
'Listen, great king, I tell you the truth—
I have dwelt here for many years.

    Till now, no one has come to meet me,
    Nor have I revealed myself to anyone,
    For fame and worldly honour are like a fire
    That consumes the forest of austerity and penance.'   (161A)

    Seeing a pleasing outward appearance, says Tulsi,
    Not just fools, but also shrewd and clever men are deceived.
    Behold the beautiful peacock—
    Its call is like nectar, but its diet is serpents.   (161B)

'That is why,' the ascetic continued, 'I stay hidden from the world—
Except for Hari, I have no need or dealings of any kind
    with anyone.
The Lord knows all without being told,
So tell me then, what is to be gained by pleasing the world?
You are pure and upright, intelligent and of sound sense, and so are
    greatly beloved of me.
You, too, have affection and faith in me.

So now, my son, if I should hide anything from you,
It would be a grievous fault on my part.'
The more the ascetic spoke of his detachment from the world,
The more the king's faith in him grew.
When he saw that the king was completely under his influence in
        thought, word and deed,
The ascetic, who was as deceitful as the stork that pretends to
        meditate while lying in wait for unwary fish, said,
'My name, friend, is Ektanu, or "one who has but one body".'[lxiii]
Hearing this, the king, once more bowing his head, said,
'Explain the meaning of this name at length
Knowing me to be your devoted servant.'

    'I was born the moment that
    Primordial creation came into existence.
    My name is Ektanu because,
    Since then, I have not taken on another body.   (162)

Hearing this, do not be astonished,
For nothing, son, is difficult to attain with penance.
It is through the power of penance that Brahma creates this world,
It is through the power of penance that Vishnu became its protector,
It is through the power of penance that Shambhu causes
        its dissolution—
Through penance, there is nothing unattainable in the world.'
Hearing this, the king felt great devotion for the ascetic,
Who then began to relate ancient tales and legends.
Through many tales of virtuous deeds and righteous action,
He discoursed upon detachment and discernment.
Of the birth of the universe, its nurturing and its dissolution,
He related at great length innumerable and marvellous stories.
Hearing these, the king was now completely under his spell

[lxiii] In other words, one not subject to transmigration

And began to reveal to him his true name.
Said the ascetic, 'King, I know you,
You deceived me, but I was pleased by that,

> For listen, monarch of the earth, it is prudent and wise
> For a king not to declare his name.
> Reflecting upon your shrewdness and wisdom,
> I feel great affection for you.   (163)

Your name is Pratapbhanu, sun of glory,
And Satyaketu, that king of men, was your father.
Through the grace of my guru, I know everything, king,
But I do not say anything, knowing that to do so will be to
    my detriment.
Perceiving your inherent simplicity and goodness, son,
Your affection and faith, your prudence and political wisdom,
Affection for you has sprung up in my heart—
And so I told you my story as you asked.
Now, have no doubt, I am pleased with you,
So ask, king, for a boon that pleases your heart.'
The king rejoiced to hear these gracious words,
And clasping the ascetic's feet, made obeisance in many ways.
'Ocean of compassion, most merciful muni, by merely being in
    your presence
I hold in my fist the four rewards of human existence.
Yet, seeing you so pleased with me, lord,
I ask for a boon otherwise impossible to attain, to become free of
    sorrow forever:

> May my body remain free of old age, death and pain,
> May no one ever defeat me in battle,
> And may I reign as supreme and undisputed monarch of
>   the earth
> For a hundred cycles of creation.'   (164)

Said the ascetic, 'King, so it will be,
But there is one difficulty—hear that too.
Even Death will bow his head at your feet,
But the one exception, lord of the earth, will be the Brahmans.
Through the power of penance, the Brahmans are ever mighty,
From their wrath, no one can protect you—
But subjugate the Brahmans, king,
And you will control even Vidhi, Vishnu and Mahesh.
But force does not work with the Brahmans—
This truth I declare, raising my arms to heaven!
Listen, monarch of the earth, unless a Brahman curses you,
You will not be killed in any age.'
The king rejoiced to hear his words.
'Now, lord, my death shall never be!
With your favour upon me, compassionate lord
All times will be fortunate and propitious for me.'

    'So shall it be,' proclaimed the false muni,
    Then craftily said,
    'If you ever tell anyone of our meeting or losing your way,
    It won't be my fault—   (165)

I warn you, king, not to do so,
For telling anyone this tale will cause you great harm.
Should this story fall into a third pair of ears,
Then, I tell you truly, it shall be your end.
Only by revealing this incident, or by a Brahman's curse—
Hear me, Pratapbhanu—can you be destroyed.
No other means or contrivance can cause your death,
Not even if Hari and Har were to rage at you in their hearts.
'It is true, my master,' said the king, clasping the hermit's feet,
'Who can protect one from a Brahman's wrath or the anger of
    one's guru?
A guru protects you even from Brahma's anger,

But against a guru's anger, there is no protector in the world.
May I be destroyed if I disregard what you say—
I care not about that.
My heart is troubled by only one fear, lord—
That a Brahman's curse is very dire!

In what way can I bring the Brahmans under my sway,
Look upon me with kindness, and tell me that too—
Except for you, merciful one,
I see no other benefactor.'   (166)

'Listen, king, there are many schemes and stratagems in the world
     by which to achieve this,
But they require great effort and are difficult to accomplish, and
     even then they may or may not be successful.
Yes, there does exist one very easy way,
Though there is one difficulty even with that.
The scheme, king, depends upon me
And it is impossible for me to go to your city,
For until this day, from the moment that I was born,
I have not entered anybody's home or village—
But if I do not go, it is detrimental to you.
This is a big dilemma for me now!'
Hearing this, the king replied in gentle tones,
'Lord, it is an accepted truth stated in the Vedas,
That the great always show affection to the small—
Thus the mountains bear grasses and tiny shrubs upon their summits,
The bottomless ocean carries the floating foam upon its crests,
And the earth eternally bears dust upon her head.'

So saying, the king clasped the hermit's feet,
'Master, be compassionate towards me!
You are ever virtuous and merciful to the humble—
So for my sake, lord, undertake this difficult task!'   (167)

Realizing that the king was under his influence,
The ascetic, so skilled in deceit, said,
'I speak truly, king, so listen to what I say—
There is nothing in this world that is difficult or impossible for me.
I will most certainly do your work,
For you are my devotee in mind, deed and word.
But magic and meditation, plans, penance and mantras are effective
And bear fruit only when they are carried out in secret.
If, king, I were to cook and prepare some food,
And you were to serve that without anyone knowing me,
Those who eat that meal
Will follow your commands.
And what's more, anyone who then eats a meal in their homes,
They too, lord of the earth, will come under your sway!
Now go, and carry out this plan, king,
And resolve for a full year

> That each day you will invite
> A hundred thousand Brahmans with their families.
> And I, for the duration of your resolve,
> Will prepare the feast each day.   (168)

In this way, king, with very little trouble,
All the Brahmans will be under your power.
The Brahmans will perform sacrifices, make offerings and serve
        the gods,
And through those, the gods, too, will easily come under your sway.
Let me tell you one more element of this plan—
I will not ever appear in this form,
But rather as your chief priest, king,
Whom I will bring away through the power of my maya,
And through the power of my penance, I will make him look like me.
I will keep him here for the length of a year,
While I, king, assuming his form,

Will arrange and manage this business in every way for you.
The night is far gone, so now get some sleep,
And you and I, king, will meet again in three days.
Through the power of my penance, I will take you and your horse
To your palace while you sleep.

> I will come to you in the form I have said,
> And you will recognize me
> When I take you aside in solitude and relate to you
> This full story.'   (169)

The king lay down, obeying the ascetic's command,
While the false sage took a seat.
The king was tired and fell into a deep sleep,
But how could that false ascetic sleep, deep as he was in
    anxious thought?
The night-wandering demon, Kalketu, came there—
It was he who as a boar had led the king astray.
He was the hermit king's greatest friend,
And knew many ways of deceit and treachery.
His hundred sons and ten brothers
Had been utter rogues, invincible, and the bane of the gods.
They had all earlier been slain in battle by Pratapbhanu,
Who had seen the grief they had caused Brahmans, saints
    and gods.
The wicked demon, nursing this earlier enmity,
Conspired with the hermit king to devise a plan
Whereby their enemy may be destroyed.
The king, under destiny's sway, knew nothing of this.

> Even if a fierce enemy be alone,
> Do not consider him insignificant—
> Rahu torments the sun and the moon
> Even today, though he has nothing left but his head.   (170)

The hermit king, seeing his friend,
Rejoiced and joyfully rose to meet him.
He related to his friend all that had happened
And the demon, greatly pleased, replied,
'Listen, king, since you have done as I had directed,
Now assume that our enemy has already been taken care of.
Throw away all anxiety and sleep in peace here—
Without medicine, Vidhi has cured the disease.
Together with his family, I will destroy our enemy by the roots
And on the fourth day from today I will come to meet you.'
Thus greatly gladdening the hermit king,
The deceitful demon, full of wrathful vengeance, left.
Pratapbhanu, with his horse,
He conveyed in an instant to the palace.
He laid the king next to his wife,
And tied up the horse in the stable.

    The king's chief priest
    He then took away,
    And kept him in a mountain cave,
    Addling his wits through his magic powers.   (171)

He himself assumed the chief priest's form,
And went and lay down upon his comfortable bed.
The king awoke before daybreak,
And acknowledged it a wonder to find himself in his own house.
Thinking and speculating about the muni's power,
He rose up quietly so that the queen did not know,
And mounting the same horse, rode back to the forest
Without being seen by any of the men and women of the city.
When two watches of the day had passed, the king returned—
Celebration and rejoicing broke out in every house.
When the king saw his chief priest,
He looked upon him with wonder, remembering what he had
    discussed with the hermit.

The three days passed like an age for the king,
His mind remained enslaved at the false muni's feet.
When it was time, the chief priest came,
And, as the hermit had told the king, related to him the full
    circumstances of their plan.

The king joyfully recognized his guru—
In the grip of delusion, he lost his wits,
And at once invited a hundred thousand eminent Brahmans
With their families.   (172)

The chief priest prepared the feast
Of six flavours and four kinds of food as prescribed in
    the Vedas.
He prepared a lavish and sumptuous banquet,
With so many condiments, seasoning and spices that they could
    not be counted.
He cooked and prepared the flesh of various animals,
But into it the rogue mixed the flesh of Brahmans.
All the Brahmans were called to eat,
Their feet were washed, and they were seated with reverence.
When the king began to serve them,
A voice from the heavens was heard—
'All you Brahmans, get up, get up and go home!
There is great harm in eating this food,
For this food has been prepared with the flesh of Brahmans!'
The Brahmans rose, heeding the voice from the sky.
The king was greatly distressed at this, but confused
    and bewildered,
And bound by destiny, he could not utter a single word.

Then cried the Brahmans in their fury,
Paying no heed to consequences,
'Be born a demon of the night, foolish king,
Along with all your family!   (173)

Vile Kshatriya, you invited Brahmans
To destroy us along with our whole community!
But the Lord preserved our faith and our honour,
And now you will perish along with your family.
Within a year you will die,
Nor will there be anyone left in your family to even pour libations
    to your spirit.'
The king, hearing the curse, became distracted with terror.
Once again the divine voice was heard from the sky,
'Brahmans, you have pronounced your curse without thinking,
The king has done no wrong!'
The Brahmans listened in astonishment to the voice from the sky.
The king hurried to where the food had been prepared,
But found neither food nor Brahman cook.
He returned, worried and deeply anxious
And related all the circumstances to the Brahmans, gods on earth—
Afraid and distressed, he threw himself prostrate upon the ground.

    'Lord of the earth, what is destined cannot be changed,
    Even though it was no fault of yours.
    A Brahman's curse is dire indeed—
    Despite every effort to undo it, it cannot be reversed.'   (174)

So saying, all the Brahmans departed.
The townsfolk heard what had happened—
Fearful and anxious, they blamed the gods,
Who, while creating a swan, had turned it into a crow.
After conveying the chief priest to his home,
The demon recounted to the hermit all that had happened.
That rogue in turn sent letters here, there and everywhere,
And all the kings to whom he had written, readied their armies for
    war and came hurrying.
Sounding their battle drums, they besieged the city,
And day after day, many long battles took place.

Pratapbhanu's warriors fought valiantly, but all were killed,
And the king, with his brother, also fell in battle.
No one from Satyaketu's line survived,
For can a Brahman's curse ever be untrue?
Having overcome their enemy, the kings re-established the city,
And returned to their own cities with victory and renown.

    Hear me, Bharadvaj, when destiny turns against someone,
    A grain of dust becomes like Meru for him,
    His own father like Jam, the god of death
    And a rope as dangerous as a snake.   (175)

And so, muni, in due course that same king
Was born as a night-wandering demon, together with his family.
He had ten heads and twenty arms,
His name was Ravan, and he was a great and formidable warrior.
The king's younger brother, whose name had been Arimardan,
Was born as the strong and mighty Kumbhakaran.
His prime minister, who had been called Dharmaruchi,
Was born of his stepmother as his younger brother—
His name was Vibhishan, which is known to all the world;
A devotee of Vishnu, he was a storehouse of wisdom and knowledge.
And as for the sons and servants of the king,
They were born as fierce and frightening demons,
Evil creatures of various kinds, who could take on any form at will,
Cruel, terrifying, without discernment of any kind.
They were all ruthless and violent, and perpetrators of every sin
    and crime—
Tormentors of all creation, they cannot be described!

    Though they had sprung from the incomparably
    Pure and unblemished clan of the Rishi Pulastya,
    Under the curse of the Brahmans,
    They were all reborn as sin personified.   (176)

The three brothers all performed various austerities,
So severe that they are difficult to describe.
When Brahma saw their penance, he went up to them and said,
'Ask of me a boon, sons, for I am pleased.'
The ten-headed one clasped his feet and humbly entreated him,
"Hear what I ask, Lord of the world—
I would not be killed by anyone,
Save the two species of monkey and man.'
'So be it, for you have done great penance,'
Brahma and I together granted him the boon.
The Lord then approached Kumbhakaran,
And seeing him, his heart was filled with dismay.
'If this rogue were to eat every day
All creation will be laid waste!' thought Brahma.
So he urged Sharada to addle his wits,
And he asked to sleep for six full months.

He then approached Vibhishan and said,
'Son, ask for a boon.'
And he asked for unblemished devotion
At the lotus feet of the Supreme Lord.   (177)

Granting them their boons, Brahma departed,
And rejoicing, the three brothers returned home.
The demon Mai had a daughter named Mandodari,
A great beauty and an ornament to womankind.
Mai brought her and gave her to Ravan,
Knowing that one day he would be lord of the demons.
Ravan rejoiced at finding such a good wife.
He then had his two brothers married.
The three-peaked mountain, Trikut, stood in the middle of
        an ocean,
Upon it was a huge and impregnable fort built by Brahma.
The Danav Mai repaired that fort.

In it stood innumerable golden palaces studded with precious stones.
Like Bhogavati, where live the serpent clans,
Like Amaravati, where resides Sakr,
More splendid and more merry than those cities was this fort,
Famed throughout the world as Lanka.

Its moat was the deep ocean,
Which surrounded it on all four sides;
Its massive ramparts were of gold, inlaid with jewels,
Of workmanship that defies description.   (178A)

In any cycle of creation, whichever mighty warrior
Is ordained by Hari to become the king of the demons,
He, of glorious majesty and incomparable strength,
Resides there with his army.   (178B)

Once, great demon warriors had lived there,
But they were all killed by the gods in war.
Now, by Sakr's command, it was occupied
By ten million guards of Kuber, king of the Yakshas.
Ten-headed Ravan came to know of this,
And, gathering his army, he surrounded the fort.
Seeing the fierce warrior and his vast army,
The Yakshas fled for their lives.
The ten-faced one then inspected the whole city—
His worries fell away and he was greatly pleased.
Considering the city to be both beautiful and naturally difficult
    of access,
Ravan made it his capital.
He assigned houses in the city to his men according to
    their rank,
And made all the demons happy.
Then one day he launched an attack against Kuber,
And came away with the flying chariot Pushpak as his trophy.

Then he went to Mount Kailash,
And, in play, lifted it up,
As though measuring the strength of his arms,
And came away, greatly pleased.   (179)

His pleasures, his wealth, the number of his sons, his army and
    his allies,
His victories, his glory, his strength, his intellect, his fame,
All increased each day,
In the same way that greed increases with every gain.
As his brother, he had the mighty Kumbhakaran,
Whose equal in war had never been born in the world.
He would drink and then sleep for six months,
But his waking would fill the three worlds with terror.
If he were to eat every day,
The whole world would quickly be laid waste,
And he was so steadfast in war that it is beyond description.
There were innumerable such mighty warriors in Ravan's city.
Meghnad, with his voice like thunder, was his eldest son,
Foremost amongst the warriors of this world,
Whom no one dared confront in battle,
And because of whom the city of the gods was in constant terror
    and turmoil.

There were also Kumukh the Ugly, Akampan the Steadfast,
    Kulisarad with teeth of adamant,
Dhumketu the Comet, Atikaya the Enormous,
And other such mighty warriors with him,
Each one capable of conquering the world alone.   (180)

All were able to assume any form at will, were skilled in every kind
    of deception,
And cared neither for dharma nor compassion even in their dreams.
Once, the ten-headed one sat in assembly,

Gazing upon his innumerable kin,
His sons, grandsons, servants and relatives gathered there,
Tribes, clans and castes of demons beyond count.
Haughty Ravan looked at his army,
And spoke in fierce tones words filled with wrath and arrogance,
'Hear me, all you companies of night-wanderers,
The gods are our enemies.
They do not fight face to face,
But seeing a strong and mighty foe, they run away.
There is one way to kill them—
Listen to me as I explain it to you.
The feasting of Brahmans, the performance of sacrifices,
    the pouring of libations into the sacred fire, and ceremonies
    to honour the dead—
Go and stop them all.

    Weak with hunger, bereft of strength,
    The gods of their own accord will come to me.
    Then I can kill them or let them go,
    After subjecting them completely to my will.'   (181)

He then summoned Meghnad
And, urging him to greater courage and enmity towards the gods,
    instructed him,
'Those gods who are in battle steadfast and strong,
And with self-respect enough to fight—
Those gods vanquish in battle and bring them here as your captives.'
The son rose, taking his father's commands upon his shoulders.
In this manner, issuing orders to all,
Ravan too went forth, mace in hand.
The earth shook as the ten-headed one stepped forth.
The thunder of his coming caused the wives of the gods to miscarry,
And hearing Ravan's wrath-filled approach,
The gods sought shelter in the caves of Mount Meru.

The lovely realms of the guardians of the ten quarters of the world,
The ten-headed one found deserted.
Again and again he would roar like a lion,
Challenging the gods and hurling abuse at them.
Intoxicated with the lust of battle, he roamed the earth
Searching for an opponent equal to himself, but did not find
    one anywhere.
The gods of the sun, moon, wind, seas and rivers, the treasures of
    the earth,
Fire, death and dharma—all those entrusted with running the world,
Kinnaras, Siddhas, men, gods and Nagas,
He determinedly pursued them all.
Every embodied being in Brahma's creation,
Every man and woman, all submitted to the ten-faced one.
Terror-stricken, they obeyed all his commands,
And daily came and fell humbly at his feet.

    Through the strength of his arms, he brought the whole
        world under his sway,
    Leaving no one free or independent.
    This king of kings, Ravan,
    Ruled according to his own will.   (182A)

    The daughters of gods, Yakshas, Gandharvas
    Men, Kinnaras and Nagas
    Innumerable beautiful and accomplished women—
    He won through the might of his arms
        and took in marriage.   (182B)

Whatever commands he gave to Indrajit[lxiv]
Were all accomplished almost before he spoke.
Now listen to the deeds of those warriors

_____

[lxiv] Meghnad

To whom he had issued instructions earlier.
Terrifying to behold and sinners all,
The demon hordes were the bane of the gods.
The Asur armies caused havoc,
Assuming countless forms through their powers of deception.
Whatever means served to uproot and destroy dharma,
They would engage in them all, in defiance of the Vedas.
Wherever they found cows or the twice-born,
That village, town or city they set on fire.
Now virtuous acts were no longer performed,
No one respected gods, Brahmans and gurus anywhere,
Nor was there devotion to Hari, the performance of sacrifices,
    austerity, or wisdom,
And the Vedas and the Puranas could not be heard even in dream.

*The chanting of mantras, meditation, detachment, penance, or offerings
    to the gods—*
If talk of these ever came to ten-headed Ravan's ears,
*He would, himself, rise and rush to attack, making sure that they
    ceased completely,*
And killing all he could lay his hands on.
Such foul and depraved behaviour pervaded the universe
That dharma was no longer heard of—
Those who dared recite the Vedas or the Puranas,
Were intimidated and terrorized and banished from the land.

The dreadful atrocities committed by these demons of the night,
Were beyond description.
Is there any limit to the sins
Of those who love violence so much?   (183)

Criminals, thieves and gamblers rose in number,
As did greedy, lecherous and lustful men who covet the wealth and
    wives of other men—

No longer respectful of mother or father or the gods,
They made the good and holy serve them.
Know all those who behave in this way, Bhavani,
To be night-wandering demons.
Seeing this excessive aversion to dharma,
The Earth grew afraid and uneasy:
'Mountains, rivers and seas do not weigh as heavily upon me
As does a single evildoer who harms and injures others.'
She saw all dharma reversed,
But terrified of Ravan, she could not speak.
After much consideration, she assumed the form of a cow,
And went where the gods and munis were hiding.
Weeping, she related her woes to them,
But none of them could help her.

Gods, munis, Gandharvas, gathering together,
All went to Viranchi's abode;
With them, in her assumed body of a cow, was poor Earth,
Grievously distressed, distracted with fear and sorrow.
The Creator understood the situation and thought to himself,
'It is beyond my power to do anything here,
He whom you serve, that Immortal Lord,
Will help both you and me.'

Then Viranchi said, 'Be patient, Earth, you who bear all,
And meditate upon Hari's feet.
The Lord understands the anguish of his devotees
And will end this terrible suffering.'   (184)

The gods all sat and pondered,
'Where shall we find the Lord so that we may put our plea before him?'
One said they should go to Vaikunth,
Another said that the Lord resides upon the Ocean of Milk.
The Lord always manifests himself in accordance

With the devotion and love in one's heart.
In that gathering, Girija, I, too, was present,
And finding an appropriate moment, I said,
'Hari pervades all places at all times equally,
And I know that he becomes manifest through love.
Tell me any place or time, any quarter of the universe,
Where the Lord is not present.
He pervades all beings, inanimate and animate, yet is separate
    and detached.
He is revealed by love as fire is revealed by friction.'
My words appealed to everyone,
And 'Excellent! Well said!' declared Brahma in praise.

Hearing me, Brahma rejoiced,
His body trembling with delight as tears of joy flowed
    from his eyes.
Then he of the steadfast mind composed himself
And, folding his hands, began to sing a song of praise.   (185)

Praise be to the Lord of the gods, who gladdens his devotees,
The supreme God, protector of those who seek his shelter;
Praise be to him, benefactor of cows and Brahmans, enemy of the Asurs,
Beloved husband of Lakshmi, the daughter of the ocean;
Protector of the gods and of the earth,
Whose deeds are marvellous, whose mysteries are known to none,
He, who is by nature compassionate, and merciful to the humble—
May he show us his favour.
Praise be to the indestructible, immortal Lord,
Present everywhere, residing in every heart, bliss supreme,
All-pervading, imperceptible, whose deeds are most pure and holy—
Mukund,[lxv] the giver of liberation, who is free of maya!
For whom long those who are free from longing,

[lxv] Vishnu, as the giver of freedom from rebirth

Whom the multitude of munis, renouncing love, fervently love,
And sing night and day of his glories—
Praise be to him, existence, consciousness and bliss combined!
He who devised Creation and brought into existence unaided
The threefold universe of gods, men and demons,
May he, destroyer of suffering and sin, take care of us,
Who know not devotion or worship.
He who destroys the fear of this existence, delights the minds of munis,
And removes the multitudinous agonies of this world—
With our hearts, words and deeds, and giving up on the cleverness upon
    which we so pride ourselves,
We come, the whole company of gods together, to seek his protection.
He whom Sharada, the Vedas, Shesh and all the rishis
Cannot comprehend,
To whom, proclaim the Vedas, are beloved the humble and needy—
May the Supreme Lord be moved to pity towards us.
He who is Mount Mandar in the ocean of worldly existence,
Who is in every way beautiful, a temple of virtue and the accumulation
    of bliss—
The munis, the Siddhas, and all the gods, distraught with fear,
Prostrate themselves at the Lord's lotus feet.

    Knowing the gods and the Earth to be afraid,
    And hearing their words full of love,
    A voice, deep and profound, came from the sky,
    And dispelled their grief and doubt.   (186)

'Do not be afraid, O sages, Siddhas and mighty gods.
For the love I bear you, I will take on human form
Along with every element of my being, and I will descend as a man
In the noble and illustrious dynasty of the sun.[63]
Kashyap and Aditi performed great penance,
And I have already given them a boon—
In the form of Dasharath and Kaushalya

They have appeared in the city of Ayodhya as the rulers of the
    kingdom of Koshal.
It is in their house that I will descend
In the form of four brothers, ornaments all, of Raghu's line.
Making Narad's words come true,
I will appear upon earth together with my supreme energy,[lxvi]
And relieve the earth's entire burden.
So be free of fear, all you company of gods!'
Having heard this divine voice from the sky with their own ears,
The gods immediately turned back, their hearts cheered
    and reassured.
Then Brahma comforted Earth—
She became free of fear, and faith and hope returned to her heart.

    Viranchi returned to his own abode
    After giving the gods these instructions:
    'Assume, each one of you, the body of a monkey, and go
        to earth
    To serve at Hari's feet.'   (187)

All the gods returned to their respective abodes,
Their minds at rest, along with Earth.
The gods received with joy
The orders that Brahma had given, and carried them out
    without delay.
Descending to earth, they took on the bodies of forest-wandering
    beings
And received incomparable strength and splendour.
With mountains, trees and claws as their weapons, all these
    valiant warriors
Steadfastly watched for Hari's coming.

[lxvi] His supreme energy personified as his consort Sita

They filled the earth in every direction—upon every mountain and
    in every forest
They settled, each gathering his own brave and valiant army.
All these good and beautiful deeds I have narrated,
But now listen to what I had left unfinished.
In the city of Avadh there reigned a jewel of Raghu's line—
The king was renowned in the Vedas, and his name was
    Dasharath.
A firm upholder of dharma, a storehouse of virtue, wise and learned,
His heart and mind were filled with devotion to bow-bearing
    Vishnu, Sarangpani.[64]

    Kaushalya and his other beloved queens
    Were all of pure and pious deportment,
    Obedient to their husband, and unwavering in their love
    And humble devotion to Hari's lotus feet.   (188)

One day, in the king's heart
Arose sadness and regret. 'I don't have a son,' he thought.
The king hastened at once to his guru's house
And fell at his feet in humble entreaty.
He related all his joys and sorrows to his guru.
Vasishtha consoled him with many words, and said,
'Take courage, for you will have four sons
Who will be renowned in the three worlds and will remove the
    fears of the faithful.'
Then Vasishtha summoned Rishi Shringi
To perform the auspicious fire-sacrifice to obtain sons.
The muni made the oblations to the sacred fire with devotion,
And Agni[lxvii] appeared holding in his hands a pot containing an
    offering of rice and milk.

[lxvii] Agni is fire personified, and through fire-sacrifices, the mediator between
    gods and men

'Whatever Vasishtha had thought of in his heart—
That purpose has been fully accomplished.
Take this offering and distribute it, O king,
Dividing it into such portions as are appropriate.'

> Then Agni, the purifying one, disappeared,
> Having instructed the whole gathering.
> The king was overwhelmed with happiness,
> He could not contain his joy within his heart.   (189)

The king immediately summoned his beloved wives,
And Kaushalya and the others went to him.
A half portion he gave to Kaushalya,
And divided the remaining portion into equal halves.
One of these portions he gave to Kaikeyi,
And what remained he again divided into two half portions;
Placing these in the hands of Kaushalya and Kaikeyi and so
    obtaining their approval,
He gave them to Sumitra and made her happy.
In this manner the queens all conceived
And their hearts were filled with great happiness.
From the day Hari entered the womb,
All the worlds were filled with bliss and prosperity.
In the palace shone all the queens,
Beautiful, virtuous and radiant with joy.
Some time thus passed in happiness—
Till the moment arrived for the Lord to become manifest.

> The conjunction of sun and moon, the zodiac sign, the
>   planetary alignments, the day, the date—
> All became favourable,
> And all beings, animate and inanimate, were steeped
>   in joy,
> For Ram's birth is the source of all bliss.   (190)

It was the ninth day of the sweet and fresh spring month of Chait,
In the bright lunar fortnight, under the asterism Abhijit, so beloved
    of Hari.
It was the middle of the day, neither very cold nor very hot,
The sacred time when the world rests.
Cool, soft and fragrant breezes began to blow,
The gods began to rejoice, and the saints were filled with
    eager longing.
The forests were full of flowers, the mountains glittered with jewels,
And all the streams and rivers flowed with nectar.
When Viranchi realized that it was time,
The gods all set out, having made ready their chariots.
The clear sky became crowded with the company of gods,
And Gandharva hosts sang in praise,
Raining down flowers in beautiful handfuls.
Drums beat and reverberated in the sky,
Nagas, munis and gods sang songs of praise,
And each, in diverse ways, offered their worship.

    The company of gods, having offered their praise,
    Returned to their respective abodes.
    And the Lord—in whom resides the Universe
    And in whom the whole world finds rest—
        became manifest.   (191)

He became manifest, the compassionate Lord,
Merciful to the lowly and Kaushalya's benefactor.
His mother, looking upon his extraordinary beauty
That could win even the hearts of munis, rejoiced.
His eye-enchanting body was as dark as a cloud heavy with rain,
And his own special weapons in his four arms he held.[65]
Adorned with jewels, with his garland of wildflowers and great eyes,
An ocean of beauty was Kharari.[lxviii]

[lxviii] Vishnu

Folding her two hands, his mother said,
'Infinite one, how should I praise you?
Beyond maya, beyond attributes, transcending knowledge, and
    immeasurable,
The Vedas and Puranas proclaim you.
Ocean of mercy and bliss, abode of all virtue,
Whom the saints and the scriptures praise—
Shri's beloved husband, who loves his devotees,
Has, for my good, become manifest.
A multitude of universes created by maya,
Are contained in every tiny hair upon his body, say the Vedas.
That this same Lord nurses at my breast,
Hearing this jest, even the most steadfast minds lose their composure.'
When this understanding dawned in his mother's mind, the Lord smiled
For he wished to perform many marvellous deeds—
He reassured his mother by relating to her the charming story of her
    previous birth,
So that in her there may arise towards him the love of a mother for a son.
Her awareness wavering, his mother spoke again and said,
'Abandon this form, my son,
And engage in those childish deeds that are so loved by a mother—
Such joy is unsurpassed.'
Hearing her words, the all-wise one began to wail—
The Lord of the gods became an infant!
Those who sing of this deed find shelter at Hari's feet
And never fall into the deep well that is this existence.

> For the sake of Brahmans, cows, gods and saints,
> He descended to earth in the form of a man,
> In a body created by his own will,
> Transcending maya, its attributes, and the senses.   (192)

Hearing the infant's cries, that beloved and most pleasing
    of sounds,
The queens all came hurrying.

Handmaidens and maidservants ran here and there in glad delight,
And all the people of the city were overwhelmed with joy.
Dasharath, hearing of his son's birth,
Was as if he had attained supreme bliss.
His heart overflowing with great love, his body trembling with joy,
He sought to rise, bidding his mind to be still.
'Merely hearing whose name leads to happiness and
        good fortune—
That same Lord has come into my home.'
The king's heart filled with supreme bliss—
He sent for musicians and commanded them to play.
He summoned his guru, Vasishtha,
Who came accompanied by Brahmans to the king's door.
He went to see the incomparable child,
The accumulation of beauty and virtue beyond description.

    The king then made ritual offerings to his ancestors and the
            household gods,
    Performed the auspicious rites and ceremonies of birth,
    And gave gifts of gold, cows, utensils and jewels
    To the Brahmans.   (193)

Flags and pennants flew all over the city, its doors and gateways
        were festooned with flowers—
The joyous decorations were beyond description.
Flowers rained down from the sky,
And all the people were full of gladness.
Crowds of women flocked together,
Hurrying forth, just as they were, in ordinary clothes
With golden pitchers and salvers piled with offerings of good omen.
Singing, they entered the king's doorway.
They performed rituals for the baby's protection,
And again and again they prostrated themselves at the infant's feet,
As poets, bards, minstrels and singers

Praised the pure virtues of Raghunayak.
Great wealth was given as alms to everyone,
And receivers did not keep these gifts but gave them away to others.
Musk, sandal and saffron collected in muddy puddles
In all the roads and lanes.

    Every home resounded with music and rejoicing,
    For the source of all beauty had been born,
    And joyful crowds of men and women
    Gathered everywhere.   (194)

When Kaikeyi and Sumitra
Also gave birth to beautiful sons,
The joy, the splendour and the lavishness of the celebration, and
    the rejoicing crowds that gathered
Could not be described even by Sharada and the serpent-king,
    Sheshnag.
The city of Avadh looked so splendid and beautiful
It seemed as though Night herself had come to see the Lord,
But upon seeing the sun still there, she had grown abashed,
And decided to turn into twilight.
The clouds of fragrant incense were like the darkness of dusk,
The flying abir, the red rays of the setting sun;
The many mansions that glittered like jewels were the stars,
The dome of the king's palace, the gentle and lustrous moon,
And in the palace, the sweet sound of the Vedas being chanted
Was like the continuous chirping of birds at dusk.
Gazing upon this spectacle, the sun forgot himself,
And a whole month passed without his knowing.

    The month became a mere day,
    But no one noticed this mystery.
    The sun stood still in his chariot,
    So how could it ever become night?   (195)

No one noticed this marvel,
And at last the jewel of the day moved on, singing Ram's praises
    as it set.
The gods, munis and Nagas, who had watched this great
    celebration,
Left for their homes, discussing their good fortune.
And further, let me tell you of a deception of mine—
Listen to it, Girija, for your mind is now firm and steadfast:
Kak Bhushundi and I were there together—
We were in human form, so no one recognized us.
Filled with supreme joy and the bliss of love
We roamed the streets, forgetting ourselves in our happiness.
Only one who receives Ram's grace
Can know of this joyful exploit of ours.
Upon this occasion, the king gave everyone who had come
Whatever their hearts desired.
Elephants, chariots, horses, gold, cows and diamonds
The king gave away, and clothes and apparel of various kinds.

    The hearts of all were satisfied
    And blessings echoed all over the land:
    'May all the boys live long!'—
    Tulsidas's beloved lords.   (196)

Several days passed by in this manner
Though no one noted the passing of day or night,
Till the king, realizing that it was time for the naming ceremony,
Sent for the wise Muni Vasishtha.
Greeting him with reverence, the king said,
'Bestow upon them, muni, the names that you have chosen.'
'Their names are many and matchless,
But I will name them, king, according to my own understanding:
He who is an ocean of bliss and happiness,
A single drop of which fills the three worlds with joy,

That abode of delight shall be named "Ram",
For he gives rest and repose to the whole universe.
He who carries upon himself the whole world, and nourishes and
    nurtures it,
His name shall be "Bharat",
And he, the very thought of whom destroys the enemy,
His name shall be "Shatrughna", renowned in the Vedas.'

> The abode of all noble qualities, beloved of Ram,
> And the mainstay of all the world—
> Upon him Guru Vasishtha bestowed
> The noble name of 'Lakshman'.   (197)

The guru gave these names after considering them carefully
    in his heart.
'The very essence of the Vedas, king, are your four sons—
They are the muni's treasures, the devotee's whole world, and the
    very breath of Shiv himself,
And still they take delight in the sweetness of their childish play.'
Looking upon him from infancy as his master and benefactor,
Lakshman devoted himself to the love of Ram's feet,
And between the two brothers, Bharat and Shatrughna,
Was love as noble as that between lord and devoted servant.
Gazing upon the two handsome pairs, dark and fair,
Their mothers broke blades of grass to keep away the evil eye.
Though all four were of pleasant disposition, abodes of
    beauty and virtue,
The greatest ocean of joy was Ram.
The kindness of his heart was as radiant as moonlight
Revealed in the heart-enchanting moonbeams of his smile.
Sometimes holding him on her lap, sometimes rocking him
    in a cradle,
His mother showered him with love, calling him her beloved
    little son.

The all-pervading Spirit of the Universe
Who is beyond the illusions of maya, without flaw, without
    form, indifferent to pleasure—
That very unborn and uncreated brahm, yielding to love and
    devotion,
Lay in Kaushalya's lap.   (198)

His dark form was as beautiful as innumerable Kamdevs
And as radiant as a blue lotus, or dark clouds laden with rain,
With pink lotus-feet and shining toenails,
Like pearls upon lotus leaves.
Upon his soles shone the auspicious marks of the thunderbolt, the
    flag and the goad,[66]
While the tinkling of his anklets captivated even the hearts
    of sages.
A girdle of tiny bells encircled his waist, his belly with the
    auspicious three folds
And a navel so deep that only those who have seen it can know it.
His long arms were adorned with innumerable ornaments,
And upon his breast hung a magnificent tiger's claw of
    exceeding beauty.
The necklace of jewels and the mark of the Brahman's foot[67]
Upon his chest lured and captivated the heart.
He had a conch-like neck and a charming chin,
A face with the radiant beauty of numberless Madans,
And two pairs of teeth and red lips.
And his nose and the tilak upon his forehead—who can describe
    their beauty?
His ears were beautiful, his cheeks were charming,
And his sweet, lisping chatter so engaging to hear.
His shining, curling hair, still untrimmed from birth,
His mother combed and arranged in many ways.
A yellow smock upon his body,
He crawls upon hands and knees, which charms and delights me.

His form neither the Vedas nor Shesh can describe:
Only he may know it who sees it in a dream.

> He who is the accumulation of bliss, beyond delusion and
>   attachment,
> Beyond knowledge and speech and the perception of the senses,
> Yielding to the supreme love of the royal couple,
> Engages in the pure and innocent deeds of a child.   (199)

In this way, Ram, father and mother of the universe,
Gladdens and delights those who reside in this city of Ayodhya
  in Koshal.
This clearly shows that those who love and adore the feet
  of Raghunath
Attain to this state, Bhavani.
But, even with immeasurable effort, how can those
Who turn their faces away from Raghupati, escape the bonds
  of worldly existence?
Though she keeps all creatures, animate and inanimate, under
  her control,
Maya, too, is afraid of the Lord,
The merest twitch of whose eyebrows makes her dance.
Tell me, turning away from such a Lord, who will you adore?
If worshipped without guile or deceit in thought, word and deed,
Raghurai bestows his grace at once.
In this way, the Lord played and frolicked as an infant,
Delighting all the residents of the city.
His mother would now pick him up and rock him in her lap
And now lay him down and rock him in his cradle.

> Absorbed in her love, Kaushalya
> Did not notice the passing of the days and nights.
> The mother, overcome by love for her little son,
> Sang constantly of his infant deeds.   (200)

One day, his mother bathed him,
And dressing him, laid him in his cradle.
She then bathed in preparation
To offer worship to her own family god.
She performed the puja and made an offering of food to the deity,
And then went to the kitchen where the food had been prepared;
Returning to where she had performed the puja,
She saw her son eating the offering.
Greatly frightened, the mother hurried to where she had left
    her child,
And saw that the little boy was still asleep in his cradle.
Returning to the place of worship again, she still saw her son there
    as before—
Her heart beat unsteadily and her mind would not be still.
'I can see two babies, one here and one there—
Is this the delusion of my mind or is there some other,
    extraordinary, reason?'
Lord Ram, seeing his mother confused and bewildered,
Laughed and sweetly smiled.

  He revealed to his mother
  His own marvellous form, indivisible, indestructible,
  In every tiny hair of which
  Are contained millions upon millions of universes.   (201)

Innumerable suns and moons, Shivs and four-faced Brahmas,
Many mountains, rivers, oceans, fields and forests,
Time, Fate, every virtue, knowledge, innate Nature,
And even things that no one had ever heard of—she saw them all.
She saw Maya, who is in every way opaque and impenetrable,
Standing with folded hands, quite terrified.
She saw the embodied soul whom Maya makes dance to her tune,
And Bhakti who releases it.
Her body trembling, she could find no words—

Closing her eyes, she laid her head at his feet.
Seeing his mother so filled with wonder,
Kharari once again took on the form of a child.
She could not even utter his praises, so overcome was she
    with terror.
'The Lord of the universe I have known as my son!'
Hari reassured his mother in many ways and said,
'Listen, Mother, on no account speak of this.'

Folding her hands, Kaushalya
Again and again entreated him,
'Never again, Lord,
May your maya overwhelm me.'   (202)

Hari performed many childlike deeds,
A source of great joy to his servants.
As time passed, the four brothers
Grew bigger, delighting those around them.
The guru then came to perform the rite of tonsure,
The Brahmans again received generous gifts and abundant alms.
The four little princes ran about,
Engaging in the most enchanting and heart-delighting deeds.
He who is imperceptible and transcends thought, deed and word,
That same Lord plays in Dasharath's courtyard.
When the king calls him to eat,
He does not come, refusing to leave the company of
    other children.
When Kaushalya goes to fetch him,
The Lord toddles away as fast as he can.
He whom the Vedas describe only as 'Not this' and of whom even
    Shiv can find no end
Is chased and picked up by his mother.
He comes, his body covered with dust,
And the king, laughing, takes him upon his lap.

Even as he eats, his mind is restless,
And as soon as he gets a chance,
He runs off again, shrieking,
His face smeared with curd and rice.   (203)

His infant deeds, so innocent and charming,
Sharada, Shesh, Shambhu and the Vedas all sing;
Those whose hearts are not captivated by them
Have been cheated by providence.
When the brothers had all left their babyhood behind and grown
    to be young boys,
Their guru and their father and mother invested them with the
    sacred threads.
Raghurai went to his guru's house to study
And acquired all knowledge in a very short time.
That Hari, whose very breath is the four Vedas,
Should have to study is cause for merriment indeed!
Accomplished in scholarship, perfect in humility, virtue and
    good conduct,
They played at being kings.
With bow and arrows in their hands, they were exceedingly
    handsome.
Seeing their beauty, all creatures, animate and inanimate,
    were captivated,
Along whichever road or path the four brothers passed,
All men and women stopped to stare at them, enraptured.

To the people of Ayodhya,
Men and woman, old and young,
Compassionate and merciful Ram
Was dearer than their own life's breath.   (204)

Calling his brothers and friends to him and taking them along,
Ram would go every day to the forest to hunt.

He would kill only the deer he knew to be most perfect and pure,
And each day bring and show them to the king.
The deer slain by Ram's arrows
Gave up their bodies and entered the abode of the gods.
Ram took his meals with his younger brothers and his friends,
And lived in accordance with the commands of his mother and father.
Whatever would make the people of the city happy,
He, the compassionate Lord, would so contrive.
He would listen to the Vedas and the Puranas with attention
And himself recite and explain them to his younger brothers.
Arising at dawn, Raghunath
Would bow his head to his mother and his father and his guru
And obtaining their permission would busy himself with the affairs
    of the city.
The king, seeing his way of life, rejoiced.

> All-pervading, indivisible, without desire, uncreated,
> Without attributes, name or form—
> For the sake of his devotees he performed
> Incomparable and marvellous deeds of many kinds.   (205)

I have sung of all these deeds,
Now listen with attention to the next part of the tale.
Vishvamitra, the great and learned muni,
Lived in the forest, knowing it to be a sacred place.
Here the muni spent his time in prayer, meditation and the
    performance of sacrifices.
But he was greatly afraid of the demons Marich and Subahu—
Seeing a fire-sacrifice, the night-wandering demons would attack
    at once,
And disturb and desecrate it, which would distress the muni.
Gadhi's son[lxix] was filled with anxiety,

[lxix] Vishvamitra

'Without Hari's help, these wicked night-wanderers cannot
     be killed.'
Then the great muni reflected,
'The Lord has descended to relieve the earth of her burdens;
Let me use this as an excuse to go into his presence
And humbly ask to bring back the two brothers Ram
     and Lakshman.
The Lord who is the abode of knowledge, detachment and
     all virtues—
Upon that Lord I will feast my eyes, filling my gaze with his image.'

     Yearning for the Lord in manifold ways,
     He left at once and did not delay on the journey.
     After bathing in the waters of the Sarayu,
     He went to the king's court.   (206)

When the king heard of the muni's arrival,
He went to receive him, taking with him a company of Brahmans.
Prostrating himself before him, he did obeisance to the muni,
And seated him upon his own throne.
Reverently washing his feet, he paid him deep homage—
'There is none today as fortunate as I.'
He served him with many kinds of foods
That greatly pleased the muni.
He then placed his four sons at the muni's feet.
Seeing Ram, the great sage was overwhelmed,
And lost himself in the radiant beauty of his face,
Like a chakor enraptured by the full moon.
The king, rejoicing in his heart, said,
'O muni, you have never favoured me thus before.
What is it that brings you here?
Tell me, so that I may do what you require without delay.'
'Hosts of demons trouble and harass me,
So I come to you, king, to ask of you a favour—

Give me Raghunath and his younger brother
To slay the night-wandering demons and protect me.

> Give them, king, with a glad heart,
> Abandon attachment and ignorance.
> Honour and fame will come to you, sire,
> And to them, great good fortune.'   (207)

When the king heard these most unwelcome words,
His heart trembled and the radiance of his countenance dimmed.
'In my old age, I have begotten four sons—
O Brahman, you have uttered these words without due reflection.
Ask me for land, cows, wealth, or treasure,
And I will give you everything I possess this very moment with
      great joy.
Nothing is more precious than one's body and one's life—
Even these, O muni, I will give in the blink of an eye.
But all my sons are as dear to me as life,
And Ram, I cannot ever give him up, sire.
The demons of the night are fierce and cruel—
And my beautiful sons are so young and tender!'
Hearing the king's words steeped in love,
The wise muni rejoiced in his heart.
Then Vasishtha reassured the king in many ways,
And dispelled his doubts and fears.
With great affection he called his two sons,
And clasping them to his heart, he gave them much advice.
'My two sons, lord, are my life,
But now, muni, you and you alone are their father.'

> The king handed his sons over to the rishi,
> Blessing them again and again.
> The Lord then went to his mother's palace,
> And after bowing his head at her feet, departed.   (208A)

Lions amongst men, the two heroes set off joyfully
To rid the muni of his fear—
Oceans of compassion, resolute and of steadfast mind,
The Creators of the whole world.   (208B)

Ram's eyes are as bright as the dawn, he is broad-chested, with
    long arms,
His body is dark-hued as a blue lotus or a tamal tree,
Around his waist is fastened a yellow cloth and a beautiful quiver,
And in his two hands, he holds a handsome bow and arrows.
One dark, the other fair-complexioned, the two brothers were
    handsome and pleasing.
In them Vishvamitra had acquired every virtue and good
    quality—
'I can see that the Lord favours Brahmans,
For upon my request the Supreme God has left his own father.'
Along the way, the muni pointed out the destruction of the forest
    on either side—
Hearing them, Taraka rushed out at them in rage.
With a single arrow Hari took her life,
But recognizing her as one in distress, bestowed upon her his own
    divine state.
Then the rishi, acknowledging Ram as his Lord
And though knowing him to be the repository of all knowledge,
    gave to him such knowledge
As protected him from hunger and thirst,
And endowed him with unequalled bodily strength and
    glowing power.

Bestowing upon him every kind of weapon,
He brought the Lord to his own hermitage.
There, with great devotion, he served him a meal of tubers,
    roots, and fruits
Recognizing in him his benefactor.   (209)

At dawn, Raghurai said to the muni,
'Go perform your fire-sacrifice without fear.'
At this, all the munis began to prepare the sacrifice,
While Ram himself remained to guard the offerings.
Hearing this, the night-wandering demon Marich,
Enemy of sages, rushed in with his troops.
Ram shot him with a blunt arrow,
That threw him across the ocean seven yojans wide.
He then slew the Rakshasa Subahu with an arrow of fire,
And his younger brother destroyed the army of night-wandering
    demons.
Thus, by killing the demons, he rendered the twice-born free
    of fear,
And hosts of gods and munis sang hymns of praise to him.
There, for a few days more, Raghurai
Remained and graced the Brahmans with his presence.
Devoutly, the Brahmans related to him many stories from
    the Puranas,
Even though the Lord already knew them.
Then the muni said with great respect,
'There is to be held a ceremony, Lord, that you should come
    and see.'
Hearing of the ceremony of the bow, the lord of the Raghu clan
Gladly went with the great muni.
Along the way, an ashram came into sight—
Neither birds, nor deer, nor any animals or living creatures were
    near it.
The Lord, seeing a strange slab of stone, asked the muni about it,
And the muni related to him the whole extraordinary tale.

'Gautam's wife, Ahalya, under the influence of a curse,
Was turned into an unmoving block of stone.
She longs for the dust of your lotus feet—
Have mercy on her, Raghubir.'   (210)

Touched by his holy feet that destroy all sorrow,
Ahalya appeared, penance personified.
Beholding Raghunayak, who gives joy to the faithful,
She stood before him with folded hands—
Overcome by love, her body trembling with joy,
She could find no words to say.
She of great good fortune fell at his feet,
With tears streaming from her eyes.
Steadying her heart, she recognized the Lord—
Her faith was renewed by Raghupati's grace.
In words pure and free of guile, she began praising him,
'Hail, Raghurai, attainable through wisdom!
I am an impure woman, Lord, and you, who are Ravan's foe,
Purify the whole world and bestow bliss upon the faithful.
O lotus-eyed one, who destroys the fear of this existence,
Save me, save me, I come to you seeking shelter.
The muni, in cursing me, has done me great good,
I take it as the greatest favour,
For I can look upon Hari who frees us from this existence, and fill
     my eyes with his image,
The ultimate blessing, as Shankar knows.
I have only one request, Lord, simple as I am,
And do not ask any other boon—
May the bee of my heart always sip
The nectar of love from the pollen of your lotus feet.
The feet from which springs the most holy and sacred river Ganga
Which Shiv bears upon his head,
Those same lotus feet which eternal Brahma adores—
The compassionate Hari has placed them upon my head.'
In this way, falling again and again at Hari's feet,
Gautam's wife departed—
Having obtained the boon most pleasing to her heart,
She left for her husband's abode full of bliss.

Such is Lord Hari, friend of the humble,
Who is compassionate without cause.
O Tulsidas, you blockhead, abandon deceit and worldly
    entanglements
And worship him alone! (211)

Ram and Lakshman went on their way with the muni
To where flowed the world-purifying Ganga.
Vishvamitra, Gadhi's son, related the story
Of the manner in which the divine river had descended to earth.[68]
Then the Lord bathed in the Ganga with the rishis,
And the Brahmans, gods of the earth, received many gifts.
Joyfully he continued on his way, accompanied by the company
    of munis,
And quickly drew near Videha's capital, Mithila.
When Ram beheld the city's pleasing splendour,
He and his younger brother were delighted.
There were many ponds, wells, streams and rivers,
With water as sweet as nectar and jewelled steps of precious stones.
Bees, drunk on nectar, softly hummed
And many-coloured birds sweetly called;
Wildflowers of many tints and hues bloomed in the woods
And cool, soft and fragrant breezes pleased and soothed.

Flower gardens, orchards and woods,
Home to innumerable birds
And full of flowers and fruit and fresh green leaves,
Adorned the city on all four sides. (212)

The beauty of this city cannot be described,
And wherever one goes within it, the heart is captivated.
Its splendid markets had handsome pavilions studded with jewels
As gorgeous as though Brahma had decorated them with his own hand.

Rich merchants, all prominent men and as wealthy as Kuber himself,
Sat displaying goods and merchandise of various kinds.
The handsome market squares lined with shops and the pretty
    lanes and alleyways
Were constantly sprinkled with fragrant water.
The houses were all prosperous and pleasing,
Brightly painted in many colours as though Rati's lord himself had
    been the painter.
The men and women of the city were all handsome, true and of
    saintly dispositions
As well as virtuous, learned and accomplished.
As for King Janak's incomparable residence—
The lavish grandeur of that palace was such that even the gods
    were astounded by it.
The mind was overcome with awe, looking at its ramparts,
Which seemed to hold within them the splendour of all the worlds.

    A dazzling white palace hung with curtains of gold,
    Embroidered with jewels in varied designs—
    It was the beautiful palace where Sita lived—
    How can its splendour be described?   (213)

At its majestic gates, all with adamantine doors,
Thronged vassal princes, tumblers, dancers, jugglers, bards
    and minstrels.
There stood vast stables,
At all times crowded with a confusion of horses, elephants
    and chariots.
The many champion warriors, ministers and army chiefs
All had mansions of a style and splendour similar to the
    king's palace.
Outside the city, by lakes and streams, and all about,
Were encamped a great many kings and princes.
Seeing a beautiful mango grove

That was safe and pleasant and in every way agreeable,
Muni Kaushik[bx] remarked, 'I like this place,
Let us stay here, O wise Raghubir.'
'Very well, lord,' replied Ram, the abode of compassion,
And made camp there with the company of munis.
'The great Muni Vishvamitra has come!'—
The news soon reached the king of Mithila.

> Taking with him his honest and loyal ministers,
> Several warriors and noble Brahmans, his guru Shatanand and
>   his kinsmen,
> The delighted king went forth
> To meet the king of munis.   (214)

The king paid him homage, placing his forehead on the sage's feet.
The great muni, pleased, gave him his blessings.
The king then reverently saluted all the company of Brahmans,
Joyfully recognizing his great good fortune.
Asking after his well-being again and again
Vishvamitra led the king to a seat.
Just then the two brothers,
Who had gone to see the flower garden, arrived.
One dark, the other fair-complexioned, the two young boys of
    tender years,
Delighted all eyes and stole the hearts of the whole world.
All stood up when Raghupati came,
And Vishvamitra seated him by his side.
Everyone was charmed and delighted upon seeing the
    two brothers—
Their eyes filled with tears, and they trembled with joy.
Beholding Ram's sweet and heart-enchanting form,
'Bodiless' Videh became truly so.[69]

[bx] Vishvamitra

Recognizing that his heart was overwhelmed with love,
The king took refuge in reason and steadied himself.
Bowing his head at the muni's feet,
He spoke, his deep voice shaking with emotion.   (215)

'Tell me, O lord, these two beautiful children—
Are they the ornaments of a muni's family or the protectors of a
    royal dynasty?
Or has brahm, the ultimate Absolute, whom the Vedas praise as
    'not this',
Taken this dual form and come here?
My heart, which by its very nature is free from worldly attachment,
Is as captivated by these children as a chakor by the moon.
That is why, lord, I question you in all sincerity—
Answer me, sire, and do not conceal anything.
When I behold them, my heart fills with great love
That forces my mind to renounce even the bliss of becoming one
    with the Absolute.'
The muni laughed and replied, 'King, you are right,
And your words are never untrue.
They are beloved of every living creature in this world.'
(Ram smiled to himself at these words.)
'They are the sons of Dasharath, jewel of the line of Raghu,
Whom the king has sent to help me.

Ram and Lakshman, these two noble brothers,
The abodes of beauty, goodness and strength,
Protected my sacrifice, as the whole world witnessed,
By defeating the Asurs in battle.'   (216)

'Muni,' said the king, 'gazing upon your feet,
I am speechless at the reward I have received for my good deeds in
    the past.
These two handsome brothers, one dark, the other fair-complexioned

Give joy to joy itself!
The pure and innocent love between them
Brings such joy to my heart as cannot be described.'
The king of Videha, enraptured, added, 'Lord,
It is like the natural love of brahm and jiva, of the Universal Spirit
　　and the individual soul.'
Again and again the sovereign of all men gazed upon the Lord,
His body trembling with joy, his heart full of glad delight.
Then, singing the muni's praises and bowing his head at his feet,
The lord of the earth brought him into the city.
To a gracious mansion that was pleasant and agreeable at all times
The king escorted him, and invited him to reside there.
After paying him further homage and attending to him in every way,
The king took his leave of the muni and went home.

　　　After Ram, the jewel of the dynasty of Raghu,
　　　Had eaten with the rishis and rested,
　　　He sat down by his brother's side.
　　　A full watch of the day still remained.　　　　　　　　(217)

In Lakshman's heart was a great longing
To go and see Janak's city—
But in awe of his brother and apprehensive of the muni
He said nothing, and only smiled to himself.
Ram understood the state of his younger brother's heart,
And his own was filled with affection towards his devotee.
Very courteously, with a shy and modest smile,
And receiving his guru's permission to speak, he said,
'Lord, Lakshman wants to see the city,
But afraid of you, sire, he hasn't said so.
If I receive your permission, lord,
I will show him the city and quickly bring him back.'
Hearing this, the great muni replied in words full of affection,
'Ram, you cannot but observe the proprieties,

For you are the protector of dharma's boundaries, son,
And give joy to your followers, bound by your love for them.

>Go see the city and return—
>The abode of all bliss are you two brothers.
>Reward the eyes of all the people
>With the sight of your beautiful faces.'   (218)

Saluting the muni's lotus feet, the two brothers
Who delight the eyes of the world, went forth.
Beholding their great beauty, a crowd of children
Followed them, eyes and hearts captivated.
Clad in yellow garments, quivers about their waists,
Handsome bows and arrows resplendent in their hands,
Their bodies adorned with sandal paste—white or red, according to
    their complexion,
One dark, the other fair—they were a heart-enchanting pair.
With shoulders like those of lions, long arms,
And beautiful strings of elephant pearls upon their chests,
With well-formed ears and bright, lotus eyes,
And faces as radiant as the moon that relieves the agony of the
    fierce flames of the three afflictions—
Pendants of gold adorned their ears
And stole the hearts of all those who looked upon them.
Their glance was charming, their eyebrows arched,
And the tilak marks upon their foreheads were as though stamped
    upon Beauty herself.

>With pretty, four-cornered caps upon their lovely heads
>Over black, curling hair,
>The two brothers were, from head to toe, beautiful to behold,
>With comeliness and grace in every limb.   (219)

'The princes have come to see the city!'
When the townsfolk heard this news,

They came running, abandoning home and work,
Like paupers rushing to loot a treasury.
Upon beholding the two brothers, so unaffectedly graceful
   and handsome,
They were overjoyed, and their eyes received their reward.
Young girls peeped out from the windows of their houses
Gazing upon Ram, in love with his beauty.
They said to each other, in words full of love,
'Friend, he surpasses in beauty innumerable Kamdevs.
Not amongst gods, men, Asurs, Nagas, or munis
Have we ever heard of such comeliness.
Vishnu has four arms, Vidhi has four heads,
Purari wears such terrifying guise and has five faces—
Another god, dear friend, there is none,
To whom his beauty may be compared.

    Of tender years, endowed with charm and beauty,
    One dark, the other fair, abodes of bliss—
    There is more beauty in their every part,
    Than in innumerable gods of love.   (220)

Tell me, dear friend, which being with shape and form
Will not be captivated upon beholding such beauty?'
Said one, in sweet tones full of affection,
'Listen, my wise friends, to what I have heard—
These two are Dasharath's sons,
This royal pair of young swans.
They are the protectors of Muni Kaushik's sacrifice,
And have killed night-wandering demons in the field of battle.
The one with the dark form and lovely lotus eyes,
Who destroyed the arrogance and false conceit of Marich
   and Subahu,
Kaushalya's son, and a treasure-house of sweetness and joy,
And who holds the bow and arrows in his hands—his name is Ram.
The fair-complexioned boy attired in the beautiful dhoti,

With the bow and arrows in his hand and who is walking behind Ram—
His name is Lakshman and he is Ram's younger brother.
His mother, dear friend, is Sumitra.

> Having helped the Brahmans,
> And on the way, rescued the muni's wife, the two brothers
> Have come here to witness the ceremony of the bow.'
> Upon hearing this, the women all rejoiced.   (221)

Seeing Ram's beauty, one of them remarked,
'This is a bridegroom worthy of Janaki.
Were the king but to see him, my friend,
He will disregard his vow and will insist upon marrying her to him.'
Another replied, 'The king has acknowledged them,
And with the muni, has received them with honour and respect.
But, my dear, the king will not give up his vow—
In the grip of destiny, he is persisting in his foolishness.'
'If providence is kind,' said another,
'And gives, as we hear, just rewards to everyone,
Then Janaki will most certainly get him as her bridegroom—
In this, my friends, there is no doubt.
Should such a union be brought about by providence,
Everyone's wishes will be fulfilled,
Oh friend, my impatience grows at the thought
That if this match be made, he may come here again some time.

> Otherwise, I tell you, my dear,
> It will be impossible for us to see him again.
> But this union will only happen
> If we ourselves have a great store of merit from our
> > past actions.'   (222)

Another said, 'You speak rightly, friend—
This marriage will benefit everyone greatly.'

Then one said, 'Shankar's bow is hard to string,
And this dark-complexioned boy has a young and slender frame.
So all is still in doubt, my wise friend!'
Hearing this, another young woman replied in sweet tones,
'Friends, I have heard some people say
That though he is small and slight to look at, his strength is
    very great.
Touched by the dust of his lotus feet,
Ahalya, who had committed such a grave offence, was saved.
How can such a one fail to break Shiv's bow?
Do not abandon this conviction or give up faith even by mistake—
Viranchi, who made Sita with such skill and care,
Deliberately created this dark-complexioned bridegroom for her.'
Hearing her words, the others were delighted—
'May it be so,' they exclaimed in sweet tones.

Their hearts full of joy, crowds of lovely women with
        beautiful eyes
Shower flowers,
And wherever the two brothers go,
There is joy supreme.   (223)

Towards the eastern part of the city went the two brothers
Where the ground had been prepared for the ceremony of
    the bow—
Upon an extensive and handsomely paved floor
A perfect vedika had been constructed.
On all four sides had been built wide golden platforms
Where the kings and princes would be seated.
Close behind, and encircling them on all sides,
Rose more platforms,
A little higher and pleasing in every way,
Where the people of the city might come and sit.
Close to these had been constructed large and beautiful pavilions,

Dazzling white, and painted in many pleasing colours,
From where all the women might view the spectacle,
Seated according to their rank and family.
The children of the city, chattering in sweet voices,
Courteously showed the Lord the preparations that
    had been made.

> On this pretext, all the children,
> Enraptured, reached out to touch his heart-enchanting form.
> Their bodies thrilling with delight, their hearts rejoicing,
> They kept gazing at the two brothers.   (224)

Ram, knowing the children were lost in love for him,
Praised with great affection all the places they had shown him.
As the children, each according to his fancy, called to them,
The two brothers would affectionately go where they
    were summoned.
Ram showed the arrangements to his younger brother,
Speaking sweet and pleasant words.
He, upon whose instructions Maya
Creates a multitude of worlds in the blink of an eye,
That same merciful Ram, for the sake of his followers,
Looked with awe upon the site prepared for the rite of the bow.
Having seen the sights, they prepared to return to their guru
With fear in their hearts, knowing that they were late.
He, of whom even Fear is afraid,
Thus showed the power of devotion,
And with sweet and gentle words
He bid the reluctant children farewell.

> With apprehension, love and humility
> And great diffidence, the two brothers
> Bowed their heads at the guru's lotus feet,
> And receiving his permission, sat down.   (225)

As night fell, at the muni's word,
They all performed the evening worship.
Two watches of the bright and beautiful night were spent
In the telling of ancient stories and legends.
The great muni then lay down to sleep,
As the two brothers began to massage his feet.
For the love of whose lotus feet,
Ascetics and holy men practise all kinds of penance and prayer—
Those same two brothers, as if conquered by love,
Affectionately pressed their guru's lotus feet.
Only upon the muni so ordering him again and again,
Did Raghubar go and lie down.
Lakshman pressed his feet, holding them close to his heart
With reverence and love, feeling supreme joy.
Again and again the Lord said, 'Sleep, dear brother,'
And so he lay down, still holding those lotus feet to his heart.

> When the night had passed, Lakshman arose
> Hearing the crowing of the cock.
> The lord of the world, all-wise Ram,
> Also awoke before their guru.   (226)

After performing all their morning rituals of purification,
    they bathed
And completing their daily rites, bowed their heads before
    the muni.
Keeping the hour in mind, and with their guru's permission,
The two brothers left to gather flowers for the morning worship.
They saw the king's beautiful garden
Where spring, captivated by its loveliness, permanently tarried.
There grew many kinds of heart-enchanting trees,
And creepers of many colours formed a beautiful canopy.
Covered with fresh new leaves, richly laden with fruit and flowers,
Their bounty put to shame even the tree of the gods.

Chataks, kokils, parrots and chakors
Sweetly cooed and peacocks danced to their song.
In the centre of the garden was a beautiful lake,
Resplendent with jewelled steps of rare and pleasing design.
In its clear waters grew lotuses and lilies of many colours.
Waterbirds called and bees hummed there.

> Beholding the garden and the lake,
> The Lord and his brother were delighted.
> Supremely delightful was this garden
> That so delighted Ram, who bestows delight on all.   (227)

They looked around and after seeking the gardeners' permission,
They began happily gathering leaves and flowers.
At that very moment, Sita arrived—
Her mother had sent her there to worship goddess Girija.
With her were her friends, all lovely and intelligent young girls,
Singing songs in sweet, melodious voices.
Near the lake, stood Girija's shining temple—
Its splendour was beyond description and captivated the heart
    upon sight.
After bathing in the lake with her friends,
She went with a glad heart to Gauri's shrine.
She performed her worship with deep love and devotion,
And asked for a handsome and suitable bridegroom.
One of her companions had left Sita's side,
And wandered off to look at the flower garden.
Reaching there, she saw the two brothers,
And, helpless with love, came back to Sita.

> Seeing her state,
> Her trembling limbs and eyes full of tears,
> The friends all asked in kind and gentle tones,
> 'Tell us, what is the cause of your joy?'   (228)

'Two princes have come to see the garden.
They are young, and in every way pleasing and handsome—
One is dark, the other fair-complexioned. But how can I describe
　　their beauty?
Speech has no eyes, and the eyes cannot speak!'
Hearing this, the friends were delighted,
Knowing the intense longing in Sita's heart.
One of them said, 'My friend, these must be the king's sons,
Who, I hear, arrived yesterday with the muni,
And who have cast such a spell with their beauty
That they have captivated all the men and women of the town,
And everywhere, everyone is talking only of their beauty—
We must certainly go and see them, for they are worth a look!'
Her words pleased Sita greatly,
For her eyes were restless to see them.
With that same dear friend leading the way, Sita followed—
No one realized that hers was an old and ancient love.

　　Recalling Narad's words, Sita[70]
　　Was filled with innocent love
　　And anxiously looked all around,
　　Like a frightened fawn.　　　　　　　　　　　　　　　　(229)

Hearing the tinkling of her bangles, girdle and anklets,
Ram thought to himself, then said to Lakshman,
'It seems as though Madan is sounding his drum,
Having set his mind on conquering the world.'
Saying this, he turned to look in that direction,
His eyes chakor birds gazing at the moon of Sita's radiant face.
His beautiful eyes grew still, he gazed unblinking,
As though Nimi, abashed, had abandoned his own territory.[71]
Seeing Sita's beauty, Ram was full of joy,
He praised her in his heart, though words he had none.
'It is as though Viranchi has made manifest in her form

All the skills with which he fashioned the world.
She makes beautiful beauty itself,
Like a flame that brightens light's abode.
All comparisons are the stale leftovers of poets—
To what shall I compare Videh's daughter?'

> Thus describing Sita's beauty to himself,
> The Lord reflected upon his own state
> And with a heart pure and innocent, said to his
>   younger brother
> These words appropriate to the moment—   (230)

'Brother, this must be Janak's daughter, the very one
For whom the ceremony of the bow is being held.
Her companions have brought her here to worship Gauri—
She wanders through the garden, lighting it up with her presence
      as she passes.
Seeing her extraordinary beauty,
My usually serene mind has grown agitated;
Only God knows the reason for this, brother,
But the right side of my body is twitching.[72]
It is the inherent nature of the dynasty of Raghu,
That no one even in thought sets foot upon the wrong path.
I have great faith in my heart
Which has never, even in a dream, look at another man's wife.
Men who never turn their backs upon their enemy in battle,
Who are never captivated by nor look at another man's wife,
And who never say no to one who asks—
Such noble men are very few in this world.'

> He thus rambled to his younger brother,
> But his heart, yearning for Sita's beauty,
> Drank in the radiance of her lovely face
> As a honeybee sips nectar from a lotus.   (231)

Sita, bewildered, was looking all around her.
'Where have the young princes gone?' she worried.
Wherever the fawn-eyed Sita turned her glance,
Quantities of shining white lotuses rained down.
Her companions then pointed out, hidden behind some vines,
The handsome youths, one dark, the other fair.
Seeing his beauty, her eyes were filled with longing,
And she rejoiced as though she had found her own treasure.
With unwavering gaze she looked upon Raghupati's radiance,
Her very eyelids forgot to blink.
In the intensity of her love, she lost all sense and awareness of
    her body
Like a chakor gazing at the autumn moon.
Through the pathway of her eyes she took Ram into her heart,
Then wisely shut the doors of her eyelids.
When her companions realized that Sita was overcome by love,
They were abashed and could not say a word.

    At that very moment, the two brothers emerged
    From the arbour of creepers and vines,
    Like two radiant moons
    Through a curtain of clouds.   (232)

'The two handsome brothers are the very pinnacles of beauty,
Their bodies are as bright and splendid as the blue lotus and
    the golden.
Elegant peacock feathers, entwined with bunches of flowerbuds
    here and there
Adorn their heads.
Upon their foreheads gleam their tilaks and drops of perspiration,
Their ears are adorned with beautiful ornaments,
With curving eyebrows, and curly hair,
And eyes as bright as new lotus buds,
And handsome chin and nose and cheeks

And charming smiles that captivate the heart—
The radiance of their faces is such that I cannot describe it:
Beholding them puts innumerable gods of love to shame.
Jewelled necklaces upon their breasts, conch-like necks
And arms strong and powerful, like the trunk of Kam's young elephant.
And the one with the cup of leaves full of flowers in his left hand—
The dark prince, my dear, is utterly enchanting.

> Slim-waisted as a lion, clad in yellow garments,
> He is the abode of beauty and grace.'
> Beholding the jewel of the solar dynasty,
> Sita's companions forgot themselves completely.   (233)

One wise friend, recovering herself
And taking Sita's hand, said to her,
'Meditate upon Gauri another time.
For now, why not look at the young princes?'
Then Sita opened her eyes shyly
And saw before her the two lions of the line of Raghu.
Beholding Ram's beauty from head to toe,
She recalled her father's vow and was greatly agitated.
When her companions saw Sita so overcome by love,
They cried in alarm, 'It is growing late!'
'We'll come again tomorrow, at this same time,'
Said one of her friends, smiling to herself.
Hearing these words, so full of meaning, Sita grew abashed.
'It is late,' she said, afraid of her mother.
With great resolve, and holding the image of Ram in her heart,
She turned away, knowing herself to be under her father's command.

> Yet, on the pretext of looking at a deer, a bird, a tree,
> She looked back again and again—
> As she gazed again and again upon Raghubir's beauty,
> Her love grew ever stronger.   (234)

Knowing how unyielding was the bow of Shiv, she left, grieving,
Holding in her heart his dark form.
When the Lord realized that Janaki,
Who held within her all happiness, love, beauty and virtue,
    was going,
He made of his great love a gentle ink
And inscribed her upon the tablet of his mind.
Sita returned to Bhavani's shrine
And offering homage at her feet, she said, with folded hands,
'All glory to you, daughter of the king of the mountains,
Glory to you, who adores Mahesh as the chakor does the moon,
Glory to you, mother of Ganesh the elephant-faced one, and of
    Skand of the six faces—
Mother of the universe, with body as bright as lightning!
You have no beginning, no middle and no end,
And even the Vedas do not understand your infinite power.
The cause of the birth, the continuation and the dissolution of
    the universe,
You enchant and captivate all creation, and amuse yourself as
    you please.

    Amongst all faithful wives,
    Mother, you have first place.
    Even a thousand Sharadas and Sheshnags
    Cannot narrate your immeasurable glory.   (235)

Serving you, the four rewards of existence are easy to attain,
Giver of boons and the beloved of Purari!
Worshipping your lotus feet, devi,
Gods, men and munis all find bliss.
You know well my heart's desire,
For you dwell eternally in every heart,
And this is the reason that I have not said it aloud.'
So saying, Vaidehi clasped her feet.

Bhavani was moved by Sita's humility and love—
A garland slipped from her image and it smiled.
Sita received the gift with great reverence.
Then spoke Gauri, her heart full of joy,
'Listen, Sita, to my blessing true:
Your heart's desire will be fulfilled.
Narad's words are always pure and true—
You will get the bridegroom upon whom your heart is set.

You will get the one your heart adores,
That sweet-natured, handsome, dark bridegroom.
He is compassionate and all-wise
And knows your virtue and your love.'
Hearing Gauri's blessing,
Sita's friends rejoiced with her,
Paying homage to Bhavani again and again,
Sita, says Tulsi, returned home, glad at heart.

> Knowing Gauri to be so well-disposed and gracious,
> Sita's heart was so full of joy as cannot be described.
> An omen of good fortune and bliss,
> Her left side began to tremble.   (236)

Admiring Sita's beauty in their hearts,
The two brothers returned to their guru.
Ram told Kaushik everything,
For his inherent nature was straightforward and honest, without
      even a touch of deceit.
Taking the flowers, the muni performed the puja
And then blessed the two brothers—
'May your heart's desires be fulfilled.'
Hearing this, Ram and Lakshman were overjoyed.
After his meal, the great and learned muni
Began to relate some ancient tales.

When the day was ended, and with their guru's permission,
The two brothers went to perform their evening rites.
A beautiful moon rose in the east—
Thinking that it resembled Sita's lovely face, Ram was glad,
But reflecting upon it further, he thought,
'That cold moon has no resemblance to Sita's countenance at all!

Born of the ocean, with poison as its brother,[73]
Pale and dim by day, with marks and blemishes upon its face—
How can that poor and wretched moon
Be compared to Sita's face?   (237)

He wanes and waxes and makes miserable women separated from
    their lovers,
And Rahu, if in conjunction, seizes and swallows him.
The cause of the kok's sorrow and the enemy of the lotus—
Moon, you have many flaws!
To compare Vaidehi's face to you
Is very wrong and completely inappropriate.'
Finding in the moon a pretext to praise Sita's beauty,
He returned to his guru, seeing that the night was far advanced.
He saluted the muni's lotus feet
And receiving his permission, lay down to rest.
When the night had passed, Raghunayak awoke,
Looked at his brother, and began to speak thus:
'Look, brother, it is dawn,
That delights the lotus, the kok birds, and all the world.'
Lakshman, folding his hands, replied
In sweet words declaring the majesty of his Lord,

'With the rising of the sun
The water-lily closes its petals and the light of the stars grows dim.
Even so, hearing of your coming,
The other princes will become powerless.   (238)

The other princes are like stars and give off light,
But they cannot dispel the deep darkness that is Shiv's mighty bow.
Just as lotuses, bees, the kok and various other birds
Rejoice at the ending of the night,
In the same manner, Lord, all your devotees
Will rejoice at the breaking of the bow.
The sun rises, and the dark is effortlessly destroyed,
The stars are obscured and the world is filled with glorious light.
The sun, on the pretext of its own rising, Raghurai,
Has shown your splendour and glory to all the princes.
This breaking of the bow been arranged only
To reveal the greatness of the might of your arms.'
The Lord smiled at his brother's words.
Then, though inherently pure, he performed the morning rituals of
    purification and bathed.
After performing his daily rites of prayer and worship, he went to
    his guru
And bowed his handsome head at his lotus feet.
Then Janak summoned the sage Shatanand, his family priest,
And sent him immediately to Muni Kaushik.
He came and related Janak's humble entreaty,
And Vishvamitra, rejoicing, called the two brothers.

    After touching Shatanand's feet,
    The Lord sat down by his guru.
    Then the muni said, 'Come, dear son, let's go,
    For King Janak has sent for us.   (239)

Let us go and see Sita's svayamvar
And whom God will give the glory.'
Lakshman said, 'The glory of breaking the bow, lord,
Can belong only to the one upon whom your favour falls.'
The sages all were was pleased to hear these noble words
And rejoicing, gave their blessings.

Then, together with the whole company of ascetics, the
    compassionate one
Set off to the place of the bow ceremony.
'The two brothers have reached the arena!'
When the townspeople heard this news,
They abandoned their homes and their chores and came running,
Young and old, children, men and women.
Janak, seeing the thronging crowds,
Called for his trusted servants and said,
'Go at once to all the people
And show each one to a suitable seat.'

    With soft and gentle words,
    They courteously seated the men and women.
    The high, the middle, the low and the humble—
    All were given seats appropriate to their station.   (240)

At that very moment, the princes arrived—
It seemed that beauty itself had taken up abode in their bodies.
Endowed with every virtue, well-bred and intelligent,
    noble heroes both,
They were handsome and charming, one dark, the other fair.
The two handsome princes shone brightly amongst the gathered nobles
Like two full moons amidst stars;
The people gathered there saw the form of the Lord
In accordance with their faith.
The brave and gallant warriors, gazing upon his form,
Saw Valour itself as having taken bodily form.
The wicked and cruel kings looked upon the Lord afraid,
For they perceived him as Dread embodied.
And then there were the Asurs deceitfully disguised as kings—
They perceived the Lord as the manifestation of death itself.
The residents of the town saw the two brothers
As the jewels of mankind that please and delight the eyes.

The women gazed upon them, rejoicing in their hearts
And each perceiving in them what she fancied most,
As though charming Passion had taken on
A form singular and incomparable.   (241)

To the wise and learned, the Lord appeared in all his divine
    splendour
With many faces, hands, feet, eyes and heads.
And how did Janak's clan and family see him?
As noble and beloved as a kinsman.
The queen, with Videha's king,
Gazed upon him with deep and indescribable love as on a child.
To the yogis he appeared as the Supreme Truth,
Calm, pure, complete and shining with innate radiance.
The devotees of Hari saw the two brothers
As their own beloved Lord, the giver of all happiness.
But the love and joy with which Sita gazed at Ram—
That is impossible to describe.
She could not express the love and joy she was feeling in her heart,
So how can any poet do so?
In this way, according to their own inherent dispositions,
Each one saw the Lord of Koshal.

Resplendent in the assembly of kings,
Were the youthful sons of the king of Koshal,
Handsome and charming, one dark, the other fair,
Stealing the eyes of the world.   (242)

Their two forms were so inherently charming,
That comparison with even a million gods of love falls short.
Their radiant faces put to shame the autumn moon,
And their lotus eyes delight the heart.
Their charming glances win even the mind of Mar himself
And so please the heart as cannot be described.

With soft cheeks, and shining earrings,
Handsome chins, perfect lips and sweet voices,
With radiant smiles that put moonbeams to shame,
Curving eyebrows and heart-enchanting noses,
Broad foreheads with gleaming tilaks,
Hair so dark and curling that even the black bees are abashed,
And, adorning their heads, yellow, four-cornered caps
Embroidered with flower-buds,
With shapely necks marked with three pleasing lines like a conch shell
As if declaring them to be the extreme of beauty in all the
    three worlds,

Around their necks beautiful necklaces of elephant-pearls,
A garland of tulsi leaves upon their breasts,
With the shoulders of a bull and the stance of a lion,
And long arms endowed with great strength,   (243)

Around their waists, quivers tied with yellow sashes,
With arrows in hand, bows on their strong and handsome
    left shoulders,
And shining yellow sacred threads,
Handsome and comely in every part, they were filled with beauty
    from head to toe.
Seeing them, everyone grew happy and blissful
And gazed at them unblinking, so that even the pupils of their eyes
    did not move.
Janak, too, rejoiced to see the two brothers.
Then, going to the muni, he clasped his lotus feet.
Paying him homage, he related to him his own story,[74]
And showed him around the whole arena.
Wherever the two handsome princes went,
Everyone looked upon them with wonder.
Each one saw Ram's face turned towards him,
Yet no one realized the divine mystery behind this.

'Excellent arrangements,' the muni said to the king,
And the king was delighted and took great pleasure in his praise.

    Of all the raised platforms there was one tier of seats
    More beautiful, bright and spacious than the others.
    There the great king seated the muni
    Along with the two brothers.   (244)

Seeing the Lord, the kings and princes all lost heart
Like stars that grow dim when the full moon rises.
In all their hearts was the firm conviction
That Ram, without doubt, would break the bow,
And that, even if Bhav's mighty bow did not break,
Sita would still place her garland upon Ram's breast.
Thinking thus they said, 'Let's go home, brothers,
Abandoning fame, glory, might and splendour.'
But other kings laughed at these words
And blinded by ignorance and arrogance, they cried,
'Even by breaking the bow it will be difficult to wed her,
So without breaking it, who can marry the princess!
Even if Death himself should oppose us,
For Sita's sake, we will defeat him in battle!'
Hearing this, other kings smiled,
Pious and sagacious men devoted to Hari, and said,

    'Ram will wed Sita,
    Shattering the arrogance of the princes.
    For who can conquer in battle
    Dasharath's valiant sons?   (245)

Do not brag and boast, and invite death unnecessarily.
Do vain fancies bear fruit or imagined sweets satisfy hunger?
Listen to our advice, sincere and free of deceit:
Know in your hearts that Sita is Jagadamba, mother of the universe,

And that Raghupati is the father of the universe.

Reflect upon this and gazing upon their beauty, fill your eyes with
　　their splendour.

Handsome, pleasing and endowed with every virtue,

These two brothers reside in Shambhu's heart.

Why do you abandon this ocean of nectar, so close at hand,

And seeing a mirage, chase after it and rush to die?

Go and do whatever pleases you,

But as for us, we have today received the fruit of this birth.'

So saying, the good kings, with deep affection,

Turned their gaze upon Ram's incomparable beauty.

The gods watched from their chariots in the sky,

Showering down flowers and singing sweet and melodious songs.

　　Then, knowing it to be the appropriate moment,
　　Janak sent for Sita.
　　Her lovely and accomplished friends,
　　With due honour, brought her there.　　　　　　　　　　(246)

Sita's radiance is impossible to describe,

For she is Jagadambika, mother of the universe, and the
　　embodiment of grace and virtue.

All comparisons seem inadequate to me,

For they are enamoured only of the limbs and bodies of ordinary
　　women.

In describing Sita, who will dare offer these same comparisons

And bring disrepute upon himself as a bad poet?

Should Sita be compared to another woman,

Where in this world would there be a maiden so beautiful?

Gira is too talkative, while Bhavani has only half a body,

Rati is very sorrowful because of her bodiless lord,

As for the goddess Ramaa, who has poison and liquor as her
　　beloved brothers,

How can Vaidehi be compared to her?[75]

Even if the ocean was filled with the nectar of beauty,
And the tortoise was grace embodied,
Even if radiance the rope, and passion Mount Mandar,
And Mar himself churned the ocean with his lotus hands,

> And even if Lakshmi, the source of beauty and bliss,
> Had been born in this manner—
> Even then the poet would shrink
> To say that she could be compared to Sita.   (247)

Her lovely attendants, singing sweet songs in heart-enchanting voices,
Led Sita to the arena.
Her delicate frame adorned with a beautiful sari,
The mother of the universe was she and her great beauty
    was unparalleled.
Jewels and ornaments graced her form—
Her handmaidens had bedecked her every limb with care.
When Sita stepped into the arena,
Seeing her beauty, men and women alike were captivated.
Rejoicing, the gods sounded their drums,
While apsaras sang and rained down flowers.
In her lotus hands glowed the garland with which she would signal
    her choice.
As she glanced quickly at all the assembled princes,
Sita, bewildered, wanted only Ram,
Though all the kings were smitten by love for her.
When she saw the two brothers by the muni,
Her eyes, finding the treasure they were seeking, were filled
    with longing.

> But, out of respect for her elders and seeing the huge gathering,
> Sita grew abashed
> And turned her gaze upon her friends,
> Having taken Raghubir into her heart.   (248)

Beholding Ram's handsome form and Sita's glowing beauty,
Men and women forgot to blink.
All of them had the same thought, but hesitating to say it aloud,
Entreated Vidhi in their hearts.
'Remove quickly, O Vidhi, Janak's foolish stubbornness
And give him our good sense!
Let the king, without hesitation, abandon his vow,
And marry Sita to Ram!
The world will speak well of him, for his decision will appeal to everyone,
But if he continues to be obstinate, his stubbornness will become
    as a fire in his heart in the end.'
All were consumed by the same ardent longing,
'The dark-complexioned one is the right groom for Janaki.'
Then Janak called his bards and minstrels,
Who came singing the glory of his line and dynasty.
The king said, 'Go and announce my vow,'
And the bards proceeded to do so with joyous hearts.

These excellent words the bards then cried aloud:
'Listen, all you kings and princes,
We raise our arms to heaven
And declare Videh's great vow.   (249)

The might of kingly arms is the moon, and Shiv's bow is Rahu,
And all know that it is heavy and hard to bend and declare it to be so.
Even Ravan and Bana, great and mighty heroes both,
Saw this bow and stealthily crept away.
The same great and unyielding bow of Purari—
Whoever in this assembly of princes breaks it today,
Will be hailed in all the three worlds,
And Vaidehi too will wed him without a thought.'
Hearing the vow, all the assembled princes were filled with desire.
Haughty warriors excessively proud of their valour,
Tightening their girdles, they rose, impatient,

And bowing their heads before their chosen gods, stepped forward.
With flushed faces, they glared at Shiv's bow and grasped it,
But could not lift it even though they tried in innumerable ways
    with all their strength.
Those kings who had some sense or discernment,
Did not go near the bow.

    Foolish kings grabbed the bow in passionate fury,
    But being unable to lift it, retired in shame.
    It was as though, upon receiving the strength of each
        successive warrior,
    The bow grew heavier and heavier.   (250)

Then ten thousand kings together
Tried to lift it, but despite their efforts, could not shift it.
Shambhu's bow could not be moved
Just as a faithful wife's heart cannot be moved by the amorous
    words of a libertine.
All those royal princes became as worthy of derision
As a sanyasi without detachment.
Their fame, victory and heroic valour,
They helplessly surrendered to the bow.
Shorn of glory, defeated at heart, the kings
Returned to sit with their attendants.
Janak looked in dismay at the princes,
And spoke words that seemed steeped in anger.
'Countless kings from every land
Have come here hearing of the vow I made.
Gods and demons, assuming the bodies of men,
And great heroes steadfast in war—all have come.

    A beautiful maiden, a grand victory,
    And most desirable fame—
    But it seems that Viranchi has not created the man
    Worthy of winning these by breaking the bow.   (251)

Tell me, who would not want these prizes?

Yet no one has been able to string Shankar's bow.

Leave along stringing it or breaking it, friends,

You could not lift it from the ground even by the height of a
    sesame seed!

Now, let no haughty warrior be outraged,

That I see the earth to be empty of heroes.

Give up your hopes and return to your homes, each of you—

Fate has not written that Vaidehi should be wed.

All the merit I have earned through virtuous acts will be lost if I
    abandon my vow,

So let the maiden remain unwed—what can I do?

My friends, had I known that the earth had no heroes left,

I would not have made myself an object of laughter and derision by
    taking this vow.'

Hearing Janak's words, all the men and women

Looked at Janaki and grew sad.

But Lakshman was furious—his eyebrows twisted into a frown,

His lips trembled, and his eyes flashed with anger.

    For fear of Raghubir he could not speak,

    But Janak's words pierced him like arrows.

    Then, bowing his head at Ram's lotus feet,

    He spoke with grave authority: (252)

'In any gathering where anyone from the line of Raghu is present

No one utters such improper words,

As Janak has just spoken

Knowing the jewel of Raghu's line to be here.

Listen, sun of the lotuses of the solar line—

I say what I truly believe and speak without arrogance.

If I but have your permission,

I can lift up this world like a ball

And shatter it like an unbaked earthen pot.

I can pull up Mount Meru by its roots like a radish

Thanks to your power and glory, divine Lord.
So what, then, of this wretched old bow?
Lord, knowing this, only give me your permission
And then witness the show that I will put on—
I will string the bow as easily as if it were a lotus stalk
And run with it for a hundred yojans.

> I will snap it, Lord, like a mushroom stalk,
> By the strength of your glory.
> And if I cannot do this, Lord, I swear by your feet
> To never hold bow or quiver again.'   (253)

When Lakshman spoke these angry words
The earth shook, the celestial elephants[76] tottered and swayed,
And all the people and the gathered kings grew afraid.
Sita rejoiced in her heart, and Janak was abashed.
The guru, Raghupati and all the sages
Were secretly delighted and trembled with joy.
But Raghupati stopped Lakshman with a sign,
And lovingly made him sit beside him.
Vishvamitra, knowing it to be the right and auspicious moment,
Spoke in tones filled with great affection,
'Rise, Ram, break Bhav's bow
And remove, son, Janak's great distress.'
Hearing his guru's words, Ram bowed his head at his feet,
Neither joy nor sorrow in his heart.
He stood up with inherent grace,
His kingly bearing putting a young lion to shame.

> Raghubar ascended the raised arena
> As the morning sun rises behind Mount Udayagiri.
> The sages were filled with joy like lotuses opening their petals
>   in the sunshine,
> While their eyes, like honey bees, rejoiced.   (254)

The hopes of the assembled kings were destroyed like the night,
And their boastful words faded away like clustered stars.
Arrogant princes wilted like water lilies that close their petals in the
    light of the sun,
And deceitful kings hid away like owls.
Munis and gods, like koks during the day, became free of sorrow
And rained down flowers in manifest adoration.
Saluting his guru's feet with deep affection,
Ram asked the sages for their permission.
The Lord of all the worlds then stepped forward with easy grace
With the gait of a noble elephant intoxicated with love.
As Ram stepped forth, all the men and women of the city
Rejoiced, their bodies quivering with joy and anticipation.
They called upon ancestors and gods, invoking their own past
    virtuous deeds,
'If the merit we have earned has any power at all,
May Ram break Shiv's bow
Like a lotus stem, Lord Ganesh!'

    Looking upon Ram with motherly love,
    And calling her companions to her,
    Sita's mother, overwhelmed by affection,
    And lamenting, spoke.   (255)

'Friends, all those watching this spectacle
Say they are our well-wishers.
But is there is no one here who will explain to his guru
That he is only a child and such insistence is not good for him?
Ravan and Banasur did not dare touch the bow,
And all other kings were defeated despite their boasts—
And now that same bow is to be given into the hands of this
    young prince?
Can a young swan lift up Mount Mandar?
The king has lost all his good sense

And Vidhi's ways, my friends, are impossible to understand!'
One wise companion replied in sweet tones,
'Do not count the strong amongst the weak, my queen.
Look at Rishi Kumbhaj, and consider the boundless ocean—
Yet he drained it, and is famed throughout the world.
The disc of the sun seems small to look at,
But when it rises, darkness flees the three worlds.

> A mantra is exceedingly small,
> But it overpowers Vidhi, Hari, Har and all the gods,
> And the mightiest elephant, though maddened and in rut,
> May be tamed by a tiny goad.   (256)

Kam, with the help of a bow and arrows made only of flowers,
Brings the whole world under his sway.
Devi, knowing this, throw away all doubt.
Ram will break the bow, my queen!'
Hearing her companion's words, the queen's faith was restored,
Her sorrow disappeared and her affection for Ram increased.
Then Vaidehi, looking only at Ram,
Anxiously implored whichever god came to mind.
Restless, she pleaded with them in her heart,
'Be gracious to me, Mahesh and Bhavani,
Make fruitful my adoration of you,
Be kind to me and lighten the weight of the bow.
Lord of Shiv's legions, divine granter of boons, Ganesh,
Until this day I have worshipped you.
Now hear my prayer, as again and again I implore you—
Lessen the heaviness of the bow.'

> Glancing again and again at Raghubir's form,
> She invoked the gods and took courage.
> Her eyes filled with tears of love,
> And her body trembled with longing.   (257)

Gazing at him, she filled her eyes with his beauty.
Then, recalling her father's vow, her heart grew restless
   once more.
'Ah, Father is determined upon his cruel vow,
With no thought for gain or loss!
His ministers are afraid, and give no counsel,
Which is not fitting for an assembly of the wise.
Here is a bow, more difficult to break than adamant,
And before it, this dark-complexioned boy, with his young and
   tender frame!
O Vidhi, how do I stay resolute and calm?
Can the delicate stalk of a siris blossom pierce a diamond?
This whole assembly has lost its mind.
So now, O Shambhu's bow, you are my only hope!
Give away to the assembled crowd your unyielding heaviness,
And, looking upon Raghupati, grow light to match his
   tender frame.'
Such was the anguish in Sita's heart
That even a fraction of an instant seemed a hundred aeons.

Glancing first at the Lord, then shyly again at the ground,
Her beautiful eyes look even more beautiful—
It seems as though a pair of Kamdev's fish[77]
Are playing in the moon.   (258)

The bumble-bee that was her voice lay imprisoned in her
   lotus mouth
It could not come out, seeing the night of her modesty.[78]
Her tears remained in the corners of her eyes,
Unspent, like a great miser's gold.
Knowing her great distress, she composed herself
And taking courage, summoned up faith in her heart.
'If in deed, thought and word, my promise is true,
And my heart is truly filled with love for Raghupati's lotus feet,

God, who resides in every heart,
Will certainly make me Raghubar's handmaiden.
Anyone who has true love for someone
Will find that one, of that there is no doubt.'
As she looked at the Lord, she was filled with love for him,
And Ram, in whom resides compassion, understood all.
He looked at Sita, and then glanced at the bow,
As Garud might glance at a tiny snake.

  Lakshman saw the jewel of Raghu's line,
  Glance at Har's great bow;
  He thrilled with joy, and spoke,
  Striking the world with his foot.   (259)

'Celestial elephants that guard the eight quarters, tortoise, snake
  and boar,[79]
Be firm and hold fast the earth so that it does not shake.
Ram wants to break Shankar's bow,
So stay alert, obeying my command!'
When Ram approached the bow,
Men and women invoked the gods, and called upon the merit of
  their past good deeds.
The doubt and ignorance of them all,
The arrogance of the foolish kings,
The weight of Bhrigupati's[lxxi] haughty pride,
The timidity of gods and munis,
Sita's distress, Janak's remorse,
The intense and burning anguish of the queens—
Finding the great ship that was Shambhu's bow
Crowded aboard all together,
Wishing to cross the boundless ocean that was Ram's strength
  of arm
Though they had no helmsman.

[lxxi] Parashuram

Ram looked at the crowd—
Everyone was as still as a painting.
The compassionate Lord then looked at Sita,
And knew her profound distress.   (260)

He saw Vaidehi's great anguish
And how a moment of time passed like an aeon for her.
If a thirsty man dies for want of water,
What use is even a lake of nectar to his corpse?
What good is rain once all the crops have withered?
What use is regret once a chance has been lost?
Thinking thus, the Lord gazed at Janaki
And was overcome with joy to see her profound love.
He paid homage to his guru in his heart
And swiftly and lightly picked up the bow.
The bow flashed like lightning when he picked it up,
Then it shone like a circle in the sky.
How he picked it up, strung it and drew it tight,
No one saw—all they saw was him standing there.
In that very instant Ram broke the bow,
And the terrible sound of its breaking filled earth, space and sky.

The harsh and terrible sound filled earth, space and sky,
The horses of the sun, startled, left their path,
The celestial elephants trumpeted, the earth shook,
The serpent, the boar and the tortoise writhed and staggered and floundered,
Gods, demons and munis covered their ears with their hands,
And all began, with great agitation, to ponder the cause.
But, says Tulsi, when they realized that Ram had broken the bow,
They broke into shouts of triumph, hailing his victory.

Shankar's bow was the ship,
The ocean was Raghubar's strength of arm,
And the whole company, that had earlier climbed aboard this vessel
In the grip of worldly attachment, was now drowned.   (261)

The Lord threw the two pieces of the bow upon the ground,
Seeing this, all the people rejoiced.
The pure ocean that is the Muni Kaushik
Filled with the clear and fathomless water that is the love he bears
    the Lord,
Seeing the full moon of Ram's form
Swelled across its wide expanse with a great tide of immense joy.
The sky reverberated with the beat of triumphant drums,
As celestial women danced and sang.
Brahma and all the other gods, the Siddhas and the great munis
Praised the Lord and gave him their blessings,
Showering down garlands of many-hued flowers
While Kinnaras sing sweet and melodious songs.
The cries and calls of victory now filled earth, space and sky
As the crash of the bow's breaking faded away.
Everywhere, delighted men and women called out,
'Ram has broken Shambhu's mighty bow!'

    Bards, minstrels and poets
    Single-mindedly sang his fame and glory
    And all the people made grateful offerings
    Of horses, elephants, money, jewels and fine clothes.　　　(262)

The pleasing sounds of cymbals, mridangs, conchs, shehnais,
Bugles, kettledrums, tabors
And many other kinds of musical instruments delighted the ear
While everywhere young women sang songs of joy.
The queen with her companions was as exultant with joy
As a parched field of rice upon which rain has fallen.
Janak abandoned worry and embraced happiness,
As a weary swimmer finds the shore.
The other kings and princes, at the breaking of the bow, lost
    their lustre,
Like lamps that lose their brilliance in the day.

But how may Sita's joy be described?
She was like a chatak that has found the rain that falls under the
    Svati nakshatra.
Lakshman gazed at Ram
As a young chakor at the moon.
Shatanand then gave the word,
And Sita approached Ram.

Accompanied by her beautiful and accomplished
    companions
Singing auspicious songs of joy,
She moved with the grace of a young swan,
Her every part endowed with infinite beauty.   (263)

In the midst of her companions, Sita shone
As does great beauty in the midst of grace.
In her lotus hands glittered the garland by which she would signal
    her choice
Glowing with the glory of victory over the world.
Her body shrinking with modesty, her heart full of gladness,
No one could see her secret love.
As she went up to Ram and saw his shining beauty,
The princess stood still, as though in a painting.
Her knowing companions, seeing her state, instructed her—
'Place the shining garland around his neck,' they said.
Hearing their words, Sita raised the garland with both hands,
But, overcome with love, she could not place it upon him.
Her raised hands shone with such grace, it seemed as though two
    lotus flowers upon their slender stems
Were timidly offering the garland to the moon itself.
Her companions, perceiving such charm and beauty, broke
    into song,
Sita then placed the garland around Ram's neck so that is rested
    upon his breast.

Seeing the garland resting upon Raghubar's chest,
The gods rained down flowers,
While the kings all shrank into themselves,
Like a cluster of lilies at the sight of the sun.   (264)

The town and the firmament resounded with music,
The wicked grew melancholy, the virtuous glad.
Gods, Kinnaras, men, Nagas and revered munis
Rejoiced and cheered and uttered blessings.
Celestial maidens danced and sang,
Showering handfuls of flowers from the sky.
Everywhere Brahmans chanted the Vedas,
While bards and minstrels sang songs of praise and glory.
It became known all over earth, and in the worlds below it and the
     heavens above it,
That Ram had broken the bow and was to wed Sita.
The men and women of the city performed arti, singing songs
     of praise,
And gave alms generously, unheeding of their means.
Sita and Ram were a radiant pair,
As though Beauty and Love had become one.
Her friends urged, 'Clasp your lord's feet, Sita!'
But Sita, greatly afraid, dared not touch them.

Recalling the release of Gautam's wife
She refrained from touching his feet with her hands.
The jewel of the Raghus smiled to himself,
Understanding her extraordinary love.   (265)

Then some of the kings, looking upon Sita, became filled
     with desire.
Cruel, degenerate fools, they were flushed with rage.
Rising, one after another, and donning armour, these
     unfortunate wretches

Began to brag and boast.
'Let us carry Sita off,' said some,
'And capture the two princes and tie them up!
He may have broken the bow, but he has still not attained
    his wish—
For who can marry the princess while we still live?
Should Videh render them any assistance,
We will defeat him in battle along with the two brothers!'
The good and virtuous kings, hearing these words, replied,
'Shame itself is shamed by this royal gathering.
Your might, glory, courage, fame
And honour all left you with the breaking of the bow.
Is it that same valour of which you are boasting, or did you find
    more somewhere?
It is because of such aberrant thinking that Vidhi blackened
    your faces!

    Look upon Ram and fill your eyes with his glory,
    Abandoning jealousy, arrogance and anger.
    Lakshman's wrath is a mighty fire—
    Know this and do not be consumed by it like moths.   (266)

Like a crow coveting the sacrifice offered to Vainateya, king of
    the birds,[lxxii]
Or a hare wanting the lion's portion,
Like one who gives way to anger without reason, wanting
    happiness and well-being,
Or an enemy of Shiv wanting prosperity,
Like a stingy, greedy man wanting sweet fame,
Or a lustful one wanting a spotless reputation,
Or one who has turned away from Hari's feet wanting salvation—
Such is your desire, lords of men!'

—————

[lxxii] Garud

Hearing the uproar, Sita grew afraid
And her companions led her to the queen.
Ram, quite unruffled, joined his guru,
Praising Sita's love in his heart.
The queen and Sita were overwhelmed by anxiety
And wondered what Vidhi now intended.
Hearing the words of the kings, Lakshman glared all about him,
But for fear of Ram, he could not speak.

> With flaming eyes and frowning brow,
> He glared, full of rage, at the kings,
> Like a young lion inflamed to fury
> Upon seeing a herd of mad elephants in rut.   (267)

Seeing the commotion, the women of the city grew uneasy,
And joining together, they all began to curse the kings.
It was at this moment, having heard that Shiv's bow had
    been broken,
That Parashuram,[80] the sun to the lotuses of Bhrigu's line, arrived.
Seeing him, the kings shrank back afraid,
Like quails hiding from a swooping hawk;
His fair body, covered with sacred ash, shone with noble
    brilliance.
Upon his broad forehead were resplendent the three lines of Shiv.[81]
His hair was matted, and his face, as handsome as the moon,
Was flushed with anger;
His brows were twisted in a frown, his eyes red with rage,
So that even his most casual glance seemed wrathful.
With the shoulders of a bull, a broad chest and mighty arms,
He wore a shining sacred thread, a string of beads, a deerskin,
And, around his waist, an ascetic's cloth made of bark, and
    two quivers.
He held a bow and arrow in his hands, and an axe upon his
    handsome shoulder.

Though in ascetic and serene attire, his deeds were harsh
    and cruel—
His appearance is impossible to describe.
It seemed as though Valour had assumed a muni's body
And come to the gathering of kings.   (268)

Beholding Bhrigupati's terrifying form,
The kings arose, made uneasy by fear.
Declaring their own names and that of their fathers,
They fell prostrate before him in obeisance.
Even those whom he glanced at casually, or in a kind or
    benevolent manner,
Thought that their life had come to an end.
Then Janak came and bowed his head before him,
And, calling Sita, made her pay him homage.
Parashuram bestowed his blessing upon her, and her friends,
    rejoicing,
Led her back to the women.
Then Vishvamitra came to meet him,
And placed the two brothers at his lotus feet,
Saying, 'These are Ram and Lakshman, Dasharath's sons.'
Parashuram, seeing the comely pair, blessed them,
But his eyes remained fixed upon Ram
Whose infinite beauty chased away the conceit of Mar himself.

Looking around him once more, he turned to Videha's king
And asked, 'Tell me, why this great crowd?'
Though knowing well the reason why, he asked like one who
    did not know,
His body filled with rage.   (269)

Janak explained the circumstances
And the reason why all the kings had come.
At his words, Parashuram turned his gaze and looked,

And saw the broken fragments of the bow thrown upon the ground.
Enraged, he cried in harsh and wrathful tones,
'Tell me, Janak, which fool has broken the bow?
Show me that idiot at once, or this very day
I will turn your kingdom upside down!'
Overcome with terror, the king gave no answer.
The crooked kings rejoiced in their hearts,
But gods, munis, Nagas, and the men and women of the town
Were filled with apprehension, and their hearts grew heavy with fear.
Sita's mother lamented in her heart,
'Vidhi has ruined all that had just been arranged so well.'
Sita, having heard of Bhrigupati's temper,
Felt half an instant pass like an aeon.

> Seeing all the people terrified
> And knowing that Janaki was frightened,
> With neither joy nor sorrow in his heart,
> Raghubir intervened and said,   (270)

'Lord, the one who has broken Shambhu's bow
Must be one of your servants.
So why not tell me, what is your command?'
Hearing this, the angry muni grew even more furious.
'A servant is one who serves,
But he who has done the deed of an enemy must be fought!
Hear me, Ram—he who has broken Shiv's bow
Is as much my enemy as was the thousand-armed Sahasrabahu.
Let him stand away from this assembly
Or else all these kings will be killed.'
Hearing the sage's words, Lakshman smiled
And mocking Parashudhar,[lxiii] spoke.
'We have broken many bows in our childhood,

[lxiii] Parashuram

But you were never before so angry, sir!
Why are you so attached to this particular bow?'
Growing even angrier at his words, the banner of the line of
    Bhrigu replied,

    'Hey, young prince in the shadow of death!
    You have no check on your tongue!
    Is any little bow like Tripurari's bow,
    Renowned throughout the world?'   (271)

Lakshman laughed and said, 'In my understanding,
Respected sir, all bows are the same.
What loss or gain is there in breaking a worn-out old one?
Seeing it, Ram mistook it for new
And it broke at his touch—it was no fault of Raghupati's.
Why then do you rage so, muni, without any cause?'
With a glance at his axe, the muni replied,
'Fool, have you not heard of my temper?
I call you a child, so I do not kill you.
You regard me, fool, only as an ascetic—
But I have practised austerity from childhood, and full of wrath,
I am famous throughout the world as the enemy of the Kshatriya clans.
By the might of my arm I have cleared the earth of kings
And given it, many times, to the Brahmans.
The axe that cut off Sahasrabahu's arms—
Take a look at it, young son of a king!

    Do not cause your mother and father
    To be overwhelmed with sorrow, young prince!
    My axe is very cruel—
    It destroys even the unborn child in the womb.'   (272)

Lakshman laughed and replied in gentle tones,
'Oho, the great muni considers himself a mighty warrior.

Again and again you show me your axe,
Hoping, with a breath, to blow away a mountain.
But there is no unripe pumpkin here
That will fall at the sight of an admonishing forefinger.
Seeing your axe, and bow and arrows
I spoke a little haughtily.
But knowing that you are of Bhṛigu's line and seeing your
    sacred thread,
I suffer whatever you say, keeping my anger in check.
In our family, we do not display our valour against
Gods, Brahmans, devotees of Hari and cows.
To kill them is sin, and to be beaten by them, dishonour,
So even if you hit me, I will fall at your feet.
Your every word is as powerful as ten million thunderbolts—
You carry your bow, arrows and axe unnecessarily.

    If seeing them, I spoke improperly,
    Forgive me, great and steadfast muni.'
    Hearing this, the jewel of Bhṛigu's line
    Wrathfully replied in a deep and rumbling voice—   (273)

'Kaushik, listen to me, this boy is a fool!
Perverse, doomed to die, he is the destroyer of his own kin!
He is a blemish on the moon of the solar clan,
Self-willed, totally uncontrollable, bereft of sense and
    utterly reckless.
In another moment, he will become a morsel in Death's mouth,
And I loudly declare that it will be no fault of mine!
Check him if you wish him to be spared
And tell him about my glory, might and wrath.'
Lakshman said, 'Muni, as long as you live,
Who else can speak of your great fame?
You, with your own mouth, your own deeds
Relate many times, in many ways.

But if you are still not satisfied, tell us some more.
Do not, by holding back your rage, suffer intolerable anguish.
You have taken the pledge of valour and are resolute and steadfast
And gain no glory by cursing and abusing.

> Heroes perform their valiant deeds in war
> And do not themselves proclaim them.
> Faced with an enemy in battle,
> Only cowards boast of their might.   (274)

You keep shouting out to Death
Summoning him, again and again, for me!'
Hearing Lakshman's harsh words
Parashuram took his dreadful axe in hand.
'Now let no one blame me—
This rude and sharp-tongued boy deserves to be killed.
Seeing that he is a child I have spared him all this while,
But now he is about to die!'
Kaushik said, 'Forgive his offence—
Sages do not count the faults and virtues of children.'
'Sharp is my axe, and without mercy my wrath,
And before me stands this sinner, my guru, Shankar's, foe.
He talks back to me, and I have let him go and not killed him
Only out of regard for you, Kaushik.
Otherwise, I would have cut him into pieces with my cruel axe
And thus, with very little effort, discharged my debt to my guru.'

> The son of Gadhi smiled and said to himself,
> 'The muni sees only greenery, as does one who loses his sight in
>   the season of rains—
> Having vanquished other Kshatriyas easily, he is blind to the
>   greatness of Ram.
> This is a sword of iron before him, not a stalk of sugarcane—
>   but even now the fool does not understand.'   (275)

Lakshman said, 'Muni, who does not know of your amiable nature?
It is renowned throughout the world.
You have become free of your debt to your mother and
    your father—
Now remains your debt to your guru, and you are most anxious
    about that.[82]
It seems that you have put that debt on to our heads—
Many days have passed, and so the interest upon it has
    grown greatly,
So now call your creditor here,
And I will immediately give him the sum owed from my own purse.'
When he heard these sharp and caustic words, the muni hefted his axe.
'Hai! Hai!' cried out the gathering in alarm.
'Bhrigubar,[lxxiv] you threaten me with your axe,
But because you are a Brahman, I spare you, enemy of princes.
You have never met great warriors, hardened by war.
Lord of the twice-born, you are mighty only in your own home.'
'That is not proper!' cried out all the people,
And Raghupati with a sign made Lakshman stop.

    Lakshman's words were like offerings of ghee
    Into the fire of Bhrigubar's wrath.
    Seeing it increase,
    The sun of the line of Raghu spoke words that, like water,
        quenched the flames of his ire.   (276)

'Lord, have pity on this child,
Naïve and barely weaned, who still has milk upon his lips. Do not
    be angry with him.
If he knew anything of your might and glory,
Would this foolish child have dared to defy you like an equal?
When a little boy is naughty,

The hearts of his guru, his mother and his father become filled
     with joy.
So have compassion on him, knowing him to be but a small child
     and your servant,
For you are an even-tempered, amiable, wise and tolerant sage.'
Hearing Ram's words, Parashuram cooled down a little,
But Lakshman said something again and grinned.
Seeing him laughing at him, he was filled with rage.
'Ram, your brother is utterly sinful!
His body is fair, but his heart is black,
It is poison, not mother's milk, that he has upon his lips!
He is by nature crooked, and resembles you not at all,
Nor does this little villain recognize me as death.'

    Lakshman said with a laugh,
    'Listen, muni, anger is the root of sin.
    Under its influence, men do wrong
    And set themselves against the world.   (277)

I am but your servant, great muni,
So abandon anger now, and show compassion—
The broken bow won't be mended by anger.
And do sit down, your feet must be aching.
If that bow is so dear to you, let us devise a plan:
Let's have it mended by calling in a skilled craftsman.'
Lakshman's words frightened Janak, who said,
'Be quiet! Such impertinence is not good!'
The men and women of the city trembled and declared,
'The younger prince is much too rude!'
Hearing those bold words again and again,
Bhrigupati's body burnt with rage and he felt his strength
     diminish.
Speaking as though doing Ram a great favour, he said,
'I spare him because he is your little brother.

His heart is dark though his body is fair,
Like a golden pot filled with poison.'

> Hearing this, Lakshman laughed again,
> But Ram looked at him reprovingly,
> And he meekly went back to his guru,
> Giving up his rude and defiant talk.   (278)

With great humility, in a voice that was sweet and gentle,
And folding his hands, Ram spoke.
'Lord, you are by nature wise—
So give no ear to a child's words.
Madmen and children have the same inherent nature,
And saints do not find fault with either.
Besides, he has not done any wrong,
It is I, lord, who is guilty of offending you.
Therefore, revered sir, whether it be grace or anger, death
        or bondage,
Direct it towards me, as you would to a slave.
Tell me quickly how your anger may be appeased,
Lord of munis, and I will do whatever is required.'
The sage replied, 'Ram, how can my anger disappear?
Even now your little brother is looking mischievously at me.
If I have not set my axe to his throat,
How effective then is my anger?

> The wives of kings miscarry
> When they hear of the terrible doings of my axe.
> My axe is here, and yet I see
> My enemy, this young prince, still alive.   (279)

My hand does not move, though my breast burns with rage,
As though my axe, this killer of kings, has become dull and lazy.
Fate has turned contrary and changed my very nature—

For when has mercy entered my heart before?
Today, compassion makes me endure this intolerable annoyance.'
Hearing this, Sumitra's son smiled and bowed his head.
'Your compassion is like a gust of wind and in accordance with
　　your nature,
You speak and it seems that flowers rain from a tree.
But if compassion so sears your body, muni,
May God keep your body when you are angry!'
'Look, Janak, this foolish boy
Persists in wanting to make Jam's realm his home!
Make haste and get him out my sight!
Though he looks small, this king's son is wicked!'
Lakshman laughed to himself.
'Shut your eyes and you will see no one.'

Parashuram then turned to Ram and said,
　　Great fury in his heart,
'You broke Shambhu's bow, you rogue,
　　And now you dare instruct me!　　　　　　　　　　　(280)

Your brother utters these sharp and biting words with your consent
While you pretend humility with your folded hands.
Either give me satisfaction in single combat
Or give up being called "Ram".
You enemy of Shiv, give up deceit and fight me,
Or I will kill you along with your brother!'
Thus Bhrigupati raved and ranted, brandishing his axe.
Ram smiled to himself, his head bowed, and thought,
'The fault is Lakshman's, yet the muni is angry with me.
Sometimes it is a great fault to be straightforward.
Everyone praises and respects one known to be crooked—
Even Rahu does not swallow the curved crescent moon.'
Aloud, Ram said, 'Revered muni, abandon your wrath.
Your axe is in your hand, and this head of mine before you.

Do whatever will calm your anger, my master,
And know me to be your devoted follower.

> How can there be war between master and servant?
> Abandon your anger, best of Brahmans.
> When he saw your attire, this boy said a few things,
> But it was not his fault.   (281)

Seeing you holding axe, bow and arrows,
The child thought you were a warrior and grew angry.
Even upon learning your name, he did not recognize you
And answered you in the manner of our clan.
Had you come like a muni and a sage,
This child would have put the dust of your feet on his head,
     respected sir.
Forgive the mistake made in ignorance,
For a Brahman's heart should be full of compassion.
What equality or rivalry, lord, can there be between us and you?
Tell me, where are the feet and where the head?
Mine is the short name, I am merely "Ram"
Yours is the long name that comes with an "axe"—with "parashu"
     preceding it, you are "Ram with the axe".
Lord, I have but a single string to my bow
While you have all the nine virtues most sacred and pure,[83]
We are defeated by you in every way,
Brahman, so forgive our offence.'

> Again and again Ram entreated Ram,
> Addressing him as 'muni' and 'noble Brahman',
> Till Bhrigupati said with a wrathful laugh,
> 'You are as contrary as your brother!   (282)

You look upon me as a typical Brahman
But let me tell you what sort of Brahman I am—

My bow is my sacrificial ladle, my arrows the offering
And my wrath the fiercely blazing sacred fire.
Entire armies complete with all four divisions[84] are the
    fragrant firewood;
And great kings have come as animals—
With this very axe have I killed them and offered them up
    as sacrifice.
I have performed countless such sacrifices in the shape of war,
    chanting the mantra of battle.
You do not know my might—
That is why, mistaking me for a mere Brahman, you speak with
    such disrespect.
By breaking the bow, your conceit has broken all bounds,
And in your arrogance, you stand as though you have conquered
    the world.'
Ram said, 'Muni, reflect before you speak—
Your anger is very great and my mistake a small one.
The old bow broke the moment I touched it,
So what reason do I have for arrogance?

    If I have shown disrespect by calling you a Brahman,
    Hear the truth, Bhrigunath, and consider—
    Before which other warrior in this world
    Would I bow my head in fear?   (283)

If anyone challenges me in battle—
Gods, demons, kings and warriors,
Whether my equal in strength or stronger than me—
I will fight him with pleasure, even if he be Death himself.
One who takes on a Kshatriya's body but shrinks from battle
Brings disgrace to his family.
I state this not as praise of my clan, but only as its natural character:
Those belonging to the line of Raghu are not afraid even of death
    in battle.

But the might and glory of those who belong to the Brahman line
    is such
That even he who fears no one, fears you.'
Upon hearing Ram's sweet and profound words,
The veil lifted from Parashudhar's mind.
He said, 'Ram, take this bow of Ramaa's lord in your hand
And draw it so that my doubts are destroyed.'
As Parashuram held it out to him, the bow went to Ram of its
    own accord
And Parashuram's heart was filled with wonder.

    He then understood Ram's majesty,
    And his body trembled with joy.
    Folding his hands, he spoke,
    His heart overflowing with love.   (284)

'Hail, sun to the profusion of lotus flowers that is the clan of Raghu,
Hail, fire that consumes the dense and impenetrable forest
    of demons!
Hail, friend of gods, Brahmans and cows,
Hail, destroyer of pride, attachment, anger and delusion!
Ocean of humility, compassion and virtue,
Hail, master of eloquence,
Who bestows happiness upon his followers, and is beautiful in
    every part,
Whose body shines with the splendour of a billion bodiless ones!
How can I praise him with but a single tongue?
Hail, swan on the Manas lake of Mahesh's heart!
In my ignorance I said much that was rude and unseemly—
Forgive me, brothers both, you in whom resides mercy.'
Proclaiming 'Hail, hail, hail to the greatest of the line of Raghu!'
Bhrigupati retired to the forest to practise penance.
The wicked kings were frightened by their own lowly fears—
The cowards fled in all directions.

The gods sounded their drums,
And showered flowers upon the Lord.
The men and women of the city all rejoiced
As their fears and doubts disappeared.   (285)

Musical instruments began to play with great noise and clamour,
And everyone began to prepare for the happy and auspicious event.
Lovely women with beautiful eyes and voices as sweet as
      the kokil's
Flocked together, singing sweet songs.
Videh's delight defied description,
As though one poor from birth had found treasure.
Sita's fears disappeared and she became as joyful
As a young chakori at the rising of the moon.
Janak paid homage to Kaushik Vishvamitra,
'It is by your grace, my lord, that Ram broke the bow—
The two brothers have accomplished my purpose.
Tell me, respected sir, what I now must do.'
Replied the muni, 'Listen, wise king of men,
Marriage was conditional upon the bow
And took effect the instant the bow broke.
Gods, men and Nagas—everyone knows it.

Even so, go and perform the wedding ceremony
According to the customs of your clan and family.
Consult the Brahmans, the elders and your guru,
About the rites and rituals prescribed in the Vedas.   (286)

Send your messengers to Avadh
And invite King Dasharath here.'
The king, rejoicing, said, 'Very well, gracious one!'
And summoning his messengers, sent them to Avadh at once.
He then summoned the merchants and all the important men of
      the city,

And they came, all of them, and with reverence bowed
    their heads.
'Markets, roads, homes and temples—
Decorate the whole town in every direction.'
Each one returned home rejoicing.
He then summoned his own servants and ordered,
'Have a handsome pavilion erected.'
Most willingly they obeyed him, and joyfully left to carry out
    his command,
Sending for hosts of skilled craftsmen
Accomplished in the art of building pavilions.
Invoking Brahma the Creator, they began to work.
They fashioned pillars of gold in the form of plantain trees,

    With leaves and fruits made of green emerald
    And flowers of rubies the colour of lotuses.
    Seeing this most rare and wonderful creation,
    Brahma himself was confused.   (287)

They fashioned stalks of bamboo, all from green emeralds,
Straight and jointed, and impossible to distinguish from the real.
From gold they fashioned betel vines
With beautiful leaves, so wonderfully crafted that they fooled
    the eye.
These vines they entwined into ropes
With strings of pretty pearls braided into them here and there.
Rubies, emeralds, diamonds and turquoises
They cut, engraved and inlaid to fashion lotus flowers.
They made bees and birds of many colours,
Which hummed and called in the breeze.
They carved figures of gods upon the pillars,
All standing with auspicious gifts in their hands.
They drew sacred ornamental squares of many kinds,
All filled in with lustrous elephant pearls.

They carved wondrously beautiful mango leaves
From blue sapphires,
With gold mango blossoms and emerald fruits
Glittering on silken cords. (288)

They wove beautiful garlands to festoon the doorways—
It seemed that the mind-born god of love himself had woven these
    snares of love.
They fashioned innumerable auspicious vessels,
And beautiful banners, flags, drapes and chowries.
The marvellous pavilion, impossible to describe,
With its countless heart-enchanting jewel-studded lamps,
The canopy meant for Vaidehi as a bride—
Which poet has the ability to describe it?
The pavilion erected for the bridegroom Ram, ocean of beauty
    and virtue,
Shone brightest in the three worlds.
Each and every house in the city reflected
The same splendour as in Janak's palace.
Even the fourteen spheres seemed small and insignificant
To him who beheld Terahuti[lxxv] at that time,
And the wealth gracing even the humblest homes was such
That looking upon it, even Indra, king of the gods, was enchanted.

Even Sharada and Shesh hesitate
To describe the splendour and grace
Of that city in which Lakshmi resides
In the secret guise of a beautiful woman. (289)

Janak's messengers reached Ram's sacred city,
And rejoiced to see the beautiful town.
At the palace gate, they announced their arrival,

[lxxv] The city of Mithila

And King Dasharath heard and sent for them.
They saluted him and gave him the letter,
The king, delighted, himself stood up to receive it.
Upon reading the letter, his eyes filled with tears,
His body trembled with joy and his breast heaved with emotion.
With Ram and Lakshman in his heart and the precious letter in
    his hand,
The king stood unable to utter a word, either sour or sweet.
Then, collecting himself, he read out the letter,
And the gathered assembly rejoiced to hear what it said.
Receiving news of the letter while at play,
Bharat came with his brother and his friends,
And asked with deep affection and humility,
'Father, where has the letter come from?

    Are my two dear brothers well?
    And tell me, what land are they in?'
    Hearing his words so steeped in love,
    The king read out the letter again.   (290)

Hearing the letter, the two brothers were overjoyed,
And could not contain their great love for Ram and Lakshman.
Seeing Bharat's pure and unalloyed love,
The entire court was especially pleased and delighted.
Then the king bade the messengers be seated near him
And said to them in sweet and pleasant tones,
'Friends, tell me, are the two boys well?
You have seen them with your own eyes, have you not?
One is dark, the other fair-complexioned, each carries a bow
    and quiver,
They are of tender years, and with Muni Kaushik.
Do you recognize them? If so, tell me how they are.'
The king, overwhelmed by love, asked thus again and again.
'Since the day that the muni took them away,

I have received firm news of them only today.
Tell me how Videh recognized them.'
Hearing these affectionate words, the messengers smiled.

    'Listen, crown jewel of kings,
    There is no one as blessed as you,
    Whose sons are Ram and Lakshman,
    The two ornaments of this world.   (291)

You do not need to inquire after your sons—
They are lions amongst men and the light of the three worlds,
Before the glowing brilliance of whose fame,
The moon seems dim and the sun cold.
You ask, lord, how they were recognized—
Does one hold a lamp in one's hand to see the sun?
At Sita's svayamvar gathered many kings and princes,
Each a warrior better than the other.
Yet no one could move Shambhu's bow,
And all those great warriors stood defeated.
Shambhu's bow broke the strength
Of the proudest warriors in the three worlds.
Even Banasur, who can lift up Mount Meru,
Acknowledged defeat in his heart and, merely circling
    the bow, departed.
And he who in play had once picked up Shiv's mountain,
Even that Ravan was defeated in that gathering.

    But there—listen well, great king of the earth—
    Ram, the jewel of the line of Raghu,
    Broke the bow without effort
    As an elephant snaps a lotus stalk.   (292)

Hearing of this, Bhrigunayak, furious, came,
And raged and threatened him in many ways.

Recognizing Ram's strength, he gave him his own bow,
Then, with humble apologies, withdrew to the forest.
King, just as Ram is unparalleled in strength,
In Lakshman too resides might and glory—
At his glance alone the other kings and princes trembled
Like elephants at a young lion's gaze.
Lord, having beheld your two sons
Our eyes can regard no one else.'
Steeped in affection, and so generous and gallant,
These words of the messengers pleased everyone greatly.
The king and his court took a great liking to them
And began to shower the messengers with gifts.
But the messengers covered their ears and cried, 'This is not right!'
Seeing their proper and decorous conduct, the gathering rejoiced.[85]

> The king rose and went to Vasishtha,
> And gave him the letter.
> Courteously summoning the messengers there,
> He related the full story to his guru.   (293)

Hearing it, the guru was overjoyed and said,
'For a good man, the world is filled with happiness.
Just as rivers flow into the ocean
Though it has no desire for them,
So happiness and prosperity come unbidden
And spontaneously to a virtuous man.
You are assiduous in the service of your guru, of Brahmans,
        cows and gods,
And Queen Kaushalya is equally pious and pure.
In this world, souls as virtuous and good as you
There are none, nor have there been or ever will be.
Who can be blessed with happiness greater than yours,
King, you who have a son like Ram?
Brave, obedient and mindful of dharma,

Your four boys are oceans of virtue.
For you, all times are propitious,
So make ready the wedding procession, sound the drums.

> And make haste!' At his guru's words,
> The king bowed his head and said, 'Very well, lord.'
> After assigning the messengers places to stay,
> The king returned to his palace.   (294)

The king summoned all the royal women
And read out Janak's letter to them.
Hearing the news, the women all rejoiced,
And the king related to them the full story.
The queens were as overjoyed at the news
As peahens hearing the rumble of rain-clouds.
The elder women of the royal household, delighted, gave their blessings,
And the three mothers were overwhelmed with happiness.
They passed the precious letter amongst themselves,
Pressing it to their bosoms to calm their hearts.
While Dasharath, noblest of all kings, recounted again and again
The glorious deeds of Ram and Lakshman.
'All this is by the grace of the muni,' said the king, departing.
The queens then summoned the gods of the earth,
And bestowed upon them gifts with great joy.
Uttering blessings in return, the noble Brahmans left.

> They then sent for the mendicants
> And gave them alms and countless gifts of many kinds.
> 'Long live the four sons of Dasharath,
> Monarch of the universe!'   (295)

Cried the mendicants as they left, attired in new clothes of
    various kinds.
The drummers, rejoicing, beat their drums loudly,

And as the news reached all the people,
Celebrations and revelry broke out in every house.
All the fourteen spheres were filled with glad delight—
'Janak's daughter is marrying Raghubir!'
Hearing these happy and auspicious tidings, the people were filled
    with joy
And began decorating roads, houses, lanes and alleyways.
Although Avadh is always a pleasant and charming place,
For it is Ram's own city, prosperous and pure,
It was made even more festive,
By the love its people bore for Ram, who is love personified.
Bright flags, pennants, banners and chowries
Made a canopy over the marketplaces in rare and wondrous fashion;
With auspicious pitchers made of gold, festoons and jewelled nets
    for doorways,
Turmeric, sacred dub grass, curds, unbroken rice and garlands
    of flowers,

    The people decorated their homes
    And made them festive and happy;
    They sprinkled the roads with fragrant perfumes,
    And at the entrances to their homes, drew auspicious squares
        filled with pretty designs.   (296)

Everywhere, crowds of women gathered,
Shining with all the sixteen adornments, glittering like lightning,
With faces as radiant as the moon, fawn-like eyes,
And beauty that made even Rati give up her pride.
They sang wedding songs in such melodious voices
That hearing their sweet tones, even the sweet-throated kokil was
    too shy to sing.
And how was the royal palace to be described?
There, a pavilion to enchant the world had been built,
Countless auspicious and heart-enchanting objects

Glittered and shone, while drums sounded deep and loud.
Here, bards and minstrels related the glory of the royal families,
While there, Brahmans chanted the Vedas.
Beautiful women sang songs of joy and good fortune
Invoking again and again the names of Ram and Sita.
The excitement was great, the palace too small to contain it—
The joy seemed to overflow in all the four directions.

> Which poet can describe
> The splendour of Dasharath's palace
> Where Ram, the jewel of the gods,
> Had descended to earth?   (297)

Then the king called Bharat to him, and said,
'Go prepare horses, elephants and chariots
And let's leave at once with Raghubir's wedding procession.'
Hearing these words, the two brothers[bxxvi] were thrilled.
Bharat sent for all the men in charge of the stables
And gave his orders. Delighted, they hastened to carry them out,
And fitted the horses with saddles and bridles that had been crafted
    with great care—
Soon, fine horses of many colours stood splendidly accoutred.
All handsome and spirited, the horses
Trod the ground as lightly as though it were burning iron.
They were of various breeds, too numerous to describe;
It seemed they wished to fly, leaving the wind behind.
Upon them mounted all the dashing young fellows,
Princes the same age as Bharat,
All handsome and comely, and all in jewelled attire,
With bows and arrows in their hands, and heavy quivers at
    their waists.

[bxxvi] Bharat and Shatrughna

All were merry, comely, graceful youths,
Chosen warriors, skilled and valiant,
And with each rider were two men on foot,
Accomplished in the use of swords.   (298)

Sworn to honour, these warriors resolute in war
Set forth and stood waiting outside the city.
Leading their clever steeds through their various paces,
They rejoiced in the sound of drums and tabors.
Charioteers made their chariots bright and colourful
With flags, pennants, gems and jewels,
And decorated them with pretty chowries and little tinkling bells
So that they robbed the sun-god's chariot of its splendour.
There were innumerable black-eared horses—[86]
These the charioteers yoked to the chariots—
All so beautiful and gorgeously adorned,
That looking at them, even a saint would be charmed.
They could race across water as if it were land,
Their hooves not sinking, so great was their speed.
After preparing the chariots with arms and equipment
The charioteers then summoned the warriors,

Who, one by one, mounted the chariots,
And the wedding procession assembled outside the city.
All saw good omens favouring the task
To accomplish which they were going.   (299)

Upon great elephants were magnificent canopies
So splendidly adorned as cannot be described.
Those mighty elephants set off, their great bells ringing
Like banks of rumbling rain clouds in the month of Savan.
There were many other kinds of conveyances—
Handsome palanquins and comfortable sedan chairs—
In which rode the companies of the learned Brahmans

As though all the verses of the Vedas had taken on bodily form.
Poets, bards, minstrels and singers of songs of praise
Went mounted on other vehicles, each according to his rank,
While heavily laden mules, camels and oxen of many breeds
Plodded along, with innumerable goods and articles upon
    their backs.
Countless porters accompanied them, bundles slung across their
    shoulders—
Who can describe the diverse articles they carried?
And crowds of servants set off in groups,
All appropriately attired and equipped.

    The hearts of all were filled with great joy,
    And their bodies trembled with excitement.
    'When will we see those two brave heroes, Ram and
        Lakshman,
    And fill our eyes with the sight?'   (300)

Elephants trumpeted, their great bells clanging loudly,
On all sides was the din of chariots and the neighing of horses,
While the rumble of drums was louder than thunder
So that no one could hear himself or another speak.
So enormous and dense was the crowd at the king's door,
That a stone thrown into it would be trampled to dust.
Women climbed onto balconies and terraces to look down at
    the scene,
Holding in their hands festive arti trays,
And singing heart-enchanting songs of many kinds—
There is so much joy as cannot be described.
Then Sumantra, the king's trusted councilor and charioteer, made
    ready two chariots
And yoked to them horses that could outrun the sun's own steeds.
He brought the two beautiful chariots to the king—
So splendid were they that even Sharada could not describe them.

One chariot was decorated with the royal insignia,
While the other glittered with fiery splendour.

> Upon this gleaming and handsome chariot
> The king joyfully seated Vasishtha.
> He himself climbed into the other chariot,
> Invoking Har, his guru, Gauri and Ganesh.   (301)

The king with Vasishtha was as glorious
As Purandar with Brihaspati.[87]
The king performed all the rites of his lineage and those prescribed
    by the Vedas,
Then, making sure that everyone was in every way ready,
Invoking Ram, and receiving the permission of his guru,
The lord of the earth set forth to the sound of the conch.
The gods rejoiced to see the wedding procession,
And rained down beautiful flowers, conferring good fortune
    upon them.
There was a tumultuous din as horses whinnied and elephants
    trumpeted
And music sounded in the sky and in the wedding procession.
Women, divine and mortal, broke out in songs of joy,
While shehnais played sweet and melodious tunes.
The clanging and ringing of bells big and small defied
    description.
Performers on foot waved swords and flags and leapt about in
    displays of martial games,
Jesters, adept in drollery and singing clever songs,
Performed merry tricks and pranks.

> Noble princes made their horses prance
> To the beat of the drums and mridangs,
> As accomplished dancers watched, astonished
> That the horses did not place a foot out of time.   (302)

The wedding procession was so splendid and grand that it
    defied description.
Beautiful and auspicious omens of good fortune were
    everywhere—
On the left, a blue-throat[88] pecked for food,
As though declaring that all was well.
Upon the right was a crow in a lush, green field,
And the mongoose, too, was seen by all.
A cool, fragrant and gentle breeze blew from the right direction,
And a beautiful woman carrying a pitcher and a baby approached.
A fox turned again and again to show itself,
While ahead, a cow nursed her calf.
A row of deer appeared on the right
Like a line of good omens.
A white-headed kite called out blessings and good fortune.
Upon the left a shyama bird was seen, perched upon a
    handsome tree.
Seen approaching in front was a man with curds and fish,
And two learned Brahmans, with books in their hands.

    All omens conferring prosperity and well-being
    And bestowing desired rewards,
    All occurred at once,
    As though to confirm their own truth.   (303)

All good and auspicious omens come easily
For him whose beautiful son is the Absolute incarnate.
With a bridegroom like Ram, a bride like Sita
And virtuous fathers-in-law like Dasharath and Janak—
Upon hearing of such a wedding, all good omens dance and say,
'Now Viranchi has proven us true!'
Thus the wedding procession set forth,
To the neighing of horses, the trumpeting of elephants and the
    beating of drums.

Knowing that Dasharath, the greatest of the solar line
    was coming,
Janak had built bridges across the rivers,
And luxurious rest-houses at intervals along the way,
As magnificent as the abode of the gods,
With good food, comfortable beds and fresh clothing
Which suited every taste and pleased everyone in the wedding
    procession.
Daily discovering new and pleasing comforts,
The guests in the wedding procession all forgot their own homes.

    Learning that the wedding procession approached
    And hearing the beating of drums,
    A welcoming party of elephants, chariots, foot soldiers
        and horses
    Went out to receive the guests.   (304)

Golden pitchers and brimming copper trays,
And beautiful vessels of many kinds
Filled with delicacies as sweet as nectar,
Of so many kinds that they cannot be described,
And fruits of many varieties, and costly and beautiful objects—
King Janak, rejoicing, sent ahead as gifts.
Jewellery, clothes and many different kinds of precious gems,
Birds, deer, horses, elephants and chariots of many sorts,
Objects of good omen and pleasing perfumes
Of many kinds the king sent,
As well as porters, who set forth with countless pots
Filled with curds and parched rice, and innumerable gifts, slung
    across their shoulders.
When the welcoming party saw the wedding procession,
Their hearts filled with joy and their bodies trembled with excitement;
And seeing the reception party and their gifts and preparations
The delighted guests beat their drums.

Some from each side set off at full gallop,
Joyfully, to meet each other.
They came together like two oceans of delight
That had abandoned their shorelines.   (305)

Celestial nymphs rained down flowers and sang melodious songs,
While the delighted gods sounded their drums.
Those who had come to receive the wedding procession placed
    their gifts before the king
And welcomed him with reverence and great affection.
The king accepted the gifts with love,
And generously distributed them amongst the poor.
Then paying them due homage and singing songs of praise,
The welcoming party conducted the wedding guests to the rooms
    prepared for them.
Rare and beautiful cloths were spread upon the floor,
So rich and costly that upon seeing them, even Kuber could no
    longer boast of his wealth.
Exceedingly pleasant and charming were the apartments
    given to them,
Where everybody was given every kind of comfort.
When Sita learnt that the wedding procession had arrived in the city,
She made known some of her own majesty.
Meditating upon them in her heart, she summoned all the
    mystical powers[89]
And sent them to attend upon the king.

All those powers, upon hearing Sita's commands,
Went to the guests' apartments
Taking with them riches and all comforts
And the pleasures and luxuries of the abode of the gods.   (306)

Beholding their apartments, the wedding guests
Found all the pleasures of the gods at hand.

No one knew the secret behind this splendour,
And everybody praised it as Janak's doing.
But Raghunayak knew Sita's power
And rejoiced in his heart to see this manifestation of her love.
The two brothers heard of their father's arrival
And could not contain their great joy in their hearts.
Though hesitant to say so to their guru,
Their hearts yearned to see their father.
Perceiving their deep humility and reverence, Visvamitra
Was greatly pleased.
Delighted, he clasped the two brothers to his heart,
He trembled with joy and his eyes filled with tears.
They set off for Dasharath's guest apartment,
Like a lake that has seen a thirsty man.

> When the king saw the muni
> Approaching with his sons,
> He rose, rejoicing, and stepped forward as one trying to assess
>   the depth
> Of this ocean of joy.   (307)

The lord of the earth prostrated himself in reverence before
    the muni,
Taking again and again the dust of his feet upon his head.
Kaushik raised up the king and clasped him to his heart,
And blessing him, asked if he was well.
Then the two brothers prostrated themselves,
And, gazing upon them, the king could not contain his happiness
    within his heart.
As he clasped his sons to his bosom, the unbearable pain of parting
    from them disappeared—
It was as though a corpse had been given the gift of life.
Then they bowed their heads at Vasishtha's feet,
And the great muni clasped them to his heart with loving delight.

The two brothers then saluted the company of Brahmans,
And received their affectionate blessings.
Bharat and his younger brother Shatrughna paid homage,
And Ram drew them up and hugged them to his heart.
Lakshman rejoiced to see his two brothers,
And embraced them, full of love.

> The citizens of Avadh, members of his household and his clan
> Dependents, ministers and friends—
> The Lord, most compassionate and gentle,
> Appropriately greeted them all.   (308)

Seeing Ram, the wedding party were soothed and comforted—
The ways of love are indescribable.
With the king his four sons looked as glorious
As though the four rewards of life had taken bodily form.
Seeing Dasharath with his sons,
The men and women of the city were delighted beyond measure.
The gods rained down flowers and beat upon their drums,
While apsaras danced and sang.
Shatanand, the company of Brahmans and ministers,
And minstrels, bards, jesters and musicians—all those who had
    gone to receive the guests,
Paid homage to the king and his wedding party,
And then, with his permission, returned.
The wedding party had arrived before the wedding date,
At which there was great rejoicing in the city.
The people, full of supreme bliss,
Entreated Vidhi to lengthen the days and nights.

> 'Ram and Sita are the pinnacles of beauty,
> The two kings, Dasharath and Janak, the pinnacles of virtue,'
> So said the people of the city to each other, men and women,
> Wherever they gathered.   (309)

'Janak's virtue has taken form as Vaidehi,
And Dasharath's piety is embodied in Ram.
No one has worshipped Shiv like these two kings,
Nor received such rewards as they.
There has never been any like them in this world,
Nor is anyone like them now, nor will there ever be.
We all, too, are the repositories of virtue,
To have been born in this world as residents of Janak's city
And to have beheld the beauty of Janaki and Ram.
Who can be more fortunate than us?
And now we will see Raghubir's wedding,
Making the best and fullest use of our eyes!'
Women with voices as sweet as the kokil's say to each other,
'O beautiful-eyed ones, there is great profit in this marriage.
By great good fortune, providence has arranged this match—
These two brothers will often come to visit, and dwell in our eyes
    as guests.

    Again and again, compelled by love,
    Janak will send for Sita,
    And the two brothers, as desirable and comely as
        innumerable Kamdevs,
    Will come to fetch her back.   (310)

They will be received and entertained in many ways—
And who, dear friend, would not love such a father-in-law?
Then, each time, gazing at Ram and Lakshman,
All the townsfolk will rejoice!
And, my friends, just as Ram and Lakshman are a pair,
With the king are two other boys exactly like them,
One dark, the other fair-complexioned, and beautiful in
    every limb—
So say all those who have seen them.'
Said one, 'I saw them today,

And they seemed as though Viranchi had fashioned them with his
    own hands.
Bharat looks just like Ram,
So that no man or woman can tell them apart at a casual glance.
Lakshman and Shatrughna look the same,
Incomparable in every part from head to foot.
They charm and enchant the heart, but the tongue is unable to
    describe them—
None in all three worlds is comparable to them.'

There is none comparable to them, so poets and wise men declare,
Says their servant Tulsi.
Oceans of strength, modesty, wisdom, virtue and beauty,
They have no equals but themselves.
The women of the city all entreated Vidhi,
And said these words to him:
'May all four brothers marry in this city
And may we sing their wedding songs!'

    Their eyes full of happy tears, their bodies trembling with joy,
    The women said to each other,
    'Friend, Purari will make all this happen,
    For the two kings are oceans of merit.'   (311)

In this manner the women all made their wishes,
And joy welled up and flooded their hearts.
The kings who had come for Sita's svayamvar,
Also rejoiced as they gazed upon the four brothers.
Praising Ram's great and unblemished glory,
The kings returned, each to his own home.
Some days passed in this manner—
The citizens and all the wedding guests were full of joy.
The auspicious day for the main wedding ceremony came—
It was the cold season, the pleasant month of Agahan,

And the planets, the date, the stars, and their conjunctions were
    all at their most propitious.
Vidhi himself calculated and fixed the auspicious moment
    with care,
And sent a note with Narad to Janak.
Janak's own astrologers had made the very same calculations,
And when the people heard this, they all declared,
'Our astrologers here are like Brahma himself!'

    It was the sacred hour before sunset, when the cows return
        home from the fields,
    The most pleasing and auspicious time of the day.
    Seeing that the omens were favourable,
    The Brahmans alerted King Janak.   (312)

The king asked the high priest,
'Now, why delay any further?'
Shatanand then summoned the ministers,
Who brought with them all the auspicious articles required for the
    ceremony.
Conches, drums and tabors sounded loudly,
Sacred pitchers and articles signifying good fortune were
    made ready,
Beautiful women in costly attire began to sing,
And pious Brahmans chanted the Vedas.
In this way, they reverently went to fetch the bridegroom's
    wedding party
From the guesthouses where they were staying.
When they beheld the king of Koshal's retinue,
Even Indra's glory appeared to them quite insignificant.
'It is time, so please do start,' they said.
At this, mighty drums resounded.
Consulting his guru, the king performed the family rites
And set off with a crowd of munis and sages.

Beholding the good fortune and splendour of the king of Avadh,
Brahma and the other gods
Began to praise him with a thousand tongues,
Regarding their own births to be worthless.   (313)

The gods, knowing that the auspicious hour had come,
Rained down flowers and sounded their drums.
Shiv, Brahma and all the great multitude of gods,
Mounted their chariots in crowds,
And overcome with love, their hearts full of gladness,
They set forth to witness Ram's wedding.
Upon seeing Janak's city, the gods were enchanted
And their own abodes now appeared insignificant to them all.
They gazed, struck with wonder, at the gorgeous pavilions
With all their marvellous adornments,
And at the men and women of the city, who were all repositories
    of beauty,
Handsome, virtuous, courteous and learned.
Beholding them, all the gods and their wives
Faded like stars in the light of the moon.
Vidhi especially was overcome with astonishment,
For nowhere could he see any of his own handiwork.

Then Shiv admonished all the gods,
'Do not lose yourself in wonder.
Recover yourselves and reflect in your hearts:
This is Sita and Raghubir's wedding,   (314)

At the mention of whose names, all evil in the world
Is destroyed at its root
And the four ends of life fall into one's hand—
They are those very Sita and Ram.' So explained Kamari[lxxvii].

[lxxvii] Shiv

Having thus admonished the gods, Shambhu
Again urged forward his noble bull.
The gods saw Dasharath setting forth joyfully,
Supreme delight in his heart.
The crowd of sadhus and Brahmans who accompanied him
Seemed like all the joys in bodily form attending upon him.
With him shone his four handsome sons
As though they were the four kinds of moksha embodied.
The gods were overcome with great love
To see the two handsome pairs—one dark, the other fair, of
    emerald and golden hue.
Then they looked upon Ram, rejoicing in their hearts,
Praising the king, and raining down flowers.

> As Uma and Purari
> Gazed again and again upon Ram's perfect form
> Beautiful from head to toe,
> They were overcome with joy and their eyes
>   filled with tears.   (315)

His dark limbs were as radiant as a peacock's throat,
His raiment of beautiful yellow outshone the lightning,
Wedding ornaments of many kinds, auspicious and
    beautifully fashioned,
Graced his form in every way.
His charming countenance was like the flawless full moon
    of autumn,
His eyes put the new-blooming lotus to the blush—
His divine beauty
Enraptured the heart, yet could not be described.
With him, resplendent, were his charming brothers
Making their swift and spirited steeds prance and trot,
The other princes, too, showed off their noble horses,
While the family bards recited the fame and glory of their line.

The horse upon which Ram was in splendour mounted,
Made Garud, the king of the birds, blush for shame with its speed.
Its beauty was beyond description in every way,
As though Kamdev himself had taken on the form of a horse.

It seemed as though the mind-born one had taken, for the love of Ram,
The form of a magnificent horse,
And its youth, strength, beauty, merits,
And gait had enraptured all the worlds.
Its saddle, encrusted with jewels, glittered
With the radiance of pearls, rubies and precious gems,
And its exquisite bridle, embellished with tiny, tinkling bells,
Captivated gods, men and munis alike.

Its heart and mind completely immersed in the Lord's will,
The horse stepped forth, resplendent.
It seemed as though a dark raincloud, adorned with stars and
    flashes of lightning,
Was making a beautiful peacock dance.   (316)

Even Sharada could not describe
The beautiful horse upon which Ram was mounted.
Shankar became so enamoured of Ram's beauty
That his fifteen eyes seemed very precious to him.
When Hari gazed upon Ram with fond affection,
He who is Ramaa's lord, and Ramaa, were enchanted.
Beholding Ram's beauty, Vidhi rejoiced
But regretted that he had only eight eyes.
Skand, commander of the divine armies, was delighted
That he had one and half times as many eyes as Vidhi.
Looking at Ram, all-wise Indra, king of the gods,
Considered Gautam's curse his greatest blessing.[90]
All the gods were envious of Indra and declared,
'No one is as fortunate as Purandar today!'

The whole company of gods rejoiced, looking at Ram,
While there was joy unparalleled amongst the retinue of
    both kings.

There was great joy amongst the royal retinue on each side
As countless drums thundered
And the gods rained down flowers, rejoicing
And calling, 'Hail, hail, hail to the jewel of Raghu's line!'
When the wedding procession was thus heard approaching,
All kinds of musical instruments were played
And the queen summoned her women
To prepare the auspicious articles for the welcoming ceremony.

They made ready all that was required for the arti
And prepared for all the auspicious ceremonies of welcome.
Then those beautiful women proceeded with graceful gait
To welcome the wedding procession.   (317)

The women, doe-eyed, and all with faces as radiant as the moon,
Robbed, with their glowing loveliness, even Rati of all pride in
    her beauty.
They were dressed in gorgeous garments of many colours,
Their bodies adorned with ornaments of every kind.
Thus auspiciously adorned in every limb,
They sang so melodiously as to put even the sweet-throated kokil
    to shame.
With tinkling bracelets, girdles and anklets,
Their swaying gait put even Kamdev's elephants to the blush.
Musical instruments of all kinds began to play,
And songs of blessing filled the sky and the town.
Shachi, Sharada, Ramaa, Bhavani
And the other divine consorts, chaste and wise,
Disguised themselves as beautiful women,
And entered the women's quarters to mingle with the royal ladies,

Singing songs of good fortune in sweet voices.
Distracted by happiness, no one realized who they were.

But who recognized anyone? Overcome with joy,
All proceeded to welcome brahm, Supreme Spirit, as bridegroom.
Soft songs and sweet-toned drums filled the air
As the gods rained down flowers. There was beauty everywhere.
Beholding the bridegroom, the source of all delight,
The women all rejoiced in their hearts.
In their lotus eyes sprang tears of happiness,
And a joyous trembling overcame their beautiful limbs.

> The bliss that arose in Sita's mother's heart
> When she beheld Ram's noble appearance
> Cannot be described in a hundred kalpas
> By a thousand Sharadas and Sheshas.   (318)

Given the auspiciousness of the occasion, the queen put aside
      her tears
And performed the welcome ceremonies with a glad heart—
The rites and rituals prescribed by the Vedas and the customs of
      her family,
The queen diligently performed them all.
The music of five kinds of instruments, the five kinds of auspicious
      sounds, and songs of joy and celebration filled the air,[91]
And carpets of every description were spread upon the floor
      in welcome.
The queen performed the arti and the sacred offering of arghya,
After which Ram entered the wedding pavilion.
Dasharath, resplendent, followed with his retinue—
Upon beholding his splendour, even the celestial guardians of the
      world were put to shame.
Again and again the gods rained down flowers
While Brahmans recited prayers for peace and harmony.

Tumultuous celebration filled the heavens and the town
So that no one could hear himself or another.
In this manner Ram arrived at the wedding pavilion,
And after the sacred libation had been poured, he was led to
    his seat.

Once he was seated, the women performed the arti—
Gazing upon the bridegroom, they were filled with delight.
Precious jewels, raiment and ornaments were showered upon him
As the women sang songs of joy and celebration.
Brahma and the other gods, disguised as Brahmans,
Observed the spectacle.
As they gazed upon the radiant splendour of the sun of the lotus line
    of Raghu,
They considered their lives fulfilled.

   The barbers, torchbearers, bards and jugglers,
   Who received the offerings that had been showered upon Ram,
   Were delighted, and bowing their heads in reverence, called
       blessings upon him.
   They could barely contain their joy within their hearts.   (319)

Janak and Dasharath met with great affection
And performed all the ceremonies prescribed in the Vedas and
    by custom.
The meeting of the two great kings was so glorious
That poets searching for a simile were embarrassed at their failure.
Finding no suitable comparison, they acknowledged defeat in their
    hearts, declaring,
'They can be likened only to themselves!'
The gods gazed with affection upon the two fathers-in-law,
And raining down flowers, began to sing their glory.
'Since the moment Viranchi created this world,
We have seen and heard of many weddings,

But two sides so comparable in pomp and grandeur
And two fathers-in-law so equal, we have seen only today.'
Upon hearing these true and gracious words of the gods,
Great love arose in both sides.
Spreading carpets for him to tread upon and pouring libations as
    they went,
Janak with reverence brought Dasharath into the wedding pavilion.

Beholding the extraordinary construction and rare elegance of the pavilion
Even munis were captivated.
Janak, wise and discerning, with his own hands
Set out seats for them all.
He paid homage to Vasishtha as though he were his own family's
    chosen deity,
And doing humble obeisance before him, received his blessings.
And the supreme love and reverence with which he paid homage
    to Kaushik
Cannot be described.

    To Vamdev and the other rishis
    The king paid glad homage.
    He gave them all seats of honour,
    And from all received their blessings.   (320)

Janak then paid homage to the king of Koshal,
Considering him equal to Ishan[lxxviii]—there was no other god like him.
Folding his hands, he humbly praised him
And recounted at great length his own glorious good fortune.
King Janak paid homage to all the guests in the wedding party
With the same respect he had given to the bridegroom's father
And conducted them all to suitable seats—
How do I, with but a single tongue, describe the intensity of his joy?

[lxxviii] Shiv

Janak honoured the bridegroom's party
With gifts, and soft and courteous words.
Vidhi, Hari, Har, the eight guardians of the world and the sun—
Who knew Raghubir's true strength and glory—
Secretly disguised themselves as noble Brahmans,
And watched the spectacle with great delight.
Janak paid them the homage due to gods
And, without recognizing them, gave them honoured seats.

But who can recognize anyone
When every person has lost even his own sense of being?
Beholding the bridegroom, the source of all bliss,
Both sides were in a state of bliss.
The all-wise Ram recognized the gods,
And worshipped them in his mind,
Assigning them seats of glory.
Beholding the Lord's innate courtesy,
The hearts of the gods were filled with delight.

As the beautiful chakor drinks the light of the moon,
So everyone's eyes with reverence drank
The radiant beauty of Ramchandra's face—
There was no dearth of love and joy in their gaze.   (321)

Seeing that the moment had come, Vasishtha called
For Shatanand, who hearing the summons, respectfully came.
'Go quickly now and bring the princess.'
Receiving the muni's command, he gladly left to fetch the bride.
The queen heard the high priest's message,
And she and her companions were filled with joy.
She sent for the Brahman wives and the elder women of the family,
And performed the family rites with songs of joy and celebration.
The noble consorts of the gods, who were disguised as women,
Were all good natured, comely and youthful.

Seeing them the other women were glad,
And even without recognizing them, held them dearer than
      their own life's breath.
Again and again the queen honoured them
As equal to Uma, Ramaa and Sharada.
The women adorned Sita, and gathering around her,
They joyously led her to the wedding pavilion.

With reverence, and auspiciously adorned, Sita was brought
To the wedding pavilion by her friends and the royal ladies.
The lovely women were adorned with all the sixteen ornaments
And moved with the graceful gait of elephants.
Hearing their sweet singing, munis abandoned their meditation
And even Kamdev's kokils were abashed,
While their toe-rings, anklets and pretty bracelets
Tinkled in rhythm with their song.

      Amidst that multitude of women,
      The naturally lovely Sita shone
      Like exceptional beauty in the form of a comely and
            alluring woman
      Amidst a crowd of beautiful women.   (322)

Sita's loveliness cannot be described,
For my ability is limited and her beauty great.
The bridegroom's party saw Sita approaching,
The epitome of beauty and in every way chaste and pure.
Everyone paid homage to her in their hearts
While upon beholding her, Ram's every wish was fulfilled.
Dasharath, with his sons, rejoiced—
The joy in his heart cannot be told.
The gods paid homage and rained down flowers
And the munis gave their blessings, the sound of their chanting
      itself the source of all well-being.

Amidst the tumult of celebration, of singing and the beating
    of drums,
Men and women were lost in the happiness of love.
In this manner, Sita arrived at the wedding pavilion,
And the noble munis, rejoicing, began chanting the prayers for peace.
All the Vedic rites and customary ceremonies required for
    the occasion
Were performed by the two family priests.

The gurus performed the rites
As the Brahmans, rejoicing, worshipped Gauri and Ganpati,
And the gods, manifesting themselves to accept the worship
And give their blessings, felt great bliss.
Whatever sacred or auspicious substances[92]
The sages needed at any particular time,
Were brought at once by servants and attendants
Who stood ready with brimming golden platters and jars.
The lineage rites were lovingly directed by the Sun himself
And were with reverence performed.
Having thus worshipped the gods,
They seated Sita on a glorious throne.
The look full of love exchanged by Sita and Ram
Was beyond anyone's ability to understand—
Beyond heart and mind and even the most eloquent language,
How can any poet express this mystery?

    At the time of the offerings, the sacred fire assumed
        bodily form[93]
    And accepted the oblations with great delight,
    And all the Vedas, in the guise of Brahmans
    Directed the performance of the wedding ceremony.   (323)

Janak's chief queen, known throughout the world,
And Sita's mother—how can one describe her?

Glory, virtue, joy and beauty—
Vidhi had brought together all these qualities in her.
When the auspicious moment came, the noble munis sent
    for her—
Hearing their call, her women with reverence brought her.
Seated on Janak's left, Sunayana shone as beautiful
As Maina seated beside Himgiri.
Golden pitchers and a beautiful jewelled basin
Filled with pure, fragrant and holy water,
The king and queen, with their own hands,
Joyfully brought and placed before Ram.
The munis recited the Vedas, and to the auspicious sound of
    their chanting,
The sky, knowing it to be an important moment, rained
    down flowers.
Gazing upon the bridegroom, the royal couple were enraptured
    by him
And began to wash his holy feet.

They began to wash his lotus feet,
Overwhelmed with love and devotion,
While in the sky and in the city, singing, drumbeats and cries of victory
Burst forth and overflowed in all directions.
The lotus feet that forever shine
On the lake that is Shiv's heart,
By meditating upon which, the mind is at once made pure
And all the impurities of the age of Kali destroyed,
At whose touch the muni's wife attained salvation
Though imbued with sin,
Whose nectar is resplendent upon Shambhu's head
And is declared by the gods to be the epitome of purity,[94]
Which the bees that are the hearts of munis and jogis
Serve to attain the states they desire—
It was those feet that the fortunate Janak washed

As all cheered and joyfully hailed him.
Joining together the hands of the bride and the groom,
The two family priests recited their lineages.
Seeing that the ceremony of the joining of the hands had been completed,
Brahma, gods, men and munis were filled with joy.
Beholding that bridegroom, source of all bliss,
The royal pair trembled with happiness, their hearts full of joy.
Then that jewel of kings, obeying worldly custom and the Vedas,
Gave his daughter away.
As Himvant had given Girija to Mahesh,
And the Ocean had given Shri to Vishnu,
In the same way did Janak give Sita to Ram
And earned sweet glory and renown anew across the world.
How was Videha's king to bow before Ram?
For Ram's dark form had made him truly 'videh'.[95]
The prescribed offerings were cast into the sacred fire, the ritual knot
was tied,
And the pair began circumambulating the sacred fire.

Hearing the sounds of rejoicing, the reciting of eulogies, the
   chanting of the Vedas,
The songs of celebration and the beating of drums,
The all-wise, knowing gods rejoiced[96]
And rained down flowers from the divine tree
   of wishes.   (324)

The prince and the princess circled the sacred fire,
And all those who looked upon them with reverence, received the
   full reward of their eyes.
The heart-enchanting pair surpasses description—
Any comparisons that I might make will fall short.
Ram and Sita's beautiful reflections
Glittered in the jewelled pillars,
As though Madan and Rati had taken on innumerable forms

To witness Ram's incomparable wedding ceremony—
Though eager to watch the ceremony, they were shy
And so appeared and disappeared again and again.
All those watching the wedding were completely absorbed in
   the sight,
And, like Janak, had lost all awareness of themselves.
Joyously, the munis made Ram and Sita circle the sacred fire,
And together with the giving of ceremonial gifts, performed all the
   customary rites.
Then Ram applied sindur to Sita's head
In a manner graceful and charming beyond description,
As if the serpent that was Ram's dark arm had filled the lotus-cup
   of his hand with red pollen
And had adorned the moon that was Sita's lovely countenance,
   longing for its nectar.[97]
Then, upon Vasishtha's direction,
The bridegroom and the bride sat together upon the same seat.

With Ram and Janaki together upon the same glorious seat,
Dasharath's heart filled with joy,
And his body trembled with happiness again and again
To see this new fruit upon the Kalpataru of his virtuous deeds.
The universe was filled with delight—
'Ram has been wed!' cried everyone.
How can I describe this joy in full?
My tongue is one, the felicity of this auspicious event unbounded.
Then Janak, with Vasishtha's permission,
Made preparations for another wedding ceremony
And summoned the princesses
Mandavi, Shrutakirti and Urmila.
His brother Kushaketu's elder daughter, Mandavi,
Who was endowed with virtue, goodness, happiness and beauty,
The king bestowed in marriage upon Bharat,
Lovingly performing every rite and ceremony.

Knowing Janaki's younger sister, Urmila,
To be the most beautiful of all beautiful women,
The king gave this young maiden in marriage,
With all honour, to Lakshman.
She who was named Shrutakirti, Kushaketu's younger daughter,
Fair of face, with lovely eyes, endowed with every virtue,
And known for her beauty and her gentle nature,
Was bestowed by the king upon Ripusudan.
Seeing each other as brides and grooms, so appropriately matched,
They shyly rejoiced in their hearts
While everyone, delighted, admired their beauty
And the gods rained down flowers.
The four beautiful brides with their handsome bridegrooms,
Resplendent beneath a single canopy,
Shone as though the four states of being
With their lords had come together in the heart of a single soul.[98]

> The king of Avadh gazed joyfully
> At all his sons with their brides—
> It was as though that jewel amongst kings
> Had found the four rewards of life and with them the means
>   to their realization.[99]   (325)

All the princes were married by the same rites
As I have described for Raghubir's wedding.
The abundant dowry defies description—
The whole pavilion was filled with gold and jewels,
Blankets, garments and rare silken cloths
Of many kinds and immense value,
Elephants, chariots, horses, male and female servants,
Cows adorned with jewels like Kamdhenu—
So many goods, beyond accounting,
Defying description, as those who saw them know.
Even the guardians of the world grew envious at the sight.

The king of Avadh accepted it all with joy.
He gave to his supplicants whatever they liked or desired
And whatever remained was taken to the guests' apartments.
Then Janak, with folded hands and addressing them in soft tones,
Honoured the bridegroom's party.

He honoured the bridegroom's party
With reverence, gifts, humility and compliments.
Then joyfully, with loving devotion, he paid homage and
    offered obeisance
To the great sages assembled there.
With bowed head, he invoked the gods
And cupping his hands, said to all,
'Gods and saints want devotion alone.
Can the ocean be satisfied by an offering of water in cupped palms?'
Folding his hands, Janak with his brother
Then addressed the king of Koshal
In sweet words
Steeped in love, courtesy and affection.
'Through our alliance with you, O king,
We have been made greater in every respect.
So look upon this kingdom and all that we possess,
With us as servants, as yours—we want nothing in return.
Consider our daughters your handmaidens,
And cherish and protect them with compassion each day renewed.
Forgive my offence—I summoned you here,
That was very presumptuous of me.'
Then the jewel of the solar race
In turn addressed the bride's father with every honour.
Their humility towards each, with their hearts full to the brim with love,
Cannot be described.
The gods rained down flowers
As Dasharath proceeded to his guest apartments
Amidst drumbeats, cheering and the chanting of the Vedas.

The sky and the city were filled with the tumult of celebration.
Then, upon receiving the command of the high priest,
The princesses' charming friends, singing auspicious songs of joy,
Conducted the bridegrooms with their brides
To the inner chamber where was enshrined the family deity.

> Again and again Sita glanced shyly at Ram,
> Though her heart was not shy,
> And her eyes, yearning with love,
> Outshone the heart-enchanting fish that glitter on
>   Kamdev's banner.   (326)

Ram's dark form is naturally beautiful—
Its radiance puts to shame countless gods of love.
Stained with auspicious red, his lotus-feet are comely
        and graceful—
Above them, bee-like, hover the minds of saints and sages.
His pure and gleaming yellow dhoti
Dims the rising sun and the lightning flash.
Around his waist is a charming belt of softly tinkling bells,
And his mighty arms are adorned with jewels and fine ornaments.
His yellow sacred thread lends great radiance to his form,
The ring upon his finger steals the heart,
And upon his broad chest, jewelled ornaments shine—
His wedding attire is splendid and shining, and looks even more
        beautiful upon him.
A yellow stole across his chest and shoulder
Is fringed at both ends with jewels and pearls.
In his face resides all beauty—
With lotus eyes, beautiful rings in his ears,
Lovely eyebrows and charming nose,
And on his forehead a gleaming tilak in which resides radiance,
And shining upon his head, a gorgeous wedding crown
Threaded with pearls and jewels.

His gorgeous wedding crown is threaded with precious jewels,
And his every limb steals all hearts.
Gazing upon the bridegroom, every mortal woman and celestial goddess
Breaks blades of grass to keep away the evil eye.
They shower him with precious gems, fine garments and ornaments,
And worship him with songs of joy and celebration.
The gods rain down flowers
As storytellers, bards and minstrels recite his fame and glory.
The women, rejoicing, led the bridegrooms with their brides
To the shrine of the family deity,
And singing songs of joy,
They began the customary rites with great affection.
Gauri guided Ram and Sharada instructed Sita
How to put into each other's mouths, the ritual morsel of food.
The women's quarters were filled with laughter and merriment—
They felt they had reaped all the rewards of this existence.
When, in the jewels upon her hands, Janaki saw
The image of Ram reflected,
She dared not move the graceful vines that were her arms nor shift
    her gaze
For fear of being separated from his presence.
The gaiety, the playfulness, the joy and the love of that moment
Surpass description though Sita's friends understood it.
Then those companions led the bridegrooms and the brides to the
    guest chambers.
At that moment, blessings were heard all around,
In the town and in the firmament there was great happiness.
'Long live the four beautiful couples!'
Declared everyone, great joy in their hearts.
Beholding the Lord, yogis, Siddhas, great munis and gods
Sounded their drums,
And raining down flowers in their delight, and with shouts and
    cheers of joy
They departed, each for their own abodes.

Then the four princes with their brides
Went up to their father—
Beauty, felicity and joy
Seemed to fill and overflow the guest chambers.   (327)

A great feast was soon made ready with dishes of many kinds,
And Janak summoned the wedding guests.
Incomparable carpets of finest cloth were spread along their way,
As King Dasharath proceeded there with his sons.
The feet of all were washed with reverence
And everyone was conducted to seats in accordance with their rank.
Janak himself washed the feet of the king of Avadh
With courtesy and affection that surpass description.
He then bathed Ram's lotus feet,
Which are forever hidden in the lotus of Har's heart.
Knowing all three brothers to be the same as Ram,
Janak washed their feet with his own hands.
The king led them all to suitable seats of honour,
And then sent for all the cooks.
With great reverence they set before the guests leaf-platters,
Their leaves made of precious gems, and fastened together with
        pins of gold.

Dal and rice, and fragrant ghee made from the milk of cows—
Pleasing to the eye, delicious and pure—
Were served in a moment to everyone
By the skilled and courteous cooks.   (328)

After the five ritual mouthfuls, the guests began to eat
And listened with amusement and delight to the bawdy songs that
        accompany a wedding feast.
Countless dishes were served,
All as delicious as nectar and defying description.
Then those accomplished cooks began to serve the guests

Viands so varied, who knows what they were called?
Four kinds of food are mentioned in culinary treatises—
There were so many dishes of each that they cannot be described.
Many kinds of seasonings were used, imparting to the food the six
    different flavours,
And of each flavour there were numberless dishes;
As the guests feasted, women sang in sweet tones their songs of
    bawdy teasing,
Mentioning by name each man and woman present.
The ribald songs were appropriate to the moment,
And the king with the entire gathering broke into laughter as
    they listened.
In this manner the guests all ate and feasted,
After which the water for washing hands and rinsing mouths was
    politely offered.

    Presenting paan to his guests, Janak
    Paid homage to Dasharath and his retinue.
    Then Dasharath, that best and greatest of kings,
    Retired, gratified, to his quarters. (329)

Each day, there were new festivities in the city,
So that days and nights passed in the blink of an eye.
The jewel of all kings, Dasharath, awoke at break of day,
As bards and minstrels began to sing his virtues.
Seeing the young princes with their lovely brides,
The joy in his heart was so great as cannot be described.
After completing the morning rites, he went to his guru
With great love and joy in his heart.
Saluting him with folded hands,
He spoke in a voice that seemed steeped in nectar,
'By your grace, king of all munis,
My every wish has been fulfilled today.
Now, lord, summon all the Brahmans

And present them with cows adorned in every way.'
Hearing this, the guru praised the great king
And then sent for the company of sages.

> Then Vamdev and the divine Rishi Narad,
> Valmiki and Jabali—
> A multitude of sages came, with Kaushik
> And other great munis and ascetics.   (330)

The king prostrated himself before them,
And paying them homage, gave them seats of honour.
He called for four hundred thousand cows,
Each as gentle and beautiful as the divine cow, Kamdhenu.
Adorning them in every way,
The earth's guardian gladly bestowed them upon the Brahmans,
     gods upon earth.
The lord of men paid them humble obeisance in many ways,
     and declared,
'Today I have reaped the reward of my existence in this world.'
Receiving the blessings of the sages, the king rejoiced.
Then summoning the beggars and mendicants,
Dasharath, that joy of the sun's line, bestowed upon them
     according to their liking,
Gold, raiment, jewels, horses, elephants and chariots.
The mendicants left, singing his praises—
'All hail to the lord of the sun's line!'
Such were the celebrations of Ram's wedding
That even Shesh cannot described them with his thousand
   tongues.

> Bowing his head again and again
> At Kaushik's feet, the king declared,
> 'All this great happiness, king of the munis,
> Is the blessing bestowed by your gracious glance.'   (331)

The king praised Janak's love and courtesy,
His magnificence and gracious behaviour, in every way.
Arising at daybreak each day, the lord of Avadh asked to take his leave,
But Janak affectionately persuaded him to stay.
Daily the honour and reverence shown to Dasharath grew anew,
Each day was Janak's hospitality manifested in a thousand ways,
There were always new and joyous festivities in the town—
No one wanted Dasharath to depart.
Many days passed in this manner,
As though the wedding guests were bound with ropes of love.
Then Kaushik and Shatanand went to Janak
And explaining, said to Videha's king,
'Now give Dasharath permission to leave
Even though your love cannot let go of him.'
'Very well, my lords,' said Janak and sent for his ministers,
Who saluted him crying 'Victory! Long life!' with bowed heads.

    Said Janak, 'The lord of Avadh wishes to depart.
    Make it known in the inner apartments.'
    Hearing these words, the ministers were overcome with emotion,
    As were priests, councillors and the king himself.   (332)

The townspeople heard that the wedding guests were leaving
And anxiously inquired of each other if it was indeed so.
Hearing that the guests were actually leaving, all grew sad
    and downcast,
Like lotuses closing their petals at dusk.
Wherever the guests were to stay on their way back,
Provisions of many kinds were sent—
Dried fruits, sweetmeats, confections
And other ingredients and condiments, of such variety that they
    cannot be described,
On the backs of heavily laden oxen and innumerable porters.
Janak also sent many fine and comfortable beds.

A hundred thousand horses and twenty five thousands chariots,
All beautifully decorated from top to bottom,
Ten thousand mighty elephants, fully caparisoned,
Which put to shame even the celestial elephants,
Wagons full of gold, raiment and precious gems,
And buffaloes, and cows, and many kinds of things.

> The boundless dowry thus given again by Videha's king
> Is beyond all telling.
> Looking upon it, even the guardians of the three worlds
> Found the riches of their realms lacking.   (333)

When all the items had in this manner been made ready,
Janak had them sent to the city of Avadh.
When the queens heard that the wedding party was leaving,
They were as distraught as fishes in shallow water.
Again and again, taking Sita in their arms,
They blessed and gave her advice.
'May you forever be beloved by your husband,
May your husband live forever—this is our blessing.
Serve your father- and mother-in-law and guru,
Observe your husband's mood, and do as he commands.'
Her experienced friends and companions, overwhelmed with love
     for her,
Taught her a woman's duty in sweet voices.
Gently instructing all the princesses,
The queens clasped them again and again to their bosoms.
Again and again the mothers embraced their daughters
And cried, 'Oh why did Viranchi create women?'

> At that very moment, accompanied by his brothers,
> Ram, the banner of the solar line,
> Gladly set forth for Janak's palace
> To take his leave and depart for home with their brides.   (334)

The four brothers were so naturally handsome
That the men and women of the city rushed to see them.
Said one, 'They want to leave us today
And King Janak has made all preparations to bid them farewell
     with their brides.
So look upon them and fill your eyes with their beauty,
Our beloved guests, the four sons of the king.
Who knows, dear friend, as reward for which past good deed
Vidhi sent them here to soothe our eyes?
Like one about to die finding life-giving amrit,
Or one who has been hungry all his life finding the divine
     Kalpataru,
Or one who resides in hell finding Hari's feet—
So is our state at the sight of these princes.
Look upon Ram and hold his radiant beauty in your heart,
Make of your heart the serpent, of his image the jewel in its crest.'
In this way, rewarding the eyes of all,
The four princes made their way to the royal palace.

> Beholding the brothers, oceans of beauty,
> The women of the palace rejoiced.
> Their delighted mothers-in-law
> Greeted them with arti and gifts.   (335)

Looking upon Ram's beauty, they were enraptured,
And overcome with love and devotion, they fell again and again at
     his feet.
They forgot all propriety, for their hearts were so full of love—
How can such artless affection be described?
They bathed him and his brothers, anointing their bodies with
     sandalwood and fragrant oils,
And with great affection, fed them a meal complete with the
     six flavours.
Then, knowing it was time, Ram spoke

In tones courteous, affectionate and modest.
'The king wishes to depart for Avadh,
And has sent us here to take our leave of you.
Mothers, give us your blessings with happy hearts,
And looking upon us as your sons, forever regard us with affection.'
Upon hearing his words, the royal women grew sorrowful,
And overcome by love, the mothers of the brides could not speak.
They clasped their daughters to their hearts,
And then with humble entreaty, gave them to their husbands.

With humble entreaty, her mother gave Sita to Ram.
Her hands folded, she said again and again,
'Son! Wise one! I am certain
That you know full well the inner state of all men
And so will know that Sita is as dear as life itself
To her family, to the people of this city, to me and to the king.
Tulsi's Lord, beholding her good nature and her love,
Accept her as your devoted handmaiden.

> You are the fulfilment of all desire, wisdom's crown,
> And love is dear to you.
> Ram, you appreciate the virtues of your devotees and destroy
>   all vices,
> For you are the abode of compassion.'   (336)

Having spoken thus, the queen clasped his feet and fell silent
As though her voice had been lost in the muddy softness of love.
On hearing her gentle words so steeped in love,
Ram paid homage to his mother-in-law in many ways.
Then, with folded hands, Ram asked for permission to leave,
Saluting her again and again.
Receiving her blessing, and once more bowing his head,
Raghurai left with his brothers.
Drawing his sweet and beautiful image into their hearts,

The queens, overcome with love, were unable to move.
Then, composing themselves, and calling their daughters,
The mothers embraced them again and again.
They would escort their daughters a little way, and then embrace
      them again—
The love between them kept growing.
Embracing each other again and again, they were at last separated
      by their friends
Like cows from their unweaned calves.

      All the townsmen and women,
      And the queens and their companions were so overwhelmed
            by love,
      It seemed as though the city of Videha had become
      The abode of sorrow and anguished partings.   (337)

The parrot and the maina that Janaki had reared
And kept in golden cages and taught to speak,
Cried out, agitated, 'Where is Vaidehi?'
Hearing them, who could remain unmoved?
If even birds and animals were so distressed,
How can I describe the state of human beings?
Then Janak came with his brother,
His eyes filled with tears of love.
Upon beholding Sita, composure deserted him
And his reputed detachment from the attachments of this world
      became but a saying.
The king clasped Janaki to his breast
And his wisdom's great restraint was destroyed.
His wise ministers admonished him,
And the king, realizing this was no time for sorrow,
      composed himself.
Embracing his daughters again and again,
He called for the beautiful palanquins that stood ready.

The whole family was overcome by love,
Yet, the king, seeing that the auspicious moment had come,
Seated the princesses in the palanquins,
Recalling Ganesh and his consort, Siddhi.   (338)

The king gave his daughters much advice
And instructed them in woman's dharma and their family's traditions.
He sent with them many maid- and menservants
Who were trusted attendants and dear to Sita.
As Sita set off, the townsfolk grew distraught,
But the stars were favourable and all good signs and auspicious
    omens were present.
Accompanied by a crowd of Brahmans and ministers,
The king went with his daughters to escort them part of the way.
Seeing that the moment had come to depart, the wedding guests
Readied chariots and elephants and horses, and music began
    to play.
Dasharath called for all the Brahmans
And giving them gifts and reverence, made them happy and
    satisfied.
The lord of the earth put the dust of their lotus feet upon his head
And receiving their blessings, rejoiced.
As he set forth, meditating upon elephant-faced Ganesh,
Innumerable auspicious omens of happiness and good fortune
    occurred.

    As the gods, rejoicing, rained down flowers
    And apsaras sang,
    The lord of Avadh departed for Avadh
    To the joyous beating of drums.   (339)

The king courteously sent back the important men of the city
And with reverence called for all the mendicants and beggars
To give them ornaments, clothes, horses and elephants,

And thus, with affection, made sure they were well looked after.
Again and again they recited the fame and glory of his clan
And holding Ram in their hearts, turned back.
Though the king of Koshal urged him again and again,
Janak, bound by love, did not wish to turn back.
The king said again in gentle tones,
'Turn back, king, you have come a great distance.'
Then, climbing down from his chariot, Dasharath stood
    firmly there,
His eyes overflowing with tears of love.
Then said Videha's king with folded hands,
In words steeped in the nectar of love,
'In what humble manner, with what words of reverence, can I
    express what I wish to say?
My lord has conferred such great honour upon me.'

    Koshal's lord paid homage in every way
    To his kinsman, his son's father-in-law.
    They embraced with great humility,
    Their love could not be contained in their hearts.   (340)

Janak bowed his head to the crowd of sages
And received blessings from them all.
He then embraced, with reverence, his sons-in-law,
The four brothers, in each of whom resided beauty, grace
    and virtue.
Folding his lotus hands so gracious,
He spoke in words that seemed born of love,
'Ram, in what way may I praise you?
The swan upon the Manas lake that is the hearts of the munis
    and Mahesh,
For whom ascetics practise asceticism and austere penance
Renouncing anger, love, attachment and desire,
The all-pervading Absolute, invisible, formless, indestructible,

The essence of consciousness and bliss, devoid of all attributes,
    but the treasure house containing every virtue;
Whom neither the mind nor speech can understand,
Whom no theorizers can reason or speculate upon,
Whose power and glory is described by the Vedas as only
    'not this',
And who remains the same in all times, past, present and future—

    You, the source of all bliss,
    Have revealed yourself to me and become visible to my eyes,
    For every joy in the world becomes accessible to the soul
    Favoured by God.   (341)

You have honoured me in every way,
And knowing me to be your devotee, you have made me your own.
If there were ten thousand Sharadas and Sheshnags
And they were to count and compute for ten million kalpas,
They could not relate the full extent of my good fortune
Or your virtues, Raghunath.
What little I dare to say, I say on the strength of my conviction
That you are pleased by even the smallest amount of love.
Again and again, with folded hands I ask,
Let my heart never leave your feet, not even by mistake.'
Hearing these noble words nourished and made stronger by love,
Ram, in whom is fulfilled all desire, was content.
He paid homage to his father-in-law with gentle courtesy,
Considering him equal to his own father, Kaushik and Vasishtha.
Then Janak humbly saluted Bharat,
Embraced him with affection, and gave him his blessings.

    Embracing Lakshman and Ripusudan
    The king gave them his blessings.
    Everyone, overwhelmed with love for one another,
    Bowed their heads again and again.   (342)

After courteously praising Janak again and again,
Raghupati departed with all his brothers.
Then Janak clasped Kaushik's feet,
Placing their dust upon his head and eyes.
'Hear me, lord of the munis, having been in your gracious presence,
I am convinced that nothing is now unattainable for me—
Whatever bliss or fame that the kings of this earth desire,
But hesitate to ask for,
Are accessible to me, lord,
For all success is consequent upon your presence.'
The king paid him humble homage, bowing again and again,
And receiving his blessings, turned back towards home.
The wedding procession departed to the beating of drums
To the delight of all those gathered there, great and small.
Upon seeing Ram, the men and women of the villages
Rejoiced, for their eyes had received their highest reward.

        Stopping and resting at various points during the journey
        And giving much joy to the people along the way,
        The wedding procession, on an auspicious day,
        Drew near Avadh.   (343)

Drums beat, and tabors resounded,
Conches sounded, horses and elephants neighed and trumpeted,
Cymbals crashed and tambourines jingled,
While shehnais played sweet and pleasing tunes.
When they heard the wedding procession approach,
The townsfolk were delighted and trembled with anticipation
        and joy.
They began, each one, to decorate their own homes
And marketplaces, streets, squares and city gates.
All the lanes were sprinkled with perfumed water,
And beautiful and auspicious squares were drawn and
        decorated everywhere.

The marketplace was so ornamented with festoons of flowers,
And banners, flags and canopies, that its description is
     beyond telling.
Areca-nut, banana and mango trees laden with fruit,
And saplings of bakul, kadamb and tamal were transplanted,
Their beautiful branches brushing the ground,
In jewelled basins finely wrought.

     Sacred pitchers were made ready and decorated in many ways,
     And placed in every house.
     Brahma and the other gods grew envious
     As they gazed upon Raghubar's city.   (344)

The king's palace, upon that occasion, was so resplendent
That its decorations captivated the heart of Madan himself.
It seemed as though auspiciousness, good omens and heart-
     enchanting loveliness,
Prosperity, plenty, and every perfection, happiness, well-being,
     gracious magnificence
And joy had all assumed graceful and beautiful forms
And come, one by one, to Dasharath's home
To look upon Ram and Vaidehi,
For tell me, who would not yearn for this sight?
Crowds of women went forth to meet them,
Each, with her beauty, putting to shame even Madan's beloved,
And all with auspicious offerings and ready to perform arti
And singing as though it were Bharati[lxxix] herself in many forms.
There was great revelry in the king's palace—
It is impossible to describe the gladness and joy of the occasion.
Kaushalya and the other mothers[100] of Ram
Were so overcome with love that they had grown unmindful even
     of their own bodies.

[lxxix] Sarasvati

They bestowed large gifts upon the Brahmans
And worshipped Ganesh and Purari.
They were as full of joy
As paupers who find the four rewards of life.   (345)

The royal mothers were all so overcome with gladness and joy
That their bodies grew weak and their feet would not move.
Longing to see Ram,
They made ready for his welcome.
Many kinds of musical instruments began to play
And Sumitra, rejoicing, made ready the auspicious offerings—
Turmeric, dub grass, curd, leaves and flowers,
Betel leaves, areca-nuts and other important items for
     good fortune,
Unbroken rice, barley shoots, gorochan, parched grain
And graceful sprigs of tulsi she laid out,
And golden vessels, beautifully painted, so resplendent
They seemed like nests made by Madan's own birds,
And auspicious offerings and perfumes beyond telling—
The queens made ready every auspicious item.
They decorated many festive platters with lamps for arti
And joyously sang sweet songs of celebration.

     With golden platters filled with auspicious offerings
     In their lotus hands, the rejoicing mothers set off
     To welcome their sons,
     Their bodies trembling with joy   (346)

The smoke of burning incense darkened the sky
As though overcast by rainclouds gathering in the month
     of Savan.
The gods rained down garlands of celestial flowers
Like rows of cranes in flight that captivate the heart.
Charming festoons of precious gems

Glittered like Indra's divine bow.[lxxx]
Upon balconies and rooftops women appeared and disappeared—
Bright and swift, they seemed like lightning flashing.
The beat of drums was like the deep rumble of rainclouds,
The musicians and minstrels called like chataks, frogs and peacocks.
The sweet perfumes that the gods rained down were like pure
    showers of rain,
And the men and women of the city, like glad fields of paddy.
Knowing it was time, the guru gave the command
And the jewel of the race of Raghu,
Meditating upon Shambhu, Girija and Ganesh,
And rejoicing greatly, entered the city with his retinue.

    Good omens appeared everywhere,
    The gods rained down flowers and beat their drums,
    Celestial women danced and, rejoicing,
    Sang sweet songs of celebration.   (347)

Minstrels, storytellers, bards, mimes and clever wags
Sang the fame and glory of the light of the three worlds.
Songs of jubilation and the pure, sweet sound of the Vedas
    being chanted,
Steeped in celebration and felicity, could be heard in all the
    ten directions.
Many musical instruments began to play,
And the gods in the sky and the people in the city were captivated.
The magnificence of the wedding party cannot be described,
They are so full of joy that their hearts cannot contain their happiness.
The residents of the city paid homage to their king
And, beholding Ram, were overcome with joy.
They showered him with gifts of jewels and raiment,
Their eyes full of tears, their bodies trembling with joy.

[lxxx] The rainbow

The women of the city, enraptured, performed the arti
And rejoiced upon beholding the four handsome young princes.
Drawing aside the beautiful curtains of the palanquins,
They beheld the brides and were overjoyed.

In this manner, giving joy and happiness to all,
They arrived at the doors of the royal palace,
Where their delighted mothers welcomed
The princes and their brides.   (348)

They perform the welcome arti again and again—
Who can describe their love and joy?—
And shower upon them in unlimited abundance
Ornaments, precious jewels and rich garments of many kinds.
Beholding their four sons with their brides,
The mothers were lost in greatest bliss.
They gazed again and again upon the radiant beauty of Sita
    and Ram
And, delighted, considered their existence upon this earth fulfilled.
Their friends looked again and again at Sita's countenance
And praised past deeds that had given them this reward.
The gods rained down flowers every instant
And, dancing and singing, they offered their homage.
Seeing the four heart-enchanting couples,
Sharada searched through all similes and metaphors,
But they all fell short, she could not find any,
And just gazed unblinkingly upon their enchanting beauty.

Performing the rites prescribed by the Vedas and the rituals
    prescribed by family custom,
And pouring libations and spreading carpets before them as
    they went,
The royal mothers welcomed their sons with their brides,
And led them into the palace.   (349)

Four magnificent thrones stood there, so beautiful
It seemed that the mind-born god of love had made them with his
    own hands.
Upon these they seated the princesses and the princes
And washed with reverence their sacred feet.
Then, in accordance with Vedic ritual, with incense, lamps and
    ritual offerings of food,
They worshipped the bridegrooms and the brides.
Again and again they performed arti,
And waved fans and pleasing chowris over their heads.
Countless gifts were showered upon them,
And the mothers, full of joy, were all as radiant
As a yogi who has discovered the highest truth,
Or a chronically ill man who has found life-restoring amrit,
Or a man poor from birth who has found the philosopher's stone,
Or a blind man who has regained the use of his eyes,
Or a mute upon whose tongue Sharada has conferred
    her eloquence,
Or a warrior who has found victory in battle—

    Greater by several million times than their happiness
    Was the joy that the royal mothers found,
    For, with his brothers, and duly married,
    The full moon of the line of Raghu had
        returned home.   (350A)

    The mothers performed the customary rituals,
    Embarrassing the bridegrooms and their brides.
    Perceiving their great love and delight,
    Ram smiled to himself.   (350B)

They worshipped gods and ancestors according to ritual,
For every desire of their hearts had been fulfilled.
Paying homage to all, they asked for the boon

Of the prosperity and well-being of Ram and his brothers.
The gods, unseen, gave their blessings
And the delighted mothers gathered them up.
Meanwhile, the king summoned all those who had joined the
    wedding procession
And gave them chariots, raiment, jewels and ornaments.
Receiving permission and keeping Ram in their hearts,
They returned rejoicing to their own homes.
The men and women of the city, too, were clothed in jewels and
    costly garments,
And songs of celebration were heard in every house.
Whatsoever the beggars and mendicants desired,
The king, rejoicing, bestowed upon them.
His attendants and countless musicians
Were all made content with gifts and courtesy.

Giving him their blessings and paying him homage,
They all sang the king's virtues.
Then, with guru and Brahmans,
The lord of men returned home.   (351)

The instructions that Vasishtha gave,
The king fulfilled with reverence, in accordance with custom and
    the Vedas.
When the queens saw the crowd of Brahmans,
They rose with respect, knowing their great good fortune.
They washed their feet and helped them perform their ritual ablutions,
While the king paid them homage and entertained them at a feast.
Gratified by his courtesy, gifts and affection,
They gave their blessings and departed with contented hearts.
The king paid homage in many ways to Gadhi's son
And said, 'Lord, there is no one as fortunate as I.'
The king praised him greatly
And with his queens, took the dust of his feet upon his head.

He gave the sage magnificent rooms inside his own palace,
Where he and the royal women kept an eye on his every wish.
He then paid homage to his own guru's lotus feet
And made him humble obeisance with a heart full of love.

> The princes with their brides,
> And the lord of the earth with all his queens,
> Bowed again and again at the guru's feet,
> And the lord of the munis gave his blessings.   (352)

The king paid him homage with great love in his heart,
And placed before him his sons and his wealth.
But the lord of the munis asked only for the customary offering
And blessed the king in many ways.
Holding Ram and Sita in his heart,
The guru, rejoicing, left for his abode.
The king then summoned the Brahman wives
And gave to them raiment and fine ornaments.
He then summoned all the married women of the city,
And gave to each clothes and jewellery keeping in mind what she liked.
All those who were entitled to receive ceremonial gifts were given
    their due—
The jewel of kings bestowed the gifts upon them according
    to their liking.
Those guests regarded as more dear and worthy of
    special reverence—
The king honoured them in every way.
The gods, who had witnessed the wedding of Raghubir,
Showered down flowers and applauded this celebration.

> Sounding their drums and rejoicing, the gods left,
> Each for his own realm,
> Relating Ram's glory to each other—
> They could scarcely contain their love in their hearts.   (353)

The king showed every possible honour to all,
And, his heart full to the brim with gladness,
He made his way to the women's apartments
And saw the young princes with their brides.
He embraced his sons with great delight—
Who can tell the joy he felt?
He lovingly took his daughters-in-law
Into his arms again and again, his heart rejoicing.
Seeing this gathering, the royal women were delighted
And bliss took up abode in their hearts.
The king then described the wedding
And everyone listened with growing delight.
King Janak's virtue, his courtesy and greatness,
His affectionate disposition and his glittering wealth,
The king recounted like a minstrel in many ways
And the queens listened, overjoyed, to his account.

　　The king bathed with his sons,
　　Then, summoning the Brahmans, his guru and his kinsmen,
　　Dined and feasted with them on a variety of dishes
　　Till five watches of the night had passed.　　　　　(354)

Beautiful women sang songs of celebration
And the heart-enchanting night became filled with joy.
Rising from the meal, they rinsed their mouths and were offered paan,
And were adorned with garlands of flowers and fragrant perfumes
　　so that they looked quite splendid.
Then, gazing at Ram, and receiving royal permission to leave,
The guests departed, their heads bowed in reverence, for their own homes.
The love, happiness, delight and glory,
A hundred Sharadas and Sheshas,
Vedas, Viranchis, Maheshas, or Ganeshas
Cannot narrate the heart-enchanting beauty of that occasion and
　　that gathering.

How, then, can I tell it—
Can an earthworm bear the earth upon its head?
The king honoured all in every way,
Then he called for his queens, and said to them in gentle tones,
'The brides are but children, come to a strange house,
Protect them as the eyelids protect the eyes.

    The boys are tired and sleepy
    Go, put them to bed.'
    So saying he retired to his own bedchamber,
    His mind fixed upon Ram's feet.   (355)

Upon hearing the king's gentle words, the queens
Made up golden beds studded with jewels
With many fine sheets as soft and white
As the froth upon a beautiful cow's milk
And pillows so fine they cannot be described.
The jewelled chamber was fragrant with flowers and perfumes.
Lit by jewelled lamps, and with an exquisitely beautiful canopy
It defied description—only those who had seen it could understand
    its splendour.
Having made ready this beautiful bed, they picked up Ram
And affectionately laid him upon it.
He had to order his brothers again and again
Before they, too, lay down upon their own beds.
Gazing upon his dark form, so soft and beautiful,
The royal mothers spoke in loving tones,
'How did you, dear son, kill on your way to the forest,
The fearful and fearsome Taraka?

    Those dreadful night-wanderers—formidable warriors
    Who fear no one in battle—
    How did you slay them, the vile Marich and Subahu,
    With all their troops?   (356)

We vow it was by the muni's grace, son,
That God averted so many calamities.
Protecting the sacrificial offerings, you two brothers
Received all knowledge by the guru's favour.
A muni's wife attained salvation at the touch of the dust of
    your feet
And your glory filled the whole world.
Shiv's bow—harder than a turtle's shell, adamant or a
    mountain peak—
You broke in the assembly of kings.
You earned the glory of having triumphed over the world and
    won Janaki
And have now returned home with your brothers, all married.
Your deeds were all more than human,
And accomplished only by Kaushik's favour.
Today our existence in this world bears fruit
When we see, son, the moon of your countenance.
And the days that went by without seeing you—
May Viranchi not take those into account!'

    Ram reassured all his mothers
    With sweet and gentle words,
    Then, meditating upon the feet of Shambhu, his guru
        and Brahmans,
    He let sleep overpower his eyes.   (357)

Even in sleep, his face was charming and radiant,
Like a red lotus that closes its petals at dusk.
In every household, women stayed awake
Singing bawdy and festive songs.
'Look, my dears, the city shines with splendour,
The night is so bright!' exclaim the queens.
The mothers-in-law fell asleep with the beautiful brides enfolded
    in their arms,

Like serpents who had hidden the jewels upon their hoods in
    their hearts.
The Lord awoke at the sacred hour of dawn,
Red-crested roosters began to crow,
Bards and minstrels sang their songs of praise,
And the people of the city gathered reverently at the gates.
Saluting Brahmans, gods, guru, mother and father,
The brothers gladly received their blessings.
Their mothers gazed upon their faces with reverence,
As they stepped outside with the king.

    Though inherently pure, they performed the customary
        morning ablutions
    And bathed in the pure and sacred river.
    Then, completing their morning worship,
    The four brothers returned to their father.   (358)

The king, seeing them, clasped them to his bosom,
And receiving his permission, they happily sat down.
Looking upon Ram, the gathered people cheered
And considered their eyes had received their greatest reward.
Then Vasishtha and Muni Kaushik came,
And were seated upon handsome thrones.
The king, together with his sons, touched their feet and paid
    them homage,
Looking upon Ram, the two gurus were overwhelmed
    with love.
Vasishtha began reciting the sacred legends,
While the king with the royal women listened.
The deeds of Gadhi's son, which are difficult even for a muni's
    mind to comprehend,
Vasishtha joyfully narrated at great length.
Said Vamdev, 'All this is true!
His glorious fame is spread across the three worlds.'

Hearing these words, everyone was glad,
But in Ram and Lakshman's heart there was even greater joy.

> There was perpetual celebration, joy and festivity,
> And in this manner, the days passed.
> Avadh filled and overflowed with bliss
> That grew greater and greater every day.   (359)

Determining an auspicious day, the pretty kangans were untied[101]
Amid great festivity, delight and celebration.
The gods, seeing daily a new happiness, grew envious
And pleaded with Brahma that they be reborn in Avadh.
Vishvamitra daily wished to depart
But remained, a prisoner to Ram's affectionate entreaties.
Seeing the king's deep love increase a hundredfold day after day,
The great muni was full of praise.
At last, when Vishvamitra asked permission to depart, the king was
    overcome with love
And stood before him with his sons.
'Lord, all my wealth is yours,
I am your servant, and with me my sons and wives.
Be ever compassionate to these boys,
And keep favouring me with your presence, muni.'
So saying, the king, with his sons and his queens
Fell at Vishvamitra's feet, unable to speak.
The Brahman gave many blessings
And departed amidst such affection as cannot be described.
Ram and all his brothers lovingly accompanied the muni,
Returning only upon receiving his command.

> Ram's beauty, the king's devotion,
> The weddings, the joy and the gladness—
> The moon of Gadhi's clan praised and lauded all these
> As he went, rejoicing, on his way.   (360)

Vamdev and the learned guru of the line of Raghu
Once more related the story of Gadhi's son.
Listening to the muni's great renown, the king mused to himself
Over the efficacy of his own good deeds.
Then, upon receiving the king's command, the people dispersed
And the king, with his sons, returned to his palace.
Everyone everywhere sang the story of Ram's wedding
And his pure fame spread throughout the three worlds.
From the moment that Ram returned home with his bride,
Every delight made its home in Avadh.
The joy and celebration at the Lord's wedding
Cannot be described even by Gira or the king of the serpents.
Knowing that the life of all poets is sanctified
By the glory of Ram and Sita, accumulation of all well-being,
I, too, have tried to relate it,
For the purpose of thus purifying my speech.

To make his own song sacred and pure,
Tulsi has sung of Ram's glory.
But Raghubir's deeds are a boundless ocean—
Which poet has ever been able to cross it?
Those who with reverence hear or sing
Of the joy and celebrations that accompanied Ram's investiture with the
    sacred thread and his wedding,
They will, by the grace of Vaidehi and Ram,
Be forever blessed with happiness.

        Those who sing or listen with love
        To the story of Sita and Ram's wedding,
        For them there is happiness forever,
        For Ram's glory is the abode of all joy.   (361)

Thus ends the first descent into the Manas lake of Ram's acts that
destroys all the impurities of the age of Kali.

Glossary

abir:	Red powder, thrown into the air in celebration.
Aditi:	The mother of the gods. In the Rig Veda, she is represented as being the mother of Daksh as well as the daughter of Daksh. She is addressed as 'the mother of the gods' and 'the mother of the world'. She gave birth to eight sons, of which she abandoned the eighth, the Sun. The other seven became the Adityas. In the Yajur Veda, she is called the wife of Vishnu, but in the Ramayana, the Mahabharata and the Puranas, Vishnu is called the son of Aditi; therefore, he is also sometimes called Aditya. In the Vishnu Purana, she is the daughter of Daksh and the wife of the sage Kashyap, by whom she was the mother of Vishnu in his Vaman, or dwarf, incarnation, and also of Indra. In the *Ramcharitmanas*, Aditi is reborn as Kaushalya and Kashyap as Dasharath, and in that form, they are the mother and father of Ram, who is Vishnu in his seventh incarnation.
Agahan:	The eighth month of the Hindu calendar equivalent to November–December.
Agastya:	A rishi, and the author of several hymns in the Rig Veda. It is said that he was born in a water-pitcher

as 'a fish of great lustre'. He is therefore also known as 'Ghatjoni' and 'Kumbhaj' or 'pitcher-born'. He is supposed to have drunk up the ocean because it had offended him, and because he wanted to help the gods in their wars with the Daityas when the latter had hidden themselves in the sea. He is therefore also called 'Samudra-chuluk' or 'ocean-drinker'.

ages of the world; yuga: The duration of the world is said to be 4,320,000,000 human years (equal to a day for Brahma); this period consists of a thousand epochs, and each epoch is made up of four ages, or yugas. These are: (i) Krit or Satyayug (the golden age); (ii) Tretayug (the silver age); (iii) Dwaparyug; (iv) Kaliyug. The first age comprises 1,728,000 years; the second 1,296,000 years; the third 864,000 years; and the fourth 432,000 years. The duration of the Dwapar is twice the length of the Kali, that of the Treta is thrice that of the Kali, and that of the Satyayug is four times that of the Kaliyug. In the current epoch, the first three ages have already elapsed, while the Kali is that in which we live. Ram's incarnation took place towards the end of the Tretayug.

Agni: Fire, one of the most ancient and sacred objects of worship in Hinduism. He appears in three places—in the sky as the sun, in air as lightning, and upon earth as ordinary fire. He is one of the chief deities of the Vedas, and, through the fire-sacrifices, the mediator between gods and men.

Ahalya: Wife of the Rishi Gautam, and a very beautiful woman. She was the first woman created by Brahma, who gave her to Gautam. Ahalya's exceptional beauty caught Indra's eye. Determined to seduce her, he enlisted the help of the moon, who turned into a cock and crowed at midnight.

Gautam, thinking it was time for his morning worship, went off to the river to bathe. Then Indra, taking the form of the rishi, entered his hermitage and seduced his unsuspecting wife. The sage, returning, caught him and in his fury cursed him. He also threw out Ahalya from the hermitage, and depriving her of the prerogative of being the most beautiful woman in the world, turned her into a block of stone. She was restored to life by the touch of Ram's feet.

Amaravati: Indra's capital city, renowned for its magnificence and splendour.

amla: The plant known as the Indian gooseberry and its fruit. The fruit is small and green and quite sour, but greatly valued for its medicinal properties. 'Holding an amla in the palm of your hand' signifies understanding something clearly and from every angle, just as the small and round amla fruit can be seen when held upon one's palm.

amrit: Nectar conferring immortality, produced at the churning of the ocean by the gods and demons.

Anasuya: The wife of the Rishi Atri, and by him, the mother of the sage, Durvasa. She was also one of the daughters of Daksh. She was exceedingly pious and practised intense austerities, which gave her miraculous powers.

anchal: The flowing, free end of a sari.

Angad: Son of Baali, the monkey king of Kishkindha.

apsara: The apsaras are the nymphs of Indra's court. They are beautiful, fairy-like beings, and are the wives or mistresses of the Gandharvas. They are also famous for their liaisons with mortal men. The

Ramayana and the Puranas attribute their origin
to the churning of the ocean. It is said that when
they appeared out of the ocean, neither the gods
nor the Asurs could have them, so they became
common to all. They are also called Suranganas,
or 'the wives of the gods'.

arghya: A libation of water and milk, flowers, kush grass
                           and other auspicious ingredients made to a deity,
                           or an honoured guest.

ark: The plant known as the crown flower. Native to
                           India and South-east Asia, it grows to about 4 m
                           in height, and has waxy white or lavender flowers.
                           Its leaves and stem gives a thick, milky sap if
                           broken. The seed follicles are small and hard.
                           The plant is poisonous, but has several medicinal
                           uses in Ayurveda. It is often grown in temple
                           compounds and is believed to be particularly liked
                           by Lord Shiva.

arti: A ceremony performed in welcome of an
                           honoured guest, by moving circularly around his
                           head a platter containing lamps, incense, flowers,
                           etc.

Arundhati: The morning star, personified as the wife of the
                           Rishi Vasishtha.

Ashvamedha: 'The sacrifice of a horse'; a sacrifice performed
                           only by the greatest and most powerful of kings.
                           It was believed that the performance of a hundred
                           such sacrifices would enable a mortal king to
                           overthrow Indra and become the ruler of the
                           universe. A horse was selected and consecrated
                           by the performance of certain ceremonies; it was
                           then let loose to wander wherever it wanted for
                           a year. The king, or his representative, followed
                           the horse with an army, and if the horse entered

another country, the ruler of that country had to either fight or submit. If the king who had released the horse was victorious over the kings through whose lands the horse passed, he would return home triumphant after a year, with the defeated kings behind him; if he failed in this, he was ridiculed and disgraced. After a king returned home successful, a great festival was held, during which the horse was sacrificed, either really or metaphorically.

Ashvins; Ashvin twins; Ashvinkumar:
Two Vedic deities, twin sons of the Sun by a nymph who concealed herself in the form of a mare (*ashva* in Sanskrit)—hence, Ashvini, and her sons, Ashvins. The Ashvins are ever young and handsome, and shine with the radiance of gold. Swift as falcons, they ride in a golden chariot drawn by horses or birds, and, as personifications of the morning twilight, they are the first bringers of light in the morning sky. They also have great healing powers, and are the physicians of heaven.

Astagiri:
This is the western mountain behind which the sun is supposed to set; it is also called Astachal.

Asur:
Literally, 'not a god', so 'enemy of the gods', or generally 'demons'. The word is used as a general term for the enemies of the gods, including Daityas and Danavs, who are descended from the sage Kashyap. It does not include the Rakshasas, who are descended from the sage Pulastya. The Asurs are in constant conflict with the gods.

Atri:
A rishi, and author of many Vedic hymns. In the Vedas, he appears in hymns in praise of Agni, Indra, and the Ashvins; later he is regarded as one of the ten Prajapatis, or lords of creation, engendered by Manu for the creation of the world; and still later, he appears as one of the mind-born

sons of Brahma. He is also one of the Saptarishi, the seven great sages who preside over the world, and as one of them, he is one of the seven stars of the Great Bear. He married Anasuya, one of the daughters of Daksh, and their son was the sage Durvasa. In the Puranas, he was also the father of Soma, the moon, and the ascetic Dattatreya by Anasuya.

Ayodhya:

The capital city of the kingdom of Koshal. It was the city from which ruled Ikshvaku, the founder of the solar dynasty. It later became the capital city of Dasharath and then of Ram. It is also the city of Ram's birth. It is also called Avadh.

Baali:

The monkey-king of Kishkindha. He was the son of Indra, and said to have been born from his mother's hair (*baal*), hence his name. He was killed by Ram, and his kingdom given to his brother, Sugriv. His wife was Tara, and his sons were Angad and Tar.

Baitarni:

'(The river) to be crossed'; it is the river that must be crossed before hell can be entered. The river is described as being filled with blood, excrement and all kinds of filth. It flows fast and with great force.

bakul:

A medium evergreen tree native to India. The tree gives thick shade and bears fragrant flowers. Its fruit is also edible and is used in traditional medicine. It is also called maulsari.

Bali:

A good and virtuous Daitya king, he was the son of Virochan, who was the son of Prahlad, the son of Kanakakasipu. Through devotion and penance, Bali became so powerful that he defeated Indra and the other gods, and extended his rule over the three worlds. The gods appealed to Vishnu for help, and he took on his Vaman or dwarf avatar to restrain the king. (See Vishnu, fifth avatar.) He asked the generous king for three steps of land. The king granted him the boon. Vishnu then stepped over the earth with his first step, the heavens with his second, and when he asked where he should place his foot for the third step, Bali offered his own head. Out of respect for Bali's goodness and generosity, Vishnu stopped short and gave him the infernal region of Patal to rule. Bali is also called Mahabali, and his capital city was Mahabalipuram.

Bana; Banasur: A powerful Daitya, the eldest son of the Daitya king, Bali; he had a thousand arms and was a devotee of Shiv and an enemy of Vishnu. He is also called Vairochi.

ber: The jujube tree and its fruit. This is cultivated as well as grows wild in India; every part of the tree has medicinal uses, and its small and somewhat acid fruit is very popular and is eaten pickled, cooked or raw. 'Holding a ber in the palm of your hand' signifies understanding something clearly and from every angle, just as the small and round ber fruit can be seen when held upon one's palm.

Bhadon: The sixth month of the Hindu calendar, equivalent to August–September.

Bhagirath: A king of the Ikshvaku dynasty, and a descendent of Sagar; he brought the sacred River Ganga to earth from heaven. King Sagar of Avadh married two women, the princess Keshini, and Sumati, the daughter of the sage Kashyap. With Keshini, he had one son, Asamanjas; through him the royal line was continued. With Sumati he had sixty-thousand sons. Now Asamanjas

grew up into such a wild and immoral man
that Sagar abandoned him. Unfortunately, the
sixty-thousand also followed in their brother's
footsteps, and became so known for their impiety
that the gods complained about them to Vishnu
and to the sage Kapil. Once, Sagar decided to
hold the Ashvamedha or horse-sacrifice. Though
the horse was guarded by his sixty-thousand sons,
it was carried off to Patal, the underworld. They
dug their way to the underworld, where they
saw the sage Kapil seated in meditation, and the
horse grazing close by. Thinking that he was the
thief, they threatened him with their weapons.
This disturbed the sage in his meditation, and
so enraged him that a single glance from him
reduced them to ashes. Their remains were
found by Anshumat, the son of Asamanjas, who
begged Kapil that his uncles be raised to heaven
through his favour. Kapil promised Anshumat's
grandson would be the means of accomplishing
this by bringing down Ganga, the river of
heaven. Anshumat returned to Sagar, who then
completed the sacrifice. The deep chasm that his
sons had dug became the ocean, which is called
'saagar' after his sons. The son of Anshumat was
Dilip, and his son was Bhagirath. Determined
to free the souls of his ancestors, Bhagirath left
his kingdom in the care of his ministers and
retreated to the Himalayas, where he practised
severe austerities in order to please Brahma. After
a thousand years of prayer and penance, Brahma
appeared before him. When Bhagirath told him
that he wanted to bring down the divine river,
Ganga, so that he may perform the appropriate
rites for his ancestors, Brahma told him to pray
to Shiv, for only he could withstand the force of
the river's descent. So Bhagirath prayed to Shiv.
The compassionate god was quickly pleased, and
agreed to help him, promising to hold the Ganga

in his matted locks and so reducing the force of her descent. Ganga agreed to come to earth, and as she fell, Shiv stood beneath her cascading waters and caught them in his hair, letting only a trickle escape. This trickle was as much as the earth could bear, and this became the mighty River Ganga upon earth. She followed Bhagirath, and he guided the river from the Himalayas, across the plains of northern India, into the sea, and from there to Patal, where the ashes of Sagar's sixty-thousand sons were washed with her waters and purified.

bhakti: A many-nuanced idea meaning at one time all or any one of the following: faith, belief; devotion, adoration, worship; attachment, devotedness, service. In the Hindu context, it means devotion to and love for a personal god. There are nine forms of bhakti, which are explained by Ram to Sabari in the Aranyakand (35-36).

Bharadvaj: An eminent rishi to whom are attributed many hymns from the Vedas.

Bharat: 'He who supports, bears, or carries'; son of Dasharath and Kaikeyi, younger brother to Ram.

Bhogavati: The magnificent, subterranean capital city of the Nagas in Patal.

Bhrigu: A Vedic sage. He is one of the Prajapatis and the great Rishis, and regarded as the founder of the race of Bhrigus or Bhargavas, in which were born Jamadagni and his son, Parashuram. He officiated at Daksh's sacrifice.

Bhringi: A sage, especially devoted to Shiv. It is said that Bhringi was so deeply devoted to Shiv that he even refused to honour Parvati, maintaining that he would worship Shiv and Shiv alone. He attempted to circle Shiv in homage, leaving out Parvati, so Shiv took Parvati upon his lap; Bhringi then turned himself into a snake and tried to slither between the two. At that, Shiv made Parvati a part of himself, taking on the form of Ardhanarishvar. Bhringi then turned himself into a bee and tried to separate the two. At this Parvati was so angry that she cursed him, so that he lost all flesh and blood and, turning into a bag of bones, collapsed upon the ground. Bhringi then realized that he could not separate Shiv from Parvati, for they were not separate, but together made up the whole. Bhringi was forgiven, and given a third leg by which to support himself.

Bhushundi;
Kak Bhushundi:

The crow, Bhushundi. He is a sage in a crow's body, and a great devotee of Ram. He is also one of the four narrators of the *Ramcharitmanas*, and relates the story of Ram to Garud.

birth, modes of:

According to Hindu tradition, there are four modes of birth: (i) born from the womb (such as man and other mammals); (ii) born of an egg (such as birds, fish and so on); (iii) engendered by heat and moisture (such worms, insects, lice, etc.); and (iv) born by sprouting or germinating (trees, plants, vegetables, etc.). From these four modes of birth are generated eighty-four lakh (1 lakh = 100,000) forms of life.

blue-throat:

The Indian roller. This bird has a blue crown and blue wings and tail, and a pale-brown breast. Though it does not have a blue throat, it is called nil-kanth (literally 'blue-throat' in Hindi), which is also a name for Shiv. It can be easily seen in India, and is believed by many to be sacred to Vishnu.

brahm: The Absolute, the Eternal, the Self-existent, the
                          divine essence and source of all being from which
                          all created things emanate and to which they all
                          return (not to be confused with Brahma who is
                          the Supreme Spirit personified as the Creator).

Brahma: The Supreme Spirit manifested as the Creator of
                          the universe. He is the first god of the Hindu triad
                          of the Creator, the Preserver and the Destroyer.
                          He is represented as red in colour, with four
                          heads. He wears a pointed beard, usually white in
                          colour. He has four arms, in which he variously
                          holds his sceptre, a spoon, a rosary of beads, a
                          waterpot, a lotus, his bow Parivita and the Vedas.
                          His consort is the goddess Sarasvati. His vehicle
                          is the hansa, or swan. Brahma is also called
                          'Aj', the unborn; Chaturanan or Chaturmukh,
                          'having four faces'; Sanat, 'the ancient'; Vidhi,
                          as providence, or the one who ordains what will
                          be; Vidhatra or Vidhata 'disposer' or 'arranger';
                          Viranchi, the Creator.

Brahman: The first of the four castes of Hinduism. It is
                          the priestly caste, though its members may not
                          necessarily be priests. In Hindu belief, a Brahman
                          is the chief of all created beings. His person
                          is inviolate, he is entitled to every honour and
                          causing harm to a Brahman results in the severest
                          consequences, in this life and the next. The chief
                          duty of a Brahman is the study and teaching of the
                          Vedas, and the performance of fire-sacrifices and
                          other ceremonies. Hindus believe that there are
                          two kinds of gods: the gods themselves, and then
                          the Brahmans who have learnt the Vedas—they
                          are gods upon earth.

chakor; chakori (f.):   A mythical bird, which is believed to subsist
                          only upon moonbeams and to eat fire at the full
                          moon.

chatak; chataki (f.): A mythical bird that subsists only on raindrops that fall in autumn, when the sun is at the same longitude as the star Svati.

Chintamani: The 'wish-jewel'. It has the power of granting all desires. It belongs to Brahma, who is himself sometimes called by this name.

Chitrakut: 'Bright peak'; one of the peaks of the Vindhya range, and the first dwelling-place of Ram and Sita during their exile.

Dadhichi: A Vedic rishi. Once, Indra had been driven out of his kingdom by the Asur, Vritra, who was invulnerable to any known weapon. Vritra also stole all the water in the world for his own use and that of his army. Indra turned to Vishnu for help, who revealed that Vritra could be defeated only by a weapon made from the bones of the sage Dadhichi, who was practising penance in the Naimisha forest. Indra and the other gods went to Dadhichi and appealed to him for help. The sage agreed, and gave up his life immediately. From his bones, Vishvakarma, the smith of the gods, fashioned the thunderbolt and other weapons, with which Indra and the gods defeated Vritra and his army.

Daityas: A race of demons and giants, the sons of Diti, daughter of Daksh, by the sage Kashyap. They warred against the gods, and were often victorious. They are very similar to their cousins, the Danavs.

Daksh: 'Competent, intelligent'; Daksh is one of the mind-born sons of Brahma, and is generally associated with male energy or creative power. Depending on the source consulted, he had twenty-four, fifty, or sixty daughters. The Ramayana and the Mahabharata agree on the larger number. According to the Mahabharata, ten of his daughters married Dharma, and thirteen married the sage Kashyap, becoming the mothers of gods and demons, men, birds, serpents and all living things. Twenty-seven married Soma, the Moon, and these became the twenty-seven Nakshatras or lunar asterisms. His daughter Sati married Shiv and killed herself because of a quarrel between her father and her husband. Daksh was also one of the Prajapatis, and is often regarded as their chief. He is also called Prajesh (lord of creatures).

damru: A small drum shaped like an hour-glass, which is held in one hand; it is said to have been created by Shiv, and by beating it, Shiv produced the very first sounds. Shiv also performs his cosmic dance of regeneration to the beat of the damru.

Danav; Danuj: A clan of demons, giants who warred against the gods; they are the sons of Danu, daughter of Daksh, by the sage Kashyap. They are associated with and very similar to the Daityas.

Dandak: A vast forest between the rivers Godavari and Narmada. Some passages in Valmiki's Ramayana describe it as beginning immediately south of the Jamuna. It is described as a wilderness, with scattered hermitages, and full of wild beasts and Rakshasas.

Dasharath: A prince of the solar dynasty, descendant of Ishkvaku, the king of Koshal, and the father of Ram and his brothers, Bharat, Lakshman and Shatrughna. Dasharath had three wives, Kaushalya, Sumitra and Kaikeyi.

Dharma: Literally, 'that which is to be held fast or kept'. It is a many-layered concept, and can variously mean statute, law, rule, or custom; customary observances of caste, sect, or social class;

prescribed course of conduct, duty, or obligation; virtue, morality, morals; righteousness, good works; religion, piety, or religious observances.

Dhruv:

The Pole star; son of Uttanapad and his wife Suniti, he was a staunch devotee of Vishnu. According to the Vishnu Purana, King Uttanapada was one of the sons of Manu Swayambhuva. He had two wives: Suruchi, who was his favourite, and was haughty and cruel, and Suniti, the second queen, who was gentle and kind. Suruchi had a son called Uttam, and Suniti's son was Dhruv. Suruchi demanded that her son Uttam should alone succeed to the throne. Uttanapad agreed, and Suniti and Dhruv left the palace for the forest. Dhruv, rejected by his father, declared he wanted no honours except those that he attained by his own actions. In his grief he meditated upon Vishnu, and in return for his unwavering devotion, Vishnu raised him up to the heavens as the Pole star.

Diti:

One of the daughters of Daksh, wife of Kashyap, and mother of the Daityas.

Durvasa:

'Ill-clothed'; a sage known for his fiery temper and irascible nature. According to some sources, he is the son of Atri and Anasuya; but some authorities say that he is a son or an emanation of Shiv. Many fell under the curse of his anger, including Indra, whom he cursed for disrespecting him, and by his curse, the gods under Indra became weak and were overpowered by the Asurs. This state of affairs ultimately led to the churning of the ocean by the gods and demons to recover amrit and other precious things.

Dushan:

A man-eating Rakshasa, the younger brother of Ravan; he was killed by Ram.

elephants, celestial:

The eight elephants who protect the earth and support it at the eight points of the compass. They are Airavat, Pundarik, Vaaman, Kumud, Anjan, Pushpadant, Sarvabhaum and Supratik. (See also guardians of the eight quarters).

food, flavours of:

There are six kinds of flavours in food. These are: sweet, sour, salt, bitter, acrid and astringent.

food, kinds of:

There are four kinds of food, classified according to the way in which they are ingested: (i) food that is chewed; (ii) food that is swallowed; (iii) food that is sucked; and (iv) food that is lapped up or drunk.

Galav:

A pupil of Rishi Vishvamitra. At the end of his studies, he asked Vishvamitra what fee he should give him. Vishvamitra refused to ask for anything, but when Galav insisted, he grew annoyed, and to get rid of him, asked him to bring him a thousand white horses with one black ear. After a long search, Galav found three kings who each had two hundred of the kind of horses he wanted. The kings, all of whom were childless, agreed to let him have the horses if he could somehow ensure they had a son. Galav appealed to Garud for help, who took him to see King Yayati. The king gave him his daughter, Madhavi, who, by a special boon, was able to bear sons and still remain a virgin. Galav gave her in marriage one after another to the three childless kings, Haryashwa, king of Ayodhya, Divodas, king of Kashi, and Ushinar, king of Bhoj; to each of the kings, Madhavi bore a son, and in return, Galav received 200 of the horses he wanted. Galav then presented Madhavi and the 600 horses to Vishvamitra. The sage accepted them and had a son by Madhavi, who was named Ashtaka. When Vishvamitra retired to the forest, he gave his hermitage and the horses

to Ashtaka. And Galav, having taken Madhavi
back to her father, also retired to the forest, like
his guru.

Gandharva: The Gandharvas are heavenly beings, who have
                          their home in the sky or atmosphere; many of
                          them live in Indra's heaven. They are entrusted
                          with the task of preparing soma for the gods,
                          are skilled in medicine, and are singers and
                          musicians.

Ganesh: Lord of the ganas, the troops of lesser deities
                          attendant upon Shiv; the son of Shiv and
                          Parvati. As the god of wisdom and the remover
                          of obstacles, he is propitiated at the beginning of
                          any endeavour. He is represented as a short man,
                          with a yellow body, four hands, and the head of
                          an elephant, with one tusk. He has a pot belly,
                          signifying his love of food. In one hand he holds
                          a shell, in another a discus, in the third a club,
                          and in the fourth a lotus. His steed is a rat. He is
                          also called Ganpati, 'chief of the ganas'; Ganraja,
                          'king of the ganas', Gajanan, 'elephant-faced';
                          Vinayak, 'leader of the Shiv's retinue' or 'remover
                          of obstacles'.

Ganga: The sacred river Ganges. According to the
                          Puranas, the river flows from the toe of Vishnu,
                          and was brought down to earth by the actions
                          of Bhagirath, to purify the ashes of the sixty-
                          thousand sons of King Sagar, who were burnt by
                          the angry glance of the sage Kapil. Thus the river
                          is also called Bhaagirathi. To save the earth from
                          the shock of her fall, Shiv caught the river upon
                          his head and checked the force of her waters with
                          his matted hair. (See also Bhagirath.) Personified
                          as a goddess, she is the daughter of Himvat
                          and Maina, and her sister is Uma, the goddess
                          Parvati.

Garud:

King of the birds and the steed of Vishnu. He is represented with the head, wings, talons and beaks of an eagle, and the body and limbs of a man. His face is white, his wings red and his body golden. When he was born, he was so bright that people mistook him for Agni. He is the son of the rishi Kashyap and Vinata, one of the daughters of Daksh. From his mother he is called Vainateya, 'Vinata's son'; as Vishnu's mount he is called 'Hariyan'; as the enemy and devourer of snakes he is called Urugari, Uragari, Pannagari, Uragad; and as king of the birds he is Khagesh, Khagapati.

Godavari:

Revered by Hindus, this is India's second-longest river after the Ganga; it rises in Trimbakeshwar in Maharashtra and flows east for 1465 kilometres to empty into the Bay of Bengal.

Gomati:

River in northern India; it is a tributary of the Sarju. It is also called the Dhenumati.

gorochan:

A bright yellow pigment, found as a bezoar in cattle; this is considered very rare and holy and has various ritual uses in Hindu practice, and is specially used for marking the foreheads of Hindus with the tilak. It is also supposed to have medicinal properties, including as a sedative and an antidote to poisons.

guardians of the eight quarters:

The eight points of the compass (the four cardinal and four intermediate points) are guarded and presided over by eight guardian deities. They are: (i) Indra, king of the gods, guards the east; (ii) Agni, or Fire, the south-east; (iii) Yama, god of death, the south; (iv) Surya, the Sun, the south-west; (v) Varun, the Sky, the west; (vi) Vayu, the Wind, the north-west; (vii) Kuber, god of wealth, the north; (viii) Soma, the Moon, the north-east. Some substitute Shiv in his form as Ishan, for Soma.

Each of these guardian deities has an elephant who helps to defend and protect the quarter; together these eight celestial elephants support the earth upon their backs. Indra's elephant at the east is Airavat; Agni's elephant at the south-east is Pundarik; Yama's at the south is Vaaman; Surya's at the south-west is Kumud; Varun's at the west is Anjan; Vayu's at the north-west is Pushpadant; Kuber's at the north is Sarvabhaum; and Soma's elephant at the north-east is Supratik.

Guha: Chief of the Nishads, and a devotee and friend of Ram.

guna: A quality, or an ingredient or constituent of nature, of which there are three in particular, viz., Sattva, Rajas, and Tamas, or 'goodness, passion, and darkness', or 'virtue, foulness, and ignorance'.

gunj seeds: The tiny, bright red and black seeds of the shrub known as the jequirity bean or the rosary pea; they form the smallest of a jeweller's weights.

Hanuman; Hanumant; Hanumat: Literally, 'he who has large jaws'; the monkey chief who helped Ram in his search for Sita and fought with him in his war against Ravan. The son of Pavan, the Wind, he was of divine origin and endowed with magical powers. His mother was Anjana, the wife of a monkey called Kesari. He was enormously strong, he could also fly and change his size at will. In his true form he is as vast as a mountain and tall as a tower. His body is yellow and glows like molten gold. His face is as red as a ruby and his tail is so long that no one can measure its length. At the end of the war with Ravan, he went back with Ram to Ayodhya; there, Ram gave him the reward of perpetual life and youth. He epitomizes devotion to Ram. He is known by many names. For setting Lanka on fire, he is called Lankadahi; as the son of the wind he has the patronymics Pavanputra, Anili and Maruti; from his mother he is called Anjaneya; for his magic powers and knowledge of the healing arts, he is called Yogachara and Rajat-dyuti, 'the brilliant'. He is also a grammarian, and rivals Brihaspati, the guru of the gods, in his knowledge of all the sciences.

Harishchandra: Son of Trishanku and king of Ayodhya, the twenty-eighth in descent from Ishkvaku, founder of the solar dynasty. He was a just and virtuous king, and famed for his generosity. There are several legends about him. The Mahabharata says that he was raised to Indra's heaven for his performance of the Rajasuya sacrifice (a fire-sacrifice that may be performed only by the greatest of kings) and his immense generosity. The Markandeya Purana gives a fuller version of the story: One day, while Harishchandra was out hunting, he heard the cries of several women in distress. The king rushed to help, but the cries were an illusion created by Vighnaraj, the god of obstacles. At that time, the sage Vishvamitra was observing strict penance in the forest. Vighnaraj, to test Harishchandra's goodness, entered his body, and the moment he did so, the king lost his temper and began to loudly curse and hurl abuse at Vishvamitra. This angered the sage, who, because of his anger lost all the power he had acquired through years of penance. Vishvamitra was now furious with Harishchandra, and the king, seeing his wrath, begged for forgiveness. In return, the sage demanded the sacrificial gift that would be due to him as a Brahman for the performance of a Rajasuya sacrifice. The king agreed, and promised to give him whatever he would choose to ask. Vishvamitra demanded that the king give him everything he possessed. The king agreed

and handed over all his material possessions to
the sage, including his kingdom and the clothes
he wore, so that he had remaining only his own
body, a garment of bark, his wife, Shaivya, and
his son, Rohit. The king, now destitute, left for
the city of Banaras. But the sage was waiting
for him there, and demanded that the gift be
completed. In despair, Harishchandra sold his
wife and his son, and handed over the proceeds to
Vishvamitra. Now there remained only himself.
Just then, Dharma, the god of justice, appeared
in the form of a low-caste Chandal, and offered
to buy him. When Vishvamitra still insisted upon
the completion of his gift, the king sold himself
to the Chandal and gave the money to the sage.
His new master put Harishchandra in charge of
a cremation ground, with strict instructions to
be always present there and to allow cremation
only after the payment of a toll. The honest king
did exactly as his master commanded. As the
months passed, his appearance grew dishevelled,
and he lost all hope of ever seeing his wife and
son again. One day, Rohit was bitten by a snake
and died. His grieving mother carried his body to
the cremation ground. The king and the queen
recognized each other, and exchanging stories,
were overcome with grief. They decided to
immolate themselves upon the funeral pyre of their
son. Harishchandra made ready a great pyre upon
which he placed Rohit's body, and once all was
done, he lost himself in contemplation of Vishnu.
At this, the gods all appeared and asked him to
stop, and bringing Rohit back to life, told him
that he, his wife and his son had all won a place
in heaven because of his steadfastness in fulfilling
his promise to Vishvamitra. But Harishchandra
was hesitant. He could not go to heaven without
his master, the Chandal's permission. At this,
the Chandal appeared and revealed himself to

be Dharma. Harishchandra still refused, saying he could not leave behind his faithful subjects, in turmoil without a king. So Indra, Dharma and Vishvamitra took the king, his wife and his son to Ayodhya. There, Vishvamitra crowned Rohit king of Koshal, after which Harishchandra and his wife Shaivya were taken to heaven.

Hataklochan: 'The golden-eyed', a powerful Daitya chief, son of Diti by the sage Kashyap, and twin brother of Kanakakasipu; he was killed by Vishnu in his third, Boar, incarnation. Hataklochan had dragged the earth to the bottom of the sea. In order to recover the earth, Vishnu took the form of a boar, and after a battle that lasted a thousand years, he killed Hataklochan and carried the earth back to the surface on his tusks. He is also known as Hiranyaksh and Kanakalochan.

Himvat; Himvant; Himalaya: 'Snow-clad'; the personification of the Himalaya mountains, husband of Maina, and father of Ganga and Uma (Parvati). He is also called Himachal, Himbhudar, Himgiri, Tuhinachal, Tuhingiri, 'snowy mountain'; Girish, 'mountain king' or 'king of the mountain', a title he sometimes shares with Shiv.

humours of the body: In the Indian Ayurvedic system of medicine, the body is regarded as having three humours (or bodily fluids) in addition to blood. The three humours are vat or (wind), pitt (bile) and kaph (phlegm). All organic disorders of the body arise from an imbalance in these humours.

Ikshvaku: Founder of the solar dynasty, and king of Ayodhya at the beginning of the Tretayug or second age of the world. He had a hundred sons, of whom one was Nimi, who founded the Mithila dynasty.

Indra: God of the firmament, personification of the
atmosphere; king of the gods. His consort is
Indrani (also known as Shachi); he has a son by
her, called Jayant. His heaven is Swarga; his capital
is Amaravati; his elephant is Airavat; and his
horse is Uchchaihsravas. His charioteer is Matali.
In the Vedas, he is one of the most important of
the gods, though he is not unbegotten/uncreated
but has a father and a mother. He is described in
the Vedas as a being of golden colour, with arms
of enormous length. His forms are infinite and he
can take any shape at will. He rides in a golden
chariot drawn by two ruddy horses with flowing
tails and manes. His weapon is the thunderbolt,
which he carries in his right hand; he also uses
arrows, a hook and a net in which he entangles
his enemies. His chief delight is soma ras, the
extremely potent juice of the soma plant, which
he drinks in enormous quantities. He controls the
weather, dispenses rain, and sends down lightning
and thunder. He is constantly at war with Vritra,
the demon of drought and bad weather, whom
he ultimately overcomes with his thunderbolts.
In the later centuries, Indra's importance decreased.
He became less than the triad of Brahma, Vishnu
and Shiv, but remained chief of all the other
gods. According to the Mahabharata, he is the
son of Aditi by Kashyap, and the foremost of the
Adityas. He is the regent of the atmosphere and
the guardian of the east quarter of the compass. He
sends the lightning and hurls the thunderbolt, and
the rainbow is his bow. He is represented as a fair-
skinned man, riding a white horse or an elephant,
and holding the thunderbolt in his hand. He is
constantly at war with the Asurs, and is often
defeated by them. He killed Vritra, but because
Vritra was a Brahman, Indra had to go into hiding
and perform penance till his guilt was purged away.
There are many stories of his lack of self-restraint.
He became infatuated with Ahalya, the beautiful

and virtuous wife of the sage Gautam, and in his arrogance, decided to seduce her. He tricked the sage to leave the hermitage, and then taking on his form, seduced the unsuspecting Ahalya. The sage returned to see him leaving his house, and in fury cursed him so that he would be covered with the marks of a thousand yonis (the female organs of reproduction). Thus he was called Sa-yoni. But these marks were later changed to eyes, because of which he is also called Netra-yoni or Sahasraksha 'the thousand-eyed'. He was defeated and carried off to Lanka by Ravan's son, Meghnad (who thus received the title of Indrajit, 'vanquisher of Indra'). Brahma and the other gods had to beg Meghnad to release him, which Meghnad did, in return for the boon of immortality. Brahma then tells Indra that his defeat was his punishment for seducing Ahalya. He is also known as Sakr, 'the powerful'; Purandar, 'destroyer of cities'; Pakripu, 'destroyer of the demon Pak'; Maghva or Maghvan, 'endowed with riches, wealthy'; Basav or Vasava, 'lord of the Vasus'.

Jabali:

A Brahman, and a priest of King Dasharath. He is also called Javall.

Jadu:

One of the sons of King Yayati, from his wife Devyani. Jadu (or Yadu) refused to relieve his father of the curse of old age passed on to him by the Rishi Sukra, and was therefore cursed in turn by Yayati that his children will not have a kingdom to rule. He was the founder of the line of Jadavas (or Yadavas), in which Krishna was born. He did ultimately receive the southern part of his father's kingdom, which the Jadavas went on to successfully rule.

Jagbalik:

A celebrated sage. To him is attributed the code of law called *Yajnavalkyasmriti* (from 'Yajnavalkya', the Sanskrit rendering of his name). He is believed to have flourished at the court of Janak, king of Videha and Sita's father.

Jam, Jamraj;   The god of death. He is the son of the sun god
Yam, Yamraj: Surya and his wife Saranyu, and twin brother
                            of the river Jamuna. He is represented as a man
                            green in colour and clothed in red; he is armed
                            with a huge mace and a noose. He rides upon
                            a buffalo, because of which he is also called as
                            Mahishesh, 'the god whose steed is a mahish, or
                            buffalo'. He is sometimes also called Shaman,
                            'the destroyer'.

jamana: From the Sanskrit *yavana*; originally denoted a
                            Greek, an Ionian, and then came to mean any
                            barbaric foreigner from the West.

jambu: The rose-apple tree, also called jamun in Hindi.

Jamuna; Yamuna: The river Jamuna (or Yamuna) is the daughter of
                            the sun god Surya and his wife Saranyu, and the
                            twin sister of Jam (or Yama), the god of death.
                            While Jamraj is death, Jamuna is life and bathing
                            in her waters absolves one of sin.

Jamvant: King of the bears. With his army of bears, he
                            helped Ram in his war against Ravan and was
                            always ready with sage advice and good counsel.
                            He is also called Jambavat.

Janak: A prince of the solar dynasty, king of Mithila/
                            Videha, and the father of Sita. Amongst his
                            ancestors are the kings Ishkvaku and Nimi. Janak
                            was known for his great knowledge and good
                            works. It is said that Janak refused to submit to
                            the hierarchical superiority of the Brahmans and
                            insisted upon his right to perform fire-sacrifices
                            without their intervention. He is also called
                            Siradhwaja, 'he whose banner is the plough',

because his daughter Sita appeared as a baby in the furrow he was ploughing in preparation for a fire-sacrifice to obtain children. He is also known as Videh, the title used for the kings of Videha. 'Janak' is also the name of a royal dynasty of Mithila to which he belonged. He is therefore also called Janakpati, or 'lord of the Janak dynasty'.

Jatayu: King of the vultures, and son of Garud, Vishnu's steed. He is a friend of King Dasharath, and became an ally of Ram. He saw Ravan carrying away Sita and tried to stop him. In the ensuing battle, he was mortally wounded. Ram found him in time to hear his dying words and learn what had happened to Sita. Ram and Lakshman performed his last rites, and he ascended to heaven in a chariot of fire.

javas: The camel thorn. A small and prickly plant, it grows to about four feet in height. It has long spines along its branches and bright pink or reddish flowers. It is said to wilt at the coming of the rains and flourish only in dry soil.

Jayant: Son of Indra, also called Jaya.

jiva: The individual soul.

jubaraj: Literally 'young king'; an heir-apparent associated with the reigning sovereign, who assumes kingly duties while the king is still living.

Kabandh: A hideous Rakshasa killed by Ram. He was originally a Gandharva, the son of the goddess Lakshmi. He is described as being covered with hair, as huge as a mountain, without head or neck, a mouth full of immense teeth in the middle of his belly and a single eye in his breast. According to some accounts, he was turned into this hideous monster as the result of a quarrel with Indra, who struck him with his thunderbolt and drove his head and thighs into his body. Another account says that he was cursed by the sage Durvasa. When mortally wounded, he asked Ram to burn him, and from that fire he came out in his original form as a Gandharva. He is also called Danu.

kadamb: A tall, evergreen tree, with fragrant, globe-shaped orange flowers which are used in the preparation of perfumes; the tree also has great mythological and religious significance in India.

Kadru: A daughter of Daksh, and one of the thirteen wives of the sage Kashyap. She is the mother of the serpents, including Sheshnag. Her offspring bear the metronymic Kadraveya.

Kaikeya: A kingdom in the west, beyond the rivers Saraswati and Beas, and from which came Dasharath's queen, Kaikeyi.

Kaikeyi: A princess of Kaikeya, King Dasharath's favourite queen, and the mother of Bharat, his second son.

Kailash: A mountain in the Himalayas, north of the Mansarovar; it is the abode of Shiv, and also of Kuber, the god of wealth.

Kalnemi: A Rakshasa, and Ravan's uncle. At Ravan's behest, he attempts to kill Hanuman.

kalpa: A period of 4,320,000,000 years, equal to a day for Brahma. This is one cosmic cycle of creation, and is made up of a thousand cycles of the four ages, or yugas. (See also 'ages of the world'.) According to the Puranas, there are innumerable such cycles of creation, and within them, in each cycle of the four yugas, there occurs one incarnation of Ram.

Kalpataru: A tree in Indra's paradise that grants all desires. It
                           is also called Kamtaru, 'tree of desire'.

Kam: Literally, wish, desire, longing; affection, love,
                           passion; sexual passion; lust; love of pleasure;
                           and personified, the god of love, Kamdev. He is
                           the son of Vishnu by Rukmini, and the husband
                           of Rati, the goddess of desire. He is lord of the
                           celestial nymphs, the apsaras. He is armed with
                           a bow and five arrows: the bow is of sugarcane,
                           the bowstring a line of bees, and each of his five
                           arrows is tipped with a particular flower (the
                           white lotus, the ashok flower, the mango blossom,
                           the jasmine and the blue lotus), which pierce the
                           heart through the five senses; his favourite arrow
                           is the one tipped with the mango blossom. His
                           helpers are Vasant or Spring, and Malayanil, the
                           southern winds or the cool and fragrant winds
                           that blow from the Malay mountain. He is usually
                           represented as a handsome young man riding on a
                           parrot, and attended by apsaras; one of the apsaras
                           bears his banner, which displays the Makar (a
                           fabulous sea creature that represents Capricorn in
                           the Hindu zodiac, and is depicted with the head
                           and forelegs of an antelope and the body and tail
                           of a fish), or a fish on a red background. He is
                           therefore also called Jhashketu, 'one with a fish
                           on his banner'. Once, as Shiv sat in meditation,
                           Kamdev inspired him with thoughts of Parvati;
                           Shiv, greatly angered by this impertinence,
                           opened his third eye and reduced Kamdev to
                           ashes. Later, Shiv relented and allowed him to
                           be reborn as feelings. Kamdev therefore does not
                           have a substantial form or body. He is thus called
                           Anang and Atanu, or 'bodiless'. He is also known
                           as Hridayniket, 'one whose abode is the heart';
                           Mayan or Madan, 'passion, lust or love (or the act
                           of intoxicating or exhilarating, or gladdening)';
                           Manmath, 'he who churns the heart'; Manobhav,
                           'mind-born'; Manoj, 'born of the mind'; Mansij,

'born or generated in the mind, mind-born, heart-born'; Mar, the passion of love, personified. As husband to Rati, he is known as Ratinath, 'Rati's lord'. He is also called Kandarp.

Kamadgiri: Literally, 'the mountain that fulfils all desires'; the hill in Chitrakut upon which Ram stayed.

Kamdhenu: 'The cow that grants all desires'; she belongs to the sage Vasishtha and was one of the fourteen precious objects recovered at the churning of the ocean.

Kanakakasipu: 'Golden-robed'; a powerful Daitya chief, son of the sage Kashyap and his wife Diti, and twin brother to Hataklochan. As the result of practising severe austerities, he obtained from Shiv sovereignty over the three worlds for a million years, as well as immunity from death by man and beast. He grew so arrogant in his power that he declared that no one may worship any god but him. When his son, Prahlad, remained steadfastly devoted to Vishnu, he punished him and tried to kill him several times, but in vain. He was finally killed by Vishnu in his fourth avatar as Narsingh or Narkeshari, who was half-man, half-lion, and thus neither man nor beast. He is also called Hiranyakashipu.

kanji: A sour drink made by steeping mustard seeds in water and letting it ferment.

Kapil: A celebrated sage, the founder of the Sankhya philosophy. He reduced the sixty-thousand sons of King Sagar to ashes with a single glance.

kapila cow: A brown or reddish-coloured cow, considered in Hinduism to be the most sacred of all cows. A number of Hindu pilgrimage sites are linked to cows, some specifically to the brown cow. Several of these sites are mentioned in the Mahabharata and the Puranas. According to the Puranas, the gift of a kapila cow is equal to the giving away of a whole world in charity and confers upon the giver an assured place in Vishnu's heaven for as many thousand years as there are hairs upon the body of that cow and her calf, and after that time is over, it guarantees rebirth into a rich and wealthy family. Gifts of land, horses, gold, etc., do not equal in virtue even a sixteenth of the gift of a kapila cow.

Karamnasa:	A river that flows through the holy city of Kashi; bathing in its waters destroys all merit (as opposed to bathing in the waters of the Ganga, which destroys all sin).
karila:	A thorny, leafless shrub that grows in arid regions.
karma:	Fate, or the certain consequence of previous acts; destiny.
Kashi:	The city of Varanasi. It is sacred to Shiv, and one of the most holy of all pilgrimage places for Hindus. It is believed that those who die in Kashi immediately attain liberation from the cycle of birth and rebirth.
Kashyap:	A Vedic sage, to whom are attributed some of the Vedic hymns. According to the Atharva Veda, he was 'self-born' and sprang into existence from Time. According to the Mahabharata, the Ramayana, and the Puranas, he was descended from Brahma. All authorities agree that he played a significant role in creation. The Mahabharata and later sources say that he married Aditi, and twelve other daughters of Daksh. From Aditi were born the celestial Adityas, headed by Indra, and also Visaswat, from whom was born Manu, the progenitor of all mankind. The Ramayana

and Vishnu Purana state that Vishnu in his dwarf incarnation was the son of Aditi and Kashyap. From Kashyap's twelve other wives were born demons, serpents, reptiles, birds and all living things. He is also one of the Saptarishi, the seven great sages.

Kaushalya: King Dasharath's chief queen, and Ram's mother.

Kaustubh: A precious jewel, obtained at the churning of the ocean and worn by Vishnu upon his breast.

Ketu: A comet or meteor, and the ninth of the planets; and in Vedic astronomy, the descending lunar node, represented by a dragon's tail. He is personified in mythology as the lower half of the Danav, Rahu. See Rahu.

Khar: A man-eating Rakshasa, the younger brother of Ravan; he was killed by Ram.

Khasiya: A tribal, hill people of northern India.

Kinnara: Literally, 'What men?' in Sanskrit; they are mythical beings with the body of a man and the head of a horse. They are singers and musicians, and live in the paradise of Kuber, the god of wealth, on Mt Kailash. According to some sources, they sprang from the toe of Brahma together with the Yakshas; but others say that they are the sons of Kashyap.

kinshuk: A tree native to India. When in bloom, it is covered with a profusion of bright red, flame-coloured flowers. It is also known as the palash, the dhak, or the flame-of-the-forest.

Kirat: A mountain tribe that lives by hunting; a man of that tribe.

kodo:

A kind of small grain (like millet), considered inferior to rice and usually eaten by the poor.

kok; koki (f.):

These birds are a symbol of love and fidelity. Legend says that they are doomed to spend every night apart because of a curse pronounced upon them by a sadhu. They spend the day together, but every night they must separate; the birds spend the night calling to each in sad and mournful tones. Since they can be together only during the day, the birds are full of joy in the light of the sun, and grow sorrowful in the light of the moon. They are also called chakravak birds, or chakwa (male) and chakwi (female). They are also identified with the rathang birds, the ruddy or Brahmany geese.

kokil; koel:

The black or Indian cuckoo. This bird is prominent in Indian poetry; its musical cry is supposed to inspire pleasing and tender emotions.

Kol:

A tribe that lives the hills and forests of central India; a man of that tribe.

kos:

A measure of distance, equivalent to about 2 miles.

Koshal:

A country on the Sarju river, with Avadh its capital city. This was the kingdom ruled by Dasharath, and later by Ram.

Kshatriya:

The second of the four castes of Hinduism. It is the regal or warrior caste.

Kuber:

The god of wealth, and the king of the Yakshas. He is also regent of the north, and the keeper of gold and silver, pearls and precious stones, and all the treasures of the earth. He is the son of Vishravas (the son of the sage Pulastya), and the half-brother of Ravan. His consort is called

Yakshi. Kuber's city is Alaka in the Himalayas, and his garden is on Mount Mandar, where he is waited upon by the Kinnaras. Some authorities place his abode on Mount Kailash, in a palace built by the divine architect, Vishvakarma. According to the Ramayana and Mahabharata, he once ruled in the city of Lanka, also built by Vishvakarma, and from which he was thrown out by Ravan. He is the owner of the self-moving flying chariot, Pushpak, given to him by Brahma. He is also the keeper of the nine Nidhis, nine treasures considered precious beyond compare. They are called padma or the lotus flower, maha-padma, sankha, makar, kachhapa, mukunda, kunda, nila, kharba. Their nature and purpose are not clearly defined. Each treasure is also personified as a spirit that is also the guardian of that particular treasure. These guardian spirits are worshipped by some tantrics. Kuber is represented as a fair-skinned man, deformed in body, with three legs and only eight teeth. His body is covered with jewelled ornaments. He receives no worship. He is also known as Dhanesh, 'god of wealth'; Dhandhari, 'holder of wealth'; and 'Dhanad, 'one who grants wealth, the munificent'.

Kumbhakaran: A Rakshasa, the son of Vishravas (the son of the sage Pulastya), and brother of Ravan. As the result of a boon (or, as variously told, a curse) by Brahma, he slept for six months at a time and remained awake for only a single day.

kush: A kind of grass used in sacrifices and rituals. It is also called darbh.

Kushaketu: King Janak's younger brother, the father of the princesses Mandavi and Shrutakirti. He is also known as Kushadhvaja.

Lakshman: 'Possessed of lucky signs or marks, fortunate,
                       prosperous'; son of Dasharath and Sumitra, Ram's
                       younger brother and Shatrughna's twin. For his
                       mother, Sumitra, he is also called Saumitri,
                       'Sumitra's son'. He is often considered to be the
                       incarnation of the celestial serpent, Sheshnag.

Lakshmi: The goddess of wealth and beauty, Vishnu's
                       consort, and the mother of Kamdev, the god of
                       love. According to the Ramayana, she sprang from
                       the the froth of the ocean, in all her beauty, when
                       it was churned by the gods and the Asurs. The
                       Vishnu Purana says that she accompanied Vishnu
                       in all his incarnations, and when Vishnu was born
                       as Ram, she became Sita. She is also known as
                       Shri; Indira; and Ramaa, 'Ram's consort'.

Lanka: Ravan's kingdom. Also known as Singhal.

life, ends, fruits, rewards of: These are four: (i) kama or sensual pleasure;
                       (ii) artha or wealth; (iii) dharma or religious merit;
                       and (iv) moksha or nirvana, i.e., liberation from
                       worldly existence and rebirth.

life, four stages of: For traditional Hindus, life is divided into four
                       stages: (i) Brahmacharya, the student life, spent in
                       study and obedience to one's guru; (ii) Grihastha,
                       the stage of a householder, the married man
                       living with his wife, and engaged in the ordinary
                       duties of everyday life; (iii) Vanaprastha, the
                       phase of a 'forest-dweller', who has discharged his
                       duties in this world, and who, handing over his
                       responsibilities to the next generation, has retired
                       to the forest to devote himself to a life of simplicity
                       and contemplation of the divine; and (iv) Sannyas,
                       the period spent as a religious mendicant, who
                       has renounced all worldly goods and desires and
                       attained complete detachment from this material
                       existence; freed from all forms and observances,

he wanders about, subsisting only on alms, and
striving for ultimate absorption into the divine.

lila:

Literally 'play, sport, pastime'. In Hindu belief, all
creation is the Lord's lila, his sport or pastime.

Madhav:

Krishna (Vishnu) in his role as presiding deity of
Prayag.

Magh:

The tenth month of the Hindu calendar,
corresponding to January–February.

Mahishasur:

Literally, 'the buffalo demon', an Asur killed
by the goddess Parvati in her form as Durga.
Through intense austerities, he received a boon
from Brahma and asked to be made immortal.
Brahma refused the boon of immortality, but
granted him the boon that no man would be able
to kill him. The gods were powerless against him
and were soundly defeated by him in battle. Then
the goddess Parvati, who was Shiv's Shakti, the
feminine manifestation of Shiv's cosmic energy,
took on one of her fierce forms and killed him.

Mai:

A Daitya, the architect of the Asurs, as Vishvakarma
was of the gods. He was the father of the demon
Mayavi, and of Mandodari, Ravan's wife.

Maina:

The wife of Himalaya, and the mother of Parvati.

Mainak:

A winged mountain.

Makar:

Makar (equivalent to Capricorn) is the tenth
sign of the zodiac, and is represented by a water-
animal with the body and tail of a fish, and the
forelegs, neck and head of an antelope.

Malaya, mountain range:

One of the seven mountain ranges mentioned in
the Puranas; they are supposedly the southernmost

mountains of the Western Ghats in peninsular India. The mountains were famous for their sandal trees, which yielded the finest sandalwood in the world.

Manas; Manas lake; Mansarovar:

A freshwater lake in modern Tibet, at the foot of Mt Kailash, the abode of Shiv. The lake is sacred to Hindus, Buddhists and Jains, and an important place of pilgrimage for them.

Mandakini:

A sacred river that flowed by the hill of Chitrakut, where Ram and Sita spent part of their forest exile. It is also called Payasvini, 'water-giving'. It is said that the river was brought down from heaven to Chitrakut by Anasuya, the wife of the sage Atri, in order to alleviate a drought.

Mandar:

The sacred mountain with which the ocean is said to have been churned by the gods and Asurs for the recovery of amrit and thirteen other precious things lost during the great flood.

Mandavi:

Sita's cousin, the eldest daughter of Janak's younger brother Kushadhvaj (Kushaketu); she was married to Bharat.

Mandodari:

The daughter of the Daitya Mai, she was Ravan's favourite wife, and the mother of Meghnad.

Manthara:

Queen Kaikeyi's hunch-backed bondswoman, who roused the queen's jealousy and set her against Ram, which led to him being banished to the forest for fourteen years.

Manu:

From the root *man*, 'to think'; this name belongs to fourteen mythological progenitors of mankind and rulers of the earth, each of whom rules for the period called a Manwantara (Manu-antara: the life or period of a Manu). There are fourteen

Manwantaras in any kalpa. The gods, the seven
great sages (Saptarishis) and Indra change from
one Manwantara to another. The first of these
Manus was Svayambhuva, who sprang from
Swayambhu, the self-existent.

Mar:

The passion of love; personified, it is another
name for Kamdev, the god of love.

Marich; Marichi:

A Rakshasa, son of Taraka; he was also one of
Ravan's ministers, and helped him to kidnap Sita
from the forest hermitage.

Maruts:
Marut

The storm gods. They are armed with thunderbolts
and ride on the whirlwind and direct the storm.
Many origins are assigned to them – they are the
sons of Rudra, the sons or brothers of Indra, sons
of the ocean, sons of the earth. Their number
varies—according to one source they are twenty-
nine in number, according to another, three times
sixty; in the *Ramcharitmanas*, Tulsi says they are
forty-nine in number. In the singular, Marut is
also the god of the wind, and the presiding deity
of the north-west quarter.

Matali:

Indra's charioteer.

maya; Maya:

Illusion, deception; the unreality of worldly
things; in Hindu belief, a deception dependent
on the power of the Supreme Being, through which
mankind believes in the existence of the world which
is in fact mere illusion without reality. Personified,
Maya is a woman, the consort of the Supreme Being,
and the immediate operative cause of the creation.
It also means magical or supernatural power, such as
that possessed by the Rakshasa, Ravan.

Meghnad:

Literally, 'the rumbling or thundering of clouds';
he was Ravan's eldest son by his chief queen,

Mandodari. When Ravan attacked Indra's forces, Meghnad accompanied him and fought most valiantly. He used the power of invisibility given to him by Shiv to capture, tie up and carry off Indra to Lanka where he kept him a prisoner. The gods, led by Brahma, went to Lanka to secure Indra's release, and Brahma gave Meghnad the title of 'Indrajit', 'conqueror of Indra'. He is also called Arindam, 'the destroyer of enemies'.

Mekal: A part of the Vindhya mountain range, in which rise the headwaters and several tributaries of the Narmada river.

Meru: A fabulous mountain in the centre of the earth, upon which is situated Swarga, Indra's heaven, containing the cities of the gods. It is also known as Sumeru.

Mithila: The capital city of Videha, the kingdom of King Janak; also known as Janakpur, or Janak's city, Tirhut, and Terahuti.

moksha: Ultimate freedom from birth and rebirth. There are four kinds of moksha possible: (i) living in the same world as the Supreme Being; (ii) living in close proximity to the Supreme Being; (iii) attaining a form similar to that of the Supreme Being; and (iv) complete union with the Supreme Being.

mridang: A double drum, broader in the middle than at the ends.

muni: A sage, a holy man who has attained almost divine status through penance and meditation. The term is also used as a title for the seven great Rishis and for other wise and learned men.

Naga:

A semi-divine being belonging to the serpent race, with a human face, the tale of a snake and the expanded neck of the cobra. The Nagas are said to have sprung from Kadru, one of the wives of the sage Kashyap, for the purpose of populating the underworld, Patal, where they rule in great splendour.

Nahush:

The son of Pururavas, and the father of Yayati; he came into conflict with the Brahmans. His story is told, with variations, in the Mahabharata and the Puranas. Nahush was a good and righteous king, and, through prayer and penance and sacred study, he acquired the sovereignty of the three worlds. Once, when Indra had temporarily gone into hiding (for having killed the demon Vritra, who was a Brahman), leaving his throne vacant, Nahush was chosen to reign in his stead. He ruled over the heavens wisely and well for many years, but as time went by, he became arrogant and haughty. One day, he caught sight of Shachi, Indra's beautiful consort, and wanted her for himself. Shachi, known for her love and fidelity to Indra, was angered and distressed by his advances, and complained to the sage Brihaspati and sought his protection. The gods remonstrated with Nahush, but blinded by desire, he refused to listen to them, and insisted upon having Shachi as his consort. Brihaspati then advised Shachi to lay down a condition—that she would accept Nahush as her husband if he would come to her in a palanquin carried by sages. Nahush, who had lost all sense of propriety and was guided only by his stubborn desire to possess Shachi, agreed at once. He somehow convinced the rishis to carry him to Shachi on his shoulders. The sages were not very strong men, and walked slowly with frequent stops. The king grew impatient, and kicked the sage Agastya, who was one of the sages carrying him. The sage cried out in anger, 'Fall, you serpent!' and Nahush fell from his palanquin and turned into a huge python. Horrified, he begged Agastya to forgive him; relenting, Agastya put a limit on the curse, saying that he would regain his human form when he had learnt how to be a good king. According to one version of the story, he was released from his curse by the eldest Pandava, Yudhishthira, who lectured him on the qualities of a good king. Nahush, understanding these at last, was released from his serpent form and ascended to heaven.

Nar and Narayan: Two ancient sages; twin sons of Dharma (Brahma's son) and his wife Ahimsa (daughter of Daksh). The brothers are considered by some to be the fourth avatar of Vishnu.

Narad: A Devarshi, or divine sage or saint akin to a demigod, to whom some of the hymns of the Rig-Veda are ascribed. Various sources have different accounts of his life. He is regarded as one of the four sons of Brahma, and one of the ten principal and original Munis or Rishis. He is also the inventor of the vina or lute and lord of the celestial musicians, the Gandharvas. He was also one of the great writers on law, the author of the *Naradiya Dharmashastra*. Later, he is connected to the legend of Krishna. He is also regarded as somewhat of a mischief-maker, causing frequent quarrels among the gods by bearing tales.

Narmada: A sacred river, said to rise from the Mekal hills, and because of which the river is also known as 'Mekal's daughter'.

Nimi: Son of Ikshvaku, and the founder of the dynasty of Mithila. According to the Vishnu Purana, he was cursed by the sage Vasishtha to lose his corporeal form, and in response, he pronounced the same curse upon the sage. Both then abandoned their bodily forms. Though Vasishtha took birth again, Nimi's corpse was embalmed and preserved in death as he had been in life. The gods offered to restore him back to life, but Nimi refused, saying that the separation of the soul from the body was so painful that he did not want to have to experience it again. The gods respected his wishes, and instead, placed him in the eyes of every living creature, because of which their eyelids are always blinking. (A blink of the eye is called 'nimish'.)

nine poetic sentiments (navras): The nine poetic sentiments or moods are: erotic, humorous, compassionate, astonishing, frightening, peaceful, disgusting, wrathful and heroic.

nirgun: Devoid of all qualities or properties, without attributes; the Supreme Being, who has no attributes of any kind.

Nishad: A forest tribe who lived along the banks of the Ganga; their main occupation was hunting and fishing.

Ocean of Milk: In Hindu cosmology, one of the seven seas surrounding directional space.

ocean, churning of: One of the most well-known stories in Indian mythology; from this was produced, amongst other things, amrit, the nectar of immortality, and Lakshmi, the goddess of wealth and beauty. Once, Indra displeased the sage Durvasa, who in his anger, cursed Indra that he and all the gods would lose their strength, energy and good fortune. Weakened by the sage's curse, the gods

were defeated in battle by the Asurs, who now
gained control over the universe. In despair, the
gods appealed to Vishnu. Vishnu directed them
to churn the ocean and thus to obtain from it
the nectar of immortality—this, if consumed,
would restore to them their strength and power.
The gods, rendered powerless by Durvasa's
curse, were unable to accomplish this task on
their own, and on Vishnu's advice, enlisted the
Asurs to help them, agreeing to divide with
them whatever was retrieved from the ocean.
Vishnu assured the gods that he would make
sure that the nectar of immortality would
remain with the gods. The ocean was then
churned, with Mount Mandar as the churning
stick, and Sheshnag, the celestial serpent as
the rope wound round it. The Asurs held the
head of the serpent, and the gods the tail, and
as they pulled back and forth on the serpent,
Mount Mandar began to sink into the waters.
So Vishnu took on the form of a kurma or
tortoise (his second avatar), and slipping into
the waters, supported Mount Mandar on his
back. From the churning of the ocean were
produced many precious objects, Lakshmi,
precious gems, the horse Uchhaishravas, and
a deadly poison (which Shiv swallowed and
held in his throat). At last, there arose from the
waters Dhanvantari (who became the physician
of the gods), bearing in his hands the pot of
amrit. The Asurs demanded their share of it,
but Vishnu's steed, Garud, grabbed the pot and
flew away with it. Then Vishnu took on the
form of the beautiful enchantress, Mohini, and
distributed the amrit amongst the gods, who
drank it and regained their strength. Only one of
the Asurs, called Rahu, managed to drink some
of the amrit, and though his head was cut off by
Vishnu as punishment, he had already attained

immortality and was thus placed amongst the
stars. (See Rahu, and Vishnu—second avatar).

paan: Betel leaves prepared with areca nuts, etc., used
                         as a mouth-freshener after a meal and served to
                         honoured guests.

pakar: The Indian fig tree, also called gular in Hindi.

Panchavati: A place in the Dandak forest, near the River
                         Godavari, where Ram lived for a long period
                         during his exile. It was here that Lakshman cut
                         off Supanakha's nose (*nasika*). Hence, it is often
                         identified with the modern city of Nasik.

Parashuram: 'Ram with the axe', the sixth avatar of Vishnu.
                         He was born in the Tretayug, as the son of the
                         Brahman, Jamadagni, to deliver the world from
                         the tyranny of the Kshatriyas. His weapon is
                         the axe. The Mahabharata relates that, at the
                         command of his father, he cut off his mother's
                         head. She had so infuriated her husband by her
                         thoughts that he had asked each of his sons
                         in turn to kill her. They had all refused, except
                         Parashuram. His obedience pleased his father so
                         much that he told him to ask a boon. Parashuram
                         asked that his mother be restored to life, and
                         that he himself become invincible in combat and
                         enjoy a long life. When his father was pitilessly
                         slain by the sons of Sahasrabahu (Kartavirya),
                         king of the Haihayas, Parashuram vowed to wipe
                         out the whole Kshatriya race. It is said that he
                         cleared the earth of Kshatriyas twenty-one times.
                         (See also 'Sahasrabahu'.) As foremost amongst
                         the descendants of Bhrigu, he is also called
                         Bhrigupati, Bhrigunath and Bhrigunayak, 'lord
                         of the Bhrigus'; and Bhrigubar, 'the best of the
                         Bhrigus'. He is also known as Parashudhar, 'he
                         who holds an axe'.

Parvati: 'Of the mountains'. She is the daughter of
                            Himvat (the Himalaya mountains personified),
                            and his wife Maina. She is the consort of Shiv,
                            the reincarnation of his first wife Sati. She is also
                            Shiv's cosmic energy or Shakti. She is worshipped
                            in different forms and is known by different
                            names. Her forms and names invoked by Tulsidas
                            include Ambika, 'the compassionate'; Aparna,
                            'deprived of leaves'; Bhavani, consort of Bhav
                            (Shiv); Gauri, 'the brilliant goddess'; Girija or
                            Shailaja, 'born of the mountain', and Girinandini,
                            'daughter of the mountain'. She is also Shakti
                            Shiv's cosmic energy; Shivaa, consort of Shiv; and
                            Uma, 'light' or 'splendour'. In her fierce, demon-
                            slaying form she is called Kalika, or Durga. As
                            the supreme goddess, she is called Jagadamba or
                            Jagadambika, 'mother of the world'.

Patal: One of the seven subterranean regions, and the
                            abode of the Nagas; hell.

pathin: A large freshwater fish native to India; it is also
                            known as the pahina or parhina fish.

Payasvini: 'Water-giving'; another name for the River
                            Mandakini.

persuasion, methods of: There are four methods of persuasion: (i) sama
                            (argument, calm words to win someone over to
                            one's own point of view); (ii) dana (inducement
                            in the form of money or gifts); (iii) danda
                            (punishment, corporal chastisement); (iv) bheda
                            (by causing dissension).

pipal: The holy fig-tree, *Ficus reliogiosa*.

Prahlad: The son of the Daitya king Kanakakasipu, and an
                            ardent devotee of Vishnu. Kanakakasipu grew so
                            powerful that he declared that his subjects must

worship him, and him alone. Prahlad refused, and continued to steadfastly worship Vishnu, despite all the punishment that his father heaped upon him. In his fourth avatar, as Narsingh or Narkeshari (half-man, half-lion), Vishnu killed Kanakakasipu, and made Prahlad king of the Daityas as a reward for his devotion. Prahlad was also given a status equal to Indra for his life, and finally united with Vishnu upon death.

Prajapati: 'lord of created beings', the ten mind-born sons of Brahma, from whom all mankind has descended.

Prayag: The modern city of Allahabad, the confluence of the rivers Ganga, Jamuna and the subterranean Sarasvati, and one of the most important places of pilgrimage for Hindus. Krishna, as Madhav, is its presiding deity. Prayag is also supposed to be the site of a banyan tree famous in legend to be imperishable.

Prithuraj: In the Vedas and the Puranas, he is the first consecrated king. He taught men agriculture and to cultivate the earth, and it is from him that the earth derives her name of Prithivi. It is said that he prayed for hearing as sharp as though he had ten thousand ears so that he could hear all of the glory of God.

Priyavrat: A son of Svayambhuva Manu and Satarupa. He was dissatisfied that only half the earth was illuminated by the sun at any one point, and so followed the sun seven times around the earth in his own flaming chariot. The ruts made by the wheels of his chariot became the seven oceans; and so the seven continents were formed.

Pulastya:

One of the Prajapatis or mind-born sons of Brahma, and one of the great Rishis. He was the medium through which the Vishnu Purana was communicated to man. He was the father of Visravas, who, through three handmaidens, became the father of Ravan and Kumbhakaran, of Vibhishan, and of Supnakha; all the Rakshasas are supposed to have sprung from him.

Purana:

Literally, 'old', hence an ancient legend or tale. The Puranas are sacred works comprising the whole body of modern Hindu theology and mythology. The Puranas come much later than the epics, and must be distinguished from them. While the epics tell the stories of heroes as mortal men, the Puranas tell of the deeds of gods. There are eighteen acknowledged Puranas. The Vayu Purana is regarded as the oldest, and dates back to the sixth century CE; other Puranas are considered to be as recent as the thirteenth or even the sixteenth century.

Pushpak:

A self-flying magical chariot, so large that it contains within it a palace or a city. Brahma gave it as a gift to Kuber, but it was carried away by Ravan, who then used it as his chief mode of conveyance. After Ravan had been defeated and killed by Ram, the latter used the Pushpak to carry himself and Sita back to Ayodhya. He then returned it to Kuber.

Raghu:

A prince of the solar dynasty. In Kalidasa's poem *Raghuvansa*, on the ancestry and life of Ram, Raghu is said to be the son of Dilip and the great grandfather of Ram; it is from him that Ram gets the patronymic Raghav, and the title Raghupati, or chief of the dynasty of Raghu.

Rahu: The ascending lunar node in Vedic astrology,
                           and the cause of eclipses. He is also considered
                           as one of the nine planets, the king of meteors
                           and guardian of the south-west quarter. In
                           mythology, Rahu is a Danav who seizes the Sun
                           and the Moon and swallows them, thus causing
                           eclipses. He is the son of Viprachitti and Sinhika,
                           and is known by his metronymic, Sainhikeya.
                           He had four arms, and his lower part ended in
                           a tail. At the churning of the ocean, amongst
                           the many precious objects that were produced
                           was amrit, the nectar of immortality. The gods
                           decided to keep this for themselves, and when
                           it was time to distribute it, the demons were
                           left out. Rahu, assuming a godlike form, seated
                           himself amongst the gods and drank some of
                           the amrit. The Sun and the Moon realized who
                           he was and informed Vishnu, who cut off his
                           head and two of his arms. But, since he had
                           already become immortal by drinking the amrit,
                           he was placed amongst the stars. His upper
                           parts, represented by a dragon's head, being
                           the ascending lunar node, and his lower parts,
                           known as Ketu and represented by a dragon's
                           tail, being the descending node. Since then,
                           Rahu wreaks his vengeance on the Sun and the
                           Moon by occasionally swallowing them. Rahu
                           and Ketu are usually paired together.

Rakshasa; Rakshasi (f.):   A race of demons, of whom Ravan was king.
                           According to some sources, they are the
                           descendants of the sage Pulastya, like Ravana
                           is himself; others say they sprang from the foot
                           of Brahma. They are usually portrayed as huge,
                           ugly, terrifying beings. They are skilled and
                           powerful warriors, with magical powers and the
                           ability to change shape at will. Most of them can
                           fly and many of them are man-eaters who haunt
                           cemeteries, forests and lonely places at night.

They disturb fire-sacrifices, harass pious men and make life difficult for mankind in all sorts of ways. There are good Rakshasas too, such as Ravan's brother, Vibhishan.

Ram; Ramchandra: 'Pleasing, beautiful, charming'; the eldest son of King Dasharath of Avadh, and his chief queen Kaushalya. His wife is Sita, princess of Mithila. He is the seventh avatar of Vishnu, and the protagonist of the Ramayana. As a descendant of the prince Raghu, he is called Raghav or Raghunandan. He is also called Raghunath or Raghupati, lord of the Raghus; Raghunayak, chief of the Raghus; Raghuraj, 'king of the Raghus', Raghubar, 'best of the Raghus'; Raghubir, 'hero of the Raghus'; Raghuchand, 'moon of the dynasty of Raghu'. As Sita's husband, he is also called Sitanath, 'Sita's lord'; Janakinath, 'Janak's lord'. Sita is the incarnation of the goddess Lakshmi, who is also called Ramaa or Shri—as her husband or beloved he is therefore also known as Ramaakant, Ramaaraman, Shrikant, Shriraman. He is also addressed by all the names of Vishnu.

Rambha: An apsara who emerged at the churning of the ocean; she is the epitome of perfect womanhood.

Rantidev: A king of the Lunar dynasty; he was renowned for his piety and generosity. He was a great devotee of Vishnu, and believed that all he had came from him. He was enormously rich and extremely generous, and offered so many cattle in sacrifice that their blood formed the Chambhal river. He saw himself as Vishnu's instrument to serve the poor and needy. According to the Mahabharata, he had 200,000 cooks and had 2000 cattle and as many other animals slaughtered daily for use in his kitchens, and had the meat fed to innumerable poor and needy people. One day, the gods visited

Vishnu in Vaikunth and in casual conversation
asked him, 'Who do you think is your greatest
devotee?' Without hesitation, Vishnu replied that
it was Rantidev. The gods, intrigued, decided
to test Rantidev's devotion, and caused a great
famine to overcome his kingdom. The king, with
his characteristic generosity and piety, opened
the royal granary and treasury to his people. But
the famine continued. The king then opened
his palace to the people, and gave away all that
he possessed. He shared whatever food he had
with them, but soon even that finished. The
people were starving, and, at his wits' end, the
king turned to Vishnu for help. Giving up all
food and drink, he began to meditate on Vishnu.
For forty-eight days he prayed and fasted. On
the forty-ninth day, his ministers persuaded him
to take some food, and brought him water and
a dish made of rice boiled in milk. Just as he
was about to eat the rice and milk, a Brahman
appeared, hungry and starving. The king gave
away part of the food to the Brahman. He was
just about to begin eating again when a poor man
appeared begging for food. The king gave away
another portion of the food to him. Just then, a
Shudra appeared before him, begging for food for
himself and his dogs. The king gave away the rest
of the food to him. He now had only water left,
just enough to slake his thirst. As he was about to
drink the water, a Chandal, an outcast, appeared
and begged for water. The king gave even that
away. The Chandal drank the water, and as he
did so, the king felt refreshed and strengthened.
He opened his eyes in surprise, to see the gods
before him. They acknowledged him as Vishnu's
greatest devotee, and reversed the famine and
its effects, restoring his kingdom to prosperity.
And Vishnu, to honour his devotee, took him
unto himself. Rantidev merged with his Lord,

thus attaining the highest state. An alternative version of the story states that Rantidev, in his generosity, would every now and then hold a great sacrifice and give away all that he possessed. On one occasion, having given away everything he owned, he and his family remained without food or water for forty-eight days. The king accepted his condition, and lived only upon what he received without asking. On the forty-ninth day, as he lay on the ground, starving and semi-conscious, he was given some water and a dish made of rice boiled in milk. As he was about to share this food with his wife and children the gods appeared to test him, in the guise of the Brahman, the Shudra, the low-born man with his dogs and the Chandal.

Rati: 'Love, desire'; the goddess of desire and sexual pleasure, the consort of Kamdev, and daughter of Daksh.

Ravan: The evil and powerful Rakshasa king of Lanka; the son of Vishravas by the Rakshasi Nikasha; grandson of the sage Pulastya. His chief queen was Mandodari. He was the half-brother of Kuber, and as Kuber was king of the Yakshas, Ravan was king of the Rakshasas. Through penance and prayer to Brahma, Ravan received the boon of invulnerability to gods and demons, but was doomed to die because of a woman. He was also able to take any form he pleased. He is described as having ten heads and twenty arms, copper-coloured eyes and teeth as bright as the moon. He was as dark as a cloud, and as enormous as a mountain. His body bore all the marks of royalty, but was marked by the scars of the wounds he had received in his battles against the gods. It was scarred by the thunderbolt of Indra, by the tusks of Indra's elephant, Airavat, and by Vishnu's discus. Tall as a mountain peak, he could stop the sun and the moon in their course across the sky. His strength was so great that he could lift up Mount Kailash in play. He terrorized gods and men with his evil deeds, till at last they appealed to Vishnu for help. Since he had been too arrogant to ask for invincibility against men, Vishnu took birth as Ramchandra, son of Dasharath, for the sole purpose of destroying him; the gods became incarnate as bears and monkeys to help him in this enterprise. For his ten heads, he is called Dashashish. He is also called Dashanan, 'ten-faced'; Dashkandhar or Dashkanth, 'ten-necked'; Dashmukh, 'ten-faced'. As the enemy of the gods, he is known as Surari; as the king of Lanka, he is called Lankesh.

riddhi; Riddhi: Prosperity, affluence, accomplishment. Riddhi is also prosperity, personified as Kuber's wife, or, in some instances, as one of Ganesh's wives. In the plural, the Riddhis refer to some of the attendants of Kuber, and signify riches.

rishi: A sage; the inspired sages to whom the hymns of the Vedas were revealed; also used as a title for the seven great sages, and other wise and learned men.

Rishyamuk: A mountain in the south, near the source of the Pampa river and the lake Pampa, upon which lived the monkey Sugriv and his followers. Ram stayed there for a while with the monkeys.

Sabar; Shabar: A tribal people of southern India.

Sabari; Shabari: A woman of the Sabar tribe (hence her name). The daughter of a hunter, she was a devotee of Ram. She sought salvation upon the death of her guru, the sage, Matanga; just before he died, Matanga assured her that she would indeed attain salvation, and that Ram himself would grant it to her. Sabari waited faithfully for Ram, living for many years as an ascetic in the forest. During his exile, Ram, hearing of her devotion to him, visited her in her hermitage. There, she offered him fruits that she had collected especially for him in the forest, and which she had tasted herself before offering to check their sweetness. Lakshman protested that since she had bitten into the fruit, Ram should not eat them. But Ram saw only her devotion and ate the fruits she offered. He then granted her salvation.

sachchidanand: Literally 'Existence (or being or entity) or truth, thought (or knowledge or consciousness), and happiness (or bliss)'—a name for the Supreme Spirit.

Sagar: A prince of the solar dynasty; king of Avadh. From Sumati, the second of his two wives, he had sixty-thousand sons. During the performance of the Ashvamedha, or horse-sacrifice, the king ordered his sixty-thousand sons to retrieve the sacrificial horse, which had been carried off to the underworld. They dug their way to Patal, where they found the horse grazing and the sage Kapil seated close by in meditation. Thinking him to be the thief, the sons of Sagar began to accuse and threaten him. This so enraged the saint that he reduced all of them to ashes. Their souls were finally liberated by the actions of Bhagirath, who brought the Ganga to earth in order to purify their ashes. Sagar finally completed his sacrifice, and gave the name 'saagar' to the chasm which this sons had dug (saagar means ocean).

sagun: 'With attributes'; possessing a form that has qualities, hence, the incarnate form of the Supreme Spirit.

Sahasrabahu: 'The thousand-armed'; he was king of the Haihaya tribe, and is better known by his patronymic, Kartavirya. As a result of penance and prayer, the divine saint Dattatreya granted him a thousand arms, a golden chariot to take him wherever he wished to go, the power of righting wrongs by dispensing justice, the conquest of the earth and the disposition to rule it righteously, invincibility and finally, death at the hands of a man renowned the whole world over. He ruled wisely and well for 85,000 years. He was a contemporary of Ravan, and when Ravan came to conquer his capital city, Mahishmati, he took him prisoner effortlessly; he let Ravan go on the request of the rishi, Pulastya. One day, when out hunting, Sahasrabahu reached the hermitage of the sage Jamadagni. The sage and the sons were out, but his wife, recognizing the king, treated him with due respect. But instead of acknowledging the hospitality he had received, the king in his arrogance carried off the calf of the sacred cow, Surabhi, which Jamadagni had acquired through penance. When Jamadagni's son, Parashuram, returned and heard what the king had done, he followed the king, cut off his thousand arms with his arrows and killed him. Sahasrabahu's sons, in retaliation, attacked Jamadagni in his hermitage and killed him. When Parashuram found his father's lifeless body, he laid it on a pyre and vowed to wipe out the whole of the Kshatriya race. He killed all the sons of Sahasrabahu, and cleared the earth of Kshatriyas twenty-one times. Sahasrabahu's death at the hands of Parashuram was as per the boon granted him—to be killed by a man renowned the world over.

samadhi: A state of profound meditation restraining the senses and confining the mind to contemplation.

Sampati:	A vulture, the eldest son of Arun, the charioteer of the Sun, and the older brother of the vulture, Jatayu.
Sanak; Sanandan; Sanatan; Sanatkumar:	The four Kumars, the four mind-born sons of Brahma; declining to create progeny, they remained forever boys, and forever pure and innocent. Sanatkumar was the most prominent of them all. They are also known by their patronymic Vaidhatra (from Vidhatra, or Brahma).
Sanjivani:	In mythology, a life-giving herb that is said to restore the dead to life.
sanyasi:	One who has renounced the world, abandoning all attachment; according to Hindu scripture, sannyasa is the last and fourth stage of life for a man.
Saptarishi:	The seven Rishis, the mind-born sons of Brahma. They form, in astronomy, the constellation of the Great Bear.
Sarasvati:	'Watery'. In the Vedas, Sarasvati is primarily a river, as sacred as the Ganga is today. Though now lost, it was the third stream that met the Ganga and the Jamuna at their confluence at Prayag. Sarasvati was also a deity, the personification of the river, and as a river goddess she was the bestower of fertility and wealth. In the Brahmanas and the Mahabharata, she is recognized as Vach, the goddess of speech and eloquence. In later times, she is the goddess of learning, inventor of the Sanskrit language and the Devanagari script, and patron of the arts and sciences. She is also the wife of Brahma. She is represented as a beautiful and graceful young woman, white in colour, wearing a crescent on her brow. She is often shown as holding the vina in

her hands. Her steed is the swan. In her form as the goddess of speech and eloquence, she is known as Bharati, 'articulate'; Brahmi or Brahmani, 'Brahma's consort'; Gira, 'speech'; Sharada, 'one who bears a vina'; Vani or Bani, literally 'sound, speech, language, voice'. As the consort of Brahma (Vidhatra), she is known as Vidhatri.

Sarju; Sarayu: A sacred river, that flows past Ram's city of Avadh; it is believed to rise from the sacred Manas lake.

Sati: A daughter of Daksh, and Shiv's first wife; she killed herself because of her father's anger against Shiv. She was subsequently reincarnated as the goddess Parvati, the daughter of Himvat and Maina.

Savan: The fifth month of the Hindu calendar, corresponding to July–August.

ser: A measure of weight, roughly equivalent to a kilogram.

Shachi: Indra's consort.

Shakti: Cosmic energy; it denotes the energy or active power of a deity personified as his consort, as Parvati of Shiv, Lakshmi of Vishnu, Sarasvati of Brahma, etc.

Shatanand: Janak's guru and family priest.

Shatrughna: 'Foe-destroyer'; he is Lakshman's twin and the youngest of Ram's three brothers. He is also called Ripusudan, Ripuhan, 'destroyer of enemies; and Ripudaman or Ripudavan, 'subduer of enemies'.

shehnai: A wind instrument, somewhat like a clarinet; its sound is considered auspicious and it is especially played at weddings.

Shesh; Sheshnag:

Shesh, or Sheshnag, is the king of the Nagas or the serpent race. His kingdom is Patal, abode of the Nagas. He is represented as a serpent with a thousand heads; his coils form the couch upon which Vishnu lies, and his thousand hoods the canopy which shelter him whilst he sleeps during the intervals of creation. He sometimes bears the entire world upon one of his heads. He is also called Anant, 'the endless', and is regarded as the symbol of eternity.

Shibi:

Shibi was a pious and generous king, famed for his large-heartedness and his upholding of dharma. One day the gods decided to put him to the test. Agni took on the form of a dove, and Indra that of a hawk, and as the king sat in court one morning, the dove flew into his lap and nestled there. The hawk followed and claimed the dove as its rightful prey. The king refused to give up the dove, since it had sought shelter with him, but he also realized the legitimacy of the hawk's demand. He offered the hawk anything he wanted in place of the dove, but the hawk would be satisfied with nothing except a piece of the king's own flesh, equal in weight to the dove. So the king had a pair of scales brought, and placing the dove on one side, he began hacking off pieces of his own flesh, which he put on the other side. But no matter how much of his own flesh he cut off, the dove was always heavier. At last, he climbed on to the scales himself and would have cut off his own head, but the gods intervened, and Agni and Indra, appearing in their own forms, acknowledged his generosity and made him whole again.

Shiv:

Auspicious, propitious, fortunate; the Destroyer, the great and powerful third deity in the Hindu triad; he is described as the destructive power, but his powers and attributes are much wider. As the great god of dissolution, he is called Rudra or

Mahakal; but in Hindu philosophy, dissolution is coupled with regeneration, so as Shiv or Shankar, he is the reproductive power that perpetually restores that which has been destroyed. He is thus also called Ishvar, and Mahadev, 'the great god'. As the restorer, he is worshipped in the form of a linga or phallus, or as the linga combined with a yoni, the female reproductive organ representative of his Shakti, or female energy. He is also the supreme ascetic, the epitome of penance and abstract meditation through which unlimited powers are acquired, the highest spiritual knowledge is gained, and union with the Supreme Absolute achieved. In this form he is represented as a naked ascetic, with matted hair, his body smeared with ashes. He is also the lord of goblins and ghosts, and in this form he wears serpents wound around his neck and a necklace of skulls. He is a handsome man, fair-complexioned, with five faces and four arms, and is usually represented sitting upon a tiger skin in profound meditation. He has a third eye in the middle of his forehead, and surmounted by the crescent moon. His third eye, if opened, has great destructive power—it reduced Kamdev, the god of love, to ashes, and periodically destroys creation in the cycle of destruction and regeneration. His matted locks are coiled upon his head, and within it is held the River Ganga, which he caught and contained as she descended from heaven upon earth (and because of which he is called Gangadhar, 'he who holds the Ganga'). He is often attired in the skin of a tiger, a deer, or an elephant. In his four hands he carries a deer, the bow Ajagav, a damru (small hour-glass–shaped drum) or the Khatwang (a club with a skull at the end), or a cord for binding offenders. He is usually accompanied by his bull, Nandi. His consort is the goddess Parvati. As lord of all creation, he is called Akhileshvar, and as lord of the universe he is called Vishvanath and Jagadish; as the Destroyer, he is also called Har. As lord of Mt Kailash, he is known as Girinath and Girish, 'lord of the mountain'. The city of Kashi is sacred to him; thus he is also called Kashinath, 'lord of Kashi'. As regent of the north-east quarter, he is called Ish or Ishan. For his action of reducing Kamdev, the god of love to ashes, he is known as Anangarati, 'enemy of Anang (Kamdev)'; Kamari, 'the foe or conqueror of Kam'; Kamripu, 'the foe of Kam'. In his androgynous form he is known as Ardhanarishvar, 'the god who is half a woman'. He has a bull (brish) on his banner (ketu), and is therefore also known as Brishketu. When vish or poison was thrown up amongst the treasures retrieved at the churning of the ocean, Shiv swallowed it and held it safely in his throat, which turned blue as a result; from this he is called Nilkanth, 'blue-throated' (See ocean, churning of). As the destroyer of the demon known as Tripurasur, he is also called Purari and Tripurari. An alternative explanation is that he destroyed the triple city known as Tripur, which belonged to a trio of demons collectively called Tripurasur. Since he bears the crescent moon on his brow, he is also called Shashibhushan, 'one who has the moon as his ornament' and Chandramauli, 'the moon-crested one'. For the garland of skulls that he wears around his neck, he is known as Kapali, 'the one who wears a necklace of skulls'. He is also known as Ashutosh, 'he who is quickly pleased'; Bhav, 'existence'; Shambhu, 'one who causes happiness'; Shankar, 'one who causes tranquillity' or 'auspicious'; Mahesh or Mahadev, 'the great god'; Sarv, 'complete, entire, universal'; Sadashiv, 'always happy or prosperous'.

shivaling: A phallic representation of Shiv.

Shringber; Shringberpur: The town of Shringber, it lay on the left bank of the Ganga. It was on the border of Koshal with

Bhil country. The area around was inhabited by the Nishad tribe; their chief was Guha. The town has been identified with modern Singraur.

Shringi:

'The deer-horned'; a hermit, and son of the sage Vibhandaka. Shringi or Rishyashringa as he was called, performed the fire-sacrifice that resulted in the birth of Ram and his brothers. One version of his story says that his mother was a doe, and he was therefore born with antlers; another version says that his mother was the apsara, Urvashi, who abandoned her infant son and his father, her lover, after the child's birth. Rishyashringa was brought up by his father in the forest, in complete isolation from all other human beings. He was endowed with magical and mystical powers. Once, when the kingdom of Anga was struck by intense drought, its king, Lomapad, was told that he must hold a sacrifice conducted by a priest who was perfectly chaste. The only such priest that could be found was Rishyashringa, who had grown up with no knowledge of women at all. He was persuaded to come to Anga and perform the sacrifice, which successfully ended the drought in Anga. Rishyashringa then married Shanta, the daughter of Lomapad. (Shanta was actually the adopted daughter of Lomapad; her real father was King Dasharath.)

Shrutakirti:

Sita's cousin, the younger daughter of Janak's younger brother Kushadhvaj (Kushaketu); she was married to Shatrughna.

Shudra:

The fourth, and lowest, of the four castes of Hinduism. This is the servile class, whose duty it was to serve the three higher castes.

Shuk; Shukdev:

An eminent rishi, he was the son of Vyas and the main narrator of the Bhagavat Purana.

Shvapach:	Literally, 'one who eats dog-meat', and thus refers to one belonging to the lowest, most degraded caste.
Siddha:	'Accomplished', a semi-divine being, of great purity and holiness, and said to be specially characterized by the eight siddhis or supernatural faculties, which he acquires by the performance of intense austerities or certain mystical rites or processes. The Siddhas, together with the Munis, and other holy and accomplished beings, inhabit the Bhuvarlok or middle region between the earth and the sun. The term 'Siddha' is also used for a great sage or ascetic who has attained the eight siddhis, usually through intense austerities and yogic practice.
Siddhi; siddhi:	Success or accomplishment personified; one of Ganesh's wives. In northern Indian tradition, Ganesh's two consorts are Siddhi (Success) and Buddhi (Wisdom). In one recounting, they are said to have been born of Brahma's mind, who then offered them to Ganesh as his brides; in another they are regarded as having been summoned by Ganesh himself, and then offered to him by Brahma. Buddhi is also sometimes called Riddhi—she is spiritual success, as opposed to the material success that is her sister Siddhi. In the plural, the siddhis are supernatural faculties. They are usually stated to be eight in number. They are: (i) anima, the faculty of making oneself infinitesimally small; (ii) mahima, the faculty of making oneself infinitely great; (iii) laghima, the faculty of becoming infinitely light; (iv) garima, the faculty of becoming infinitely heavy; (v) prapti, the faculty of obtaining whatever one wishes; (vi) prakamya, the faculty of doing whatever one wishes; (vii) ishitva, the power of absolute supremacy; (viii) vashitva, the power of absolute subjugation.

sindur:	Vermilion; applied on the head of a woman it indicates that she is married; it is applied to the head of the bride for the first time by the bridegroom upon the completion of the wedding rites.
sinsupa:	The ashok tree.
siris blossom:	The flower of the tree Acacia sirissa; the flower is exceptionally fragile and delicate-looking, with pale, slender filament-like petals.
Sita:	'A furrow'; in the Vedas, Sita is the furrow, or farming personified and is worshipped as the goddess of agriculture and fruits. In the Ramayana, she is the daughter of Janak, the king of Videha, and the wife of Ram. Remnants of old Vedic belief can still be seen in the story of her birth. It is related that one day, as King Janak was ploughing the field in preparation for a great fire-sacrifice to obtain children, there sprang from his plough a baby girl, whom he adopted. He named her 'Sita', which means 'furrow', and took her home to his palace, where she grew up as his beloved daughter. From her father, she is known as 'Janaki'. So, from the manner of her birth, Sita is also called Avanikumari, 'daughter of the earth'. She is also known as Vaidehi, 'daughter of Videh, king of Videha' or 'princess of Videha'; and Maithili, 'princess of Mithila'.
sixteen ways of honouring a guest:	In Hindu tradition, a guest is considered equal to a god, and he is honoured by being given the following sixteen things: (i) asana, a seat; (ii) arghya, a libation of water with milk, flowers, etc.; (iii) padya, water to wash the feet; (iv) achamaniya, water to drink; (v) snaniya, water to bathe and for ablutions; (vi) gandhakshak, sandal paste and rice grains; (vii) vastra, fresh clothes; (viii) pushpa,

flowers; (ix) dhupa, incense; (x) dipa, light or
lamps; (xi) naivedya, food; (xii) mukhasta jal,
water to rinse the mouth with; (xiii) tambula, betel
leaves; (xiv) dakshina, a gift; (xv) pradakshina,
circumambulation; and (xvi) nirajana, a worship
with lighted lamps.

Skand:

The god of war, the planet Mars, and the
commander of the divine armies. He was born
miraculously from the seed of Shiv, for the
express purpose of destroying the Asur Tarak.
It is said that Shiv cast his seed into fire, and
it was afterwards received by the river Ganga.
From her waters came forth Skand, in the form
of a beautiful baby boy. He was found by the six
Krittikas (the Pleiades), and each claimed the
baby for herself, and each wanted to nurse him. In
order to please them, Skand grew six heads. He is
shown as riding on a peacock, with a bow in one
hand and an arrow in the other. He is also known
as Shanmukh, 'one with six-faces'.

Sone:

A river in central India, it is a tributary of the
Ganga.

spheres, fourteen:

According to Hindu scripture, the universe is
divided into fourteen spheres, seven ascending
and seven descending. The seven higher spheres,
in ascending order, are: Bhuh, Bhuvah, Svah,
Mahah, Janah, Tapah and Satyam; the lower
sphere, in descending order, are: Atal, Vital,
Sutal, Talatal, Mahatal, Rasatal, Patal.

states of being, four:

The four states of being are: (i) jagrat or waking;
(ii) svapna or sleeping/dreaming; (iii) sushupti or
deep repose; and (iv) turiya or the state in which
the soul has become one with the Supreme Spirit.
These four feminine states are each paired with
a male consort; these are: (i) vishva or creation;

(ii) tejas or power; (iii) pragya or wisdom; and (iv) brahm, the universal Absolute.

Subahu: A Rakshasa. He defiled and interrupted the fire-sacrifices of the sage Vishvamitra; for this, he was killed by Ram.

Sugriv: King of the monkeys, and brother of Baali. He is also called Sukanth.

Sukarkhet: A town, identified with the town of Soron in northern India. It is located on the river Ganga, about thirty-two miles south of modern-day Ayodhya. It is an important place of pilgrimage for Hindus.

Sumantra: Dasharath's trusted minister and charioteer.

Sumitra: One of Dasharath's queens, the mother of the twins Lakshman and Shatrughna.

Supnakha; Surpanakha: Literally, 'having finger-nails like winnowing fans'; a Rakshasi, Ravan's sister.

Surasa: A goddess, the mother of the Nagas, she was asked by the gods to test Hanuman's strength and courage as he flew across the ocean to Lanka.

Sutikshna: A hermit who lived in the Dandak forest and met Ram and Sita during their exile. He was a disciple of the sage Agastya.

Svati: The star Arcturus, as forming the fifteenth nakshatra, or lunar asterism. According to popular belief, the rain that falls under this lunar asterism is endowed with special properties including the attribute that if a drop of it falls into a seashell, it becomes a pearl. The chatak subsists only on the rain that falls during autumn, under the influence of this nakshatra.

svayamvar:

The public ceremony of a young girl or princess selecting a husband of rank from an assembled gathering of suitors; this ceremony is usually restricted to the Kshatriya caste. Sometimes, a task may be set by the bride's family for her suitors to accomplish, as in the case of Sita's svayamvar, where the successful suitor had to string and break Shiv's bow.

tamal:

A tree found across India; it has very dark bark and white blossoms.

Tamas; Tamasa:

A tributary of the Ganga.

Tara:

Wife of Baali, king of the monkeys, and the mother of Angad. After Baali was killed by Ram, she was taken by Baali's younger brother, Sugriv, as his wife.

Tarak:

A Daitya, whose austerities made him formidable to the gods, and for whose destruction Shiv's son, Skand, the god of war, was born.

Taraka:

The daughter of the Yaksha, Suketu; turned into a Rakshasi by the sage Agastya, she lived in the forest at the confluence of the Ganga and the Sarju and ravaged the surrounding land and terrorized the rishis in the forest. Vishvamitra wanted Ram to kill her, to stop her from doing further harm. But Ram was reluctant to kill a woman. So deciding to deprive her of the power to do harm, he cut off her two arms. Lakshman cut off her nose and ears. But using her magic powers, she pelted Ram and Lakshman with a shower of rocks and boulders, so that finally, at

Vishvamitra's command, Ram killed her with a single arrow. Her son was the Rakshasa Marich, who later helped Ravan in his abduction of Sita.

three afflictions or   These are mental and physical distress, distress
the triple fires: caused by the acts of God, and distress caused by
                           others.

tilak: A ceremonial mark made with vermilion or sandalwood paste upon the forehead between the eyebrows upon installation to office, coronation of a king, betrothal, etc.

triveni: 'Triple-braid'; the confluence of the three sacred rivers Ganga, Jamuna and the subterranean Sarasvati at the city of Prayag (modern Allahabad). The waters of the Jamuna are dark, and of the Ganga light. The stream of the Sarasvati is invisible.

Trijata: A Rakshasi who befriended Sita when she was Ravan's prisoner in Lanka. She is also called Dharamagya.

Trishanku: The name given to Satyavrata, a prince of the solar dynasty, and king of Avadh. Satyavrata was a good king, but in his arrogance he decided to ascend to heaven in corporeal form. He therefore asked the sage Vasishtha to perform the sacrifice by means of which he could attain this end. Vasishtha declined to perform the ceremony, declaring that what the king wanted was impossible. Satyavrata then appealed to Vasishtha's sons, who refused, saying that he wanted to make trouble between them and their father and, for his presumption, cursed him to become a Chandal. While in Chandal form, and having nothing to eat one day, Satyavrata killed Vasishtha's cow, the Kamadhenu, and ate her. For these three sins, of pride, making trouble between father and sons, and killing a cow, Vasishtha gave him the name 'Trishanku' (from *tri* or 'three', and *shanku* or 'sin'). He then turned to Vishvamitra, who agreed to perform the sacrifice and send him to heaven in his current body. The sons of Vasishtha opposed the sacrifice, for which Vishvamitra reduced them all to ashes. He then began the sacrifice, but as Trishanku ascended to heaven, Indra and the other gods opposed his entry and hurled him down to earth. Trishanku fell head first, and hung upside down in the sky, midway between the earth and heaven. It was finally agreed that that is where he should stay. He can still be seen in the sky, as the constellation Trishanku in the southern hemisphere. The saliva that dropped from his mouth is said to be the River Karamnasa, the waters of which, if touched, destroy all religious merit.

Trishira: Literally, 'three-headed'; a Rakshasa, and a brother, son, or friend of Ravan, killed by Ram.

twice-born: A man of any one of the three upper Hindu castes (but particularly a Brahman), whose investiture with the sacred thread upon puberty constitutes, religiously and metaphorically, his second birth.

Udayagiri: This is the eastern mountain from behind which the sun is supposed to rise; it is also called Udayachal.

Urmila: Janak's and Sunayana's daughter, Sita's younger sister; she was married to Lakshman.

Vaikunth: The paradise or heaven of Vishnu; its site is sometimes described as in the Northern Ocean, sometimes it is said to be located on the eastern peak of Mount Meru. Vishnu himself is also sometimes designated by this term.

Valmik; Valmiki:

The author of the Sanskrit Ramayana. Regarded as the first, or original poet, he is said to have invented poetry when he began to compose the Ramayana. Tradition maintains that before he became a sage and the author of the Ramayana, Valmiki was the dacoit Ratnakar, who would waylay travellers and then rob and mercilessly kill them. One day, he ran into the sage Narad, who asked him why he did what he did. Ratnakar replied that it was for his family; Narad asked him whether his family appreciated the burden of sin that he was accumulating for their sakes and whether they would share it. Ratnakar staunchly replied that they would, but when he asked his wife and children, they refused to accept the burden of his crimes. Ratnakar realized the folly of his ways and begged for forgiveness. Narad then gave him the mantra of Ram's name, but since this was a mantra that could not be given to thieves and murderers, Narad told him to recite it backwards. Ratnakar did so, and meditated on the name, sitting so still and for so long that anthills grew around him. He continued his penance for many long years, till finally a divine voice declared him to be free of the guilt of his crimes, and renamed him Valmiki, or 'the one born of anthills'.

Vamdev:

A prominent rishi, attached to Dasharath's court.

Varun:

Amongst the oldest of the Vedic gods, Varun is the personification of the sky, the maker of earth and heaven. He is described as being furnished with snares and nooses, with which he seizes and binds evildoers. No mortal can escape from Varun's snares.

Vasishtha:

A celebrated Vedic sage, to whom many hymns are ascribed. According to the Vishnu Purana, he was the family priest of the house of Ishkvaku; he was contemporary not only with Ishkvaku himself, but with his descendants down to the sixty-first generation, including Dasharath and Ram.

Veda; Vedas:
From *vid*, 'know'; hence 'divine knowledge'. The Vedas, composed in verse in an ancient form of Sanskrit some time between 1500 and 1000 BCE (though opinions vary considerably about their age, and many scholars believe that they can be pushed back at least another thousand years), are the foundation of Hindu belief and practice. It is believed that the Vedas emanated as the breath of the Supreme Being. It is agreed that they were revealed orally to the sages whose names they bear, and thus the whole body of the Veda—the entire body of divine knowledge—is known as 'Sruti' or 'what was heard'. The Vedas are four in number: Rig, Yajur, Sama, Atharva. The Rig Veda is the oldest; in fact, it is the original Veda, from which the Yajur and Sama Vedas are mostly derived. The Atharva Veda was composed much later.

Vedant:
'End of the Veda'; name of the complete Veda; name of a certain system of philosophy and theology based particularly on the Upanishads; and of works concerning this philosophy and in support of it.

Vedashira:
One of the seven great rishis (Saptarishi), associated with the fourth Manwantara. (See Manu.)

vedi:
A quadrangular space, with the sacred fire in the centre, where wedding rites are conducted.

vedika:
Ground prepared for a sacrifice or ceremony, usually consisting of a raised floor or platform and covered with a roof supported by pillars.

Vena:
Son of Anga by his queen, Sunita, and a descendant of Manu Swayambhuva. Vena grew up to be a cruel and vicious man, so much so that his father, unable to bear his atrocities, left the kingdom and disappeared, no one knew where. Seeing the kingdom without a king, the sages decided to put Vena upon the throne. Royal power made him worse, and in his arrogance, he banned offerings and performance of sacrifices to the gods, declaring that he alone was worthy of such worship. The sages reasoned with him, but he refused to listen; they admonished him more strongly, but he would not change his mind. Finally, they killed him with blades of consecrated grass. After his death, the sages saw clouds of dust in the distance, and were told that these were raised by men who had begun to loot and plunder because the country was now without a king. Since Vena was childless, the sages rubbed his left thigh to produce a son; from this arose a short, dark man with a flat nose. He was asked to sit, 'nishida'; he did so and thus became a Nishad, from which sprang the tribe living in the Vindhya mountains. The sages then rubbed the right hand of Vena, and from this came forth his son Prithu. (See Prithuraj.) Vena's story is told a little differently in the Padma Purana. This states that Vena was a good king at the start of his rule, but soon turned to the teachings of the Jains. For this heresy, the sages attacked and beat him, till from his left thigh came forth the Nishad tribe, and from his right arm came Prithu. Being freed of sin by the birth of the Nishad, he gave up his kingdom and retired to an ashram on the Narmada, where he engaged in penance. For this, Vishnu forgave him and made him one with himself.

Vibhishan:
'The terrible'; a younger brother of Ravan, and ally of Ram. He was raised to the throne of Lanka by Ram after the defeat and death of Ravan.

Videh: 'Bodiless'; the title born by the kings of the
                            kingdom of Videha, including King Janak, Sita's
                            father.

Videha: The kingdom of King Janak, Sita's father. Its
                            capital city was the city of Mithila.

vina: An ancient multi-stringed musical instrument; it
                            is supposed to have been invented by Narad.

Vinata: A daughter of Daksh, one of the thirteen wives
                            of the sage Kashyap, and mother of Garud. From
                            her were born all the birds.

Viradh: Also known as Tumburu, he was a Gandharva
                            cursed by Kuber to become a horrible, man-eating
                            Rakshasa. He is described as being as tall as a
                            mountain peak, deformed, of dreadful aspect, clad
                            in a tiger's skin, smeared with fat, soaked in blood,
                            like death with an open mouth, bearing three
                            lions, four tigers, two wolves, ten deer and the
                            great head of an elephant with tusks on the point
                            of an iron pike. He had obtained from Brahma the
                            boon of invulnerability. Ram, with Lakshman and
                            Sita, encountered him in the Dandak forest. (This
                            incident is told in detail in Valmiki's Ramayana.)
                            Viradh cursed and taunted the brothers, and
                            grabbed Sita. Ram and Lakshman shot him with
                            their arrows, proving that he was not invulnerable.
                            But he caught them and throwing them over his
                            shoulder, ran off with them as easily as if they had
                            been children. They broke both his arms, beat
                            him with their fists and threw him to the ground,
                            but they could not kill him. So they dug a deep
                            hole and buried him alive. Then there arose from
                            the earth a beautiful form, who said he was a
                            Gandharva cursed by Kuber to take on the form
                            of a Rakshasa. Ram released him from the curse
                            and sent him back to his own realm.

Vishnu:

From *vish*, to pervade. The preserver and restorer, he is the second of the Hindu triad. He is also called Hari. In the Rig Veda, Vishnu is the manifestation of solar energy, and does not have the importance he acquired later as the great preserver of the universe. In the Puranas and the Mahabharata, he is the embodiment of mercy and goodness, which manifests itself as the preserving power, which is self-existent and all-pervading. He is therefore associated with water, which was everywhere before the creation of the world. He is represented in human form as reclining upon the serpent Shesh, and floating upon the Ocean of Milk. He is therefore also called Narayan or 'floating upon the waters'. His consort is Lakshmi, the goddess of wealth and beauty. The river Ganga is said to spring from his toe. Vishnu is represented with four hands; one holds the Panchajanya, a shankha or conch-shell; the second the Sudarshan or Vajranabha, which is a chakra or discus; the third holds Kaumodaki, a gada or club; and the fourth holds a Padma, or lotus. As the husband of Lakshmi (who is also known as Shri, Ramaa and Kamla), he is known as Shripati, Ramapati and Kamlapati; as the one who dwells with Lakshmi, he is known as Shrinivas, Ramanivas and Ramaniket. He is also known as Sarangpani, 'the one who bears the bow called Sarang'. As the slayer of the demon Khar in his incarnation as Ramchandra, he is known as Kharari, 'enemy of Khar'; as the slayer of the demons Madhu and Kaitabh he is known as Madhusudan and Kaitabhajit respectively. As the giver of liberation, he is called Mukund. He is also known as Anant, 'the infinite'. Vishnu has 'descended' to earth, or taken incarnate form several times. His 'descents', or avatars, are usually said to be ten in number, though the Bhagavata Purana says that they are twenty-two, or innumerable. Vishnu's ten avatars are as follows: (i) Matsya, 'the fish': this avatar is connected with the Hindu legend of the flood. The objective was to save Vaivaswata, the seventh Manu, who became the progenitor of all mankind. One day Manu found in the water he used for his ablutions a little fish which spoke to him and warned him of a great flood that was coming which would destroy all living creatures, and said that it would save him. The fish grew and grew till it was so huge that it had to be put into the ocean. The fish then instructed Manu to build a ship, and to take refuge in it when the flood came. Manu did so, and when the flood came, Manu embarked in the ship. The fish then swam to Manu, who, using the serpent Sheshnag tied the ship to the fish's horn, and was towed to safety; (ii) Kurma, 'the tortoise': when the great flood subsided, the gods realized that many valuable things had been lost at the bottom of the ocean. So Vishnu appeared as a tortoise, and placed himself at the bottom of the Ocean of Milk, and took upon his back the mountain Mandar. The gods and demons wound the serpent Vasuki around the mountain. The gods took one end of the serpent, the demons the other, and in this way they churned the ocean until they recovered the lost objects; (iii) Varah, 'the boar': a Daitya called Hataklochan had dragged the earth to the bottom of the sea. In order to recover the earth, Vishnu took the form of a boar, and after a battle that lasted a thousand years, he killed the Daitya and carried the earth back to the surface on his tusks; (iv) Narsingh, Narhari, or Narkeshari 'the man-lion': Vishnu took on the form of half-lion, half-man to deliver the world from the Daitya Kanakakasipu. Kananakasipu's son, Prahlad, was a devotee of Vishnu, and refused to obey his father's order that he should worship him and not Vishnu. When

Prahlad declared that Vishnu was all-pervading and everywhere, Kanakakasipu demanded to know if he was present even in the stone pillar in the hall of his palace. At this, to avenge Prahlad, Vishnu appeared out of the pillar in the form of Narsingh, half-man, half lion, and therefore neither man nor beast, and killed Kanakakasipu. The first four avatars are said to have taken place during the Satyayug, the first age of the world; (v) Vaman, 'the dwarf': in the Tretayug (the second age of the world), the Daitya king Bali became so powerful that he became king of the three worlds. The gods asked Vishnu to help them, so that may once again regain their pre-eminence in the world. So Vishnu descended to earth as a dwarf, and the son of Kashyap and Aditi. The dwarf begged Bali to give him as much land as he could cover in three strides. Bali, with his characteristic generosity, agreed. The dwarf took two strides by which he covered heaven and earth. Recognizing Bali's virtue, he refrained from taking the third step, and left Patal, or the underworld to Bali. This avatar is also known as Tribikram or Trivikrama, literally 'three strides'; (vi) Parashuram, 'Ram with the axe': he was born in the Tretayug, as the son of the Brahman Jamadagni, and his wife, Renuka. From his father's side he was descended from Bhrigu. He appeared in the world for repressing the tyranny and violence of the Kshatriya or warrior caste. Though he appeared in this world before Ramchandra, Vishnu's seventh avatar and the hero of the Ramayana, they were both living in this world at the same time. His weapon was the parashu or axe; (vii) Ram, or Ramchandra, the hero of the Ramayana and of Tulsi's *Ramcharitmanas*, he was born in the Tretayug to destroy the demon Ravan. He was the son of Dasharath, king of Ayodhya; (viii) Krishna, 'the dark': he is considered to be the most perfect of all of Vishnu's avatars. He is often regarded not as an avatar, but as Vishnu himself, when his elder brother Balram takes his place as the eighth avatar; (ix) Buddha: Buddha's far-reaching influence as a religious leader caused the Hindu Brahmins to adopt him as an avatar of Vishnu, who encourages wicked men to disregard the Vedas and the gods, and so bring about their own destruction. In eastern India, the ninth avatar is Jagannath, 'lord of the world', a form of Krishna; (x) Kalki, 'the white horse': the last and tenth avatar is yet to come. Vishnu will appear at the end of the Kaliyug, the last and fourth age, mounted on a white horse, and carrying a fiery sword. He will finally destroy the wicked and rid the world of evil, and the cycle of creation will begin again with piety restored.

Vishvakarma: A son of Brahma, and the chief architect and artist of the gods.

Vishvamitra: A celebrated sage, and the companion and counsellor of the young Ram. He was born a Kshatriya, and was the king of Kanauj, but through long and intense austerities, successfully elevated himself to the caste of Brahman and became one of the seven great Rishis. According to the Rig Veda, he was the son of a king named Kushika, because of which he is called Kaushik. Later sources make him the son of Gadhi, king of Kanyakubja and a descendant of Puru. He is therefore also called Gadhij, 'born of Gadhi' or, Gadhinandan, 'Gadhi's son'.

Vyas: Literally, 'an arranger', this title is common to many ancient authors, but is especially applied to Veda Vyas, the arranger of the Vedas. The name is also given to the compiler of the Mahabharata, and the arranger of the Puranas.

Yaksha:

Yakshas are semi-divine beings who protect forests and other wild places, and are generally harmless, though they may, on rare occasions, be evil. They are the attendants of the god of wealth, Kuber.

Yayati:

Son of Nahush, and the fifth king of the Lunar dynasty. He had two wives, Devyani and Sarmishtha. From Devyani was born his son Yadu, and from Sarmishtha his son Puru, the respective founders of the Yadavas and the Pauravas. In all he had five sons, the three others being Druhyu, Turvasu and Anu. Yayati was fond of women, and for his infidelity to Devyani, he was cursed with old age and infirmity by her father, Shukra. This curse Shukra consented to transfer to any of his sons who would agree to bear it. All refused, except Puru, who gave up his youth to his father and took on his curse of decrepitude. Yayati spent a thousand years enjoying the pleasures of the senses, after which he restored his youth to Puru and made him his successor. This story is told in the Mahabharata, as well as in the Vishnu Purana. The version in the Padma Purana is different. Yayati was invited to heaven by Indra, who sent his charioteer Matali to fetch him. On the way, they had a philosophical discussion, which had such an impact on Yayati that when he returned to earth, he, by his virtuous rule, made all his subjects free from passion and decay. Yama, the god of Death, complained that men no longer died. So Indra sent Kamdev, the god of love, and his daughter, Asruvindumati, to tempt Yayati with desire. They succeeded, and Yayati, deeply enamoured of the youthful Asruvindumati and in order to become a fit husband for her, asked each of his sons to exchange their youth for his old age. All refused, except Puru, who gave his manly vigour to his father and assumed his decrepitude. After some

time, Asruvindumati persuaded Yayati to return
to heaven, and he then gave Puru back his youth.
According to the Mahabharata, King Yayati, at
the end of his life, gave up his throne to Puru and
retired to the forest to lead the life of an ascetic.
There, the king lived on fruits and roots for some
time, and practised austerities, attaining complete
control of his mind and his senses. He also
performed fire sacrifices to honour his ancestors
and the gods, and followed every prescribed
rite and tradition for one in the third or forest-
dwelling stage of life (See four stages of life). He
then lived on scattered seeds that he gathered
for a thousand years, and then for another year
observing the vow of silence and living upon air
alone and without sleep. He passed another year
practising the most severe austerities, with four
fires burning around him and the sun above, and
then, living upon air alone, stood upon one leg for
six months. These austerities earned him a place
in heaven. He lived in heaven for a long time,
where he was held in great reverence by the gods
and other celestial beings. One day, Yayati went
to meet Indra, the king of the gods, and in the
course of conversation, Indra asked him to whom
he was equal in the austerities he had practised.
Yayati's boastful answer, that he did not, in the
matter of austerities, behold any who was his equal
amongst men, gods, Gandharvas and rishis, led
to a diminishing of his virtues, and he was hurled
from the heavens back into the world of men.

yojan: A measure of distance, equivalent to 4 kos or
                      about 9 miles.

Acknowledgements

Many people have stood by me in the five long years it has taken to complete this translation. Of these, my thanks first and foremost to R. Sivapriya, who made this project possible, and to Ambar Sahil Chatterjee, who has seen this through from the very beginning to the end. My gratitude also, to Shantanu Rai Chaudhuri, for his patient and meticulous editing.

I would also like to thank my teacher, Mrs Chandrakanta Chandra, who first introduced me to the literary genius of Tulsidas and the wonders of medieval Hindi literature in school, and whose help, in resolving nuances of language or understanding points of Tulsi's philosophy or ideology, has been invaluable to me on this journey of discovery and translation.

As always, my profound thanks to Dr Rupert Snell, my guru and guide, without whose encouragement I may not have had the courage to take up this project, and who has been ever present with help, advice, and support every step of the way.

My very special thanks to my daughters, Vipasha Bansal and Vidisha Jain, who bore the brunt of my obsession with this work. Vipasha patiently rescued me from innumerable tangles of grammar and syntax, and Vidisha was unfailing in her encouragement and support.

And finally, to my long-suffering family and friends—in particular Usha Bubna, Dr Asha Maheshwari, Anil Ratti and Shaiontoni Bose—for their patience and support, my undying gratitude.

Notes

Introduction

1. Though even at the time that Valmiki composed his epic, two other, very different, tellings of the Ram story existed—one was the Buddhist *Dasaratha Jataka*, in which Ram and Sita are brother and sister and rule as consorts, and the other the Jain *Paumchariya* by Vimalasuri, who sets the story in the court of the historical king Srinika and depicts the Rakshasas not as demons, but as normal human beings.
2. This reference to Tulsi is found in the *Bhaktamal*, a collection of short biographies composed by Nabhadas, possibly around 1585.
3. For a detailed discussion on the spread and circulation of the *Ramcharitmanas*, see Philip Lutgendorf, 'The Quest for the Legendary Tulsidas', *According to Tradition: Hagiographical Writing in India*, edited by Winand M. Callewaert and Rupert Snell.
4. For a discussion on available biographies of Tulsidas, see Philip Lutgendorf, 'The Quest for the Legendary Tulsidas', *According to Tradition: Hagiographical Writing in India*, edited by Winand M. Callewaert and Rupert Snell.
5. *Balkand*, 34.
6. *Balkand*, 30A, 31.
7. *Balkand*, 14D.
8. *Balkand*, Mangalacharan 7.
9. The relevant passages are contained in Book 3, *Aranyakand*, 24, where Sita conceals herself in the fire and substitutes her shadow; and in Book 6, *Lankakand*, 108–09, where the shadow Sita is destroyed and the real Sita steps forth out of the fire.

10. *Balkand*, 16.
11. *Balkand*, 14.
12. *Balkand*, 227–36.
13. Philip Lutgendorf, *The Life of a Text: Performing the* Ramcaritmanas *of Tulsidas*, University of California Press, 1991, p. 7.
14. *Aranyakand*, 34–36.
15. *Balkand*, 30.
16. *Balkand*, 124A.
17. For a more detailed discussion on the title, see Philip Lutgendorf, *The Life of a Text: Performing the* Ramcaritmanas *of Tulsidas*, University of California Press, 1991, pp. 19–20.
18. *Balkand*, 35–36.
19. *Balkand*, 36–37.
20. As an example, see *Uttarkand*, 113.
21. *Ayodhyakand*, 0; this doha, numbered 0, is the first doha after the Sanskrit mangalacharan; from this the Avadhi text of the second book begins.

Book I: BALKAND (CHILDHOOD)

1. The crescent moon is associated with Shiv, who wears it upon his forehead; and therefore, even though it is imperfect, it is honoured everywhere. The full moon, on the other hand, is worshipped in its own right.

2. Siddhanjan is a magical collyrium that is said to make a man able to see things buried underground or that cannot be seen otherwise.

3. The four rewards of existence are i) kama or sensual pleasure, ii) arth or wealth, iii) dharma or religious merit, and iv) moksh or liberation from worldly existence.

4. Nectar or amrit and wine or sura, both emerged from the churning of the ocean.

5. Bathing in the River Ganga frees one from sin; bathing in the Karamnasa destroys the merit of all of one's good deeds. Both rivers flow through the holy city of Kashi.

6. All three practised deception at some point in their lives, but were all discovered, with disastrous consequences for them. Kalnemi, upon Ravan's command, disguises himself as an ascetic in order to kill Hanuman, but Hanuman discovers the truth and seizing him by the feet, flings him unceremoniously all the way to Lanka, where he falls before Ravan's throne in the council room. Ravan appears before Sita in the forest disguised as a mendicant begging for alms and when Sita steps forward with the alms,

he throws off his disguise, seizes her and carries her off to Lanka. He is defeated and killed by Ram. The demon Rahu takes on the appearance of a god in order to receive the amrit at the churning of the ocean. He manages to fool Vishnu for a while, but is finally recognized by the Sun and the Moon, and is decapitated by Vishnu.

7. The lunar fortnight during which the moon wanes is known as the 'krishna paksh', the 'dark fortnight', in the Hindu calendar, while the fortnight in the which the moon waxes is called the 'shukla paksh', or bright fortnight—from 'krishna', which means dark or black, and 'shukla', which means light or bright.

8. Svati is the fifteenth nakshatra or lunar asterism; according to popular belief, the rain that falls under this asterism is endowed with special properties including the attribute that if a drop of it falls into a seashell, it becomes a pearl.

9. Khar, a man-eating rakshasa, was the younger brother of Ravan; he was killed by Ram. The literal meaning of his name is 'hard, rough, harsh'.

10. Dushan was another rakshasa who fought as one of Ravan's generals and was also killed by Ram. The literal meaning of his name is 'fault, defect, blemish, vice'. Dushan is associated with Khar. Sometimes they are referred to as brothers and cousins of Ravan.

11. 'Mantras and incantations in the common tongue' or 'sabar mantras'; these are popular amongst Tantrics and usually consist of a string of meaningless sounds and syllables.

12. Here Tulsi refers to an important event mentioned in the seventh book of Valmiki's Ramayana that occurred after the return of Ram and Sita to Ayodhya from Lanka: some of the townspeople doubt Sita's character, saying that she had, after all, spent almost a year in the house of another man. When Ram hears of this incident, out of respect for his subjects' feelings, he exiles Sita to the forest. Though Tulsi refers to this event here, he does not describe it later in the *Ramcharitmanas*.

13. Though Kaushalya had given birth to him, all the queens of King Dasharath looked upon Ram as their son, and are regarded as his mothers.

14. As distinguished from the name Ram being borne by Parashuram, the sixth avatar of Vishnu, and Balram, Krishna's older brother, who is often regarded as Vishnu's eighth avatar.

15. The three letter-sounds of the name 'Ram' are the 'bija mantra' or 'seed-letters' that represent the god of Fire, the Sun god and the Moon god. In some traditions, each letter-sound of the Sanskrit alphabet is regarded as representing one or more of the gods of the Hindu pantheon; Tantric

tradition believes that these letters, if joined with other spells sacred to a
particular deity and repeated with due ceremony a fixed number of times,
can result in the manifestation of the deity before the worshipper.

16. Hindus believe that those who die in Kashi attain freedom from rebirth at
    once. This, says Tulsi, is due to the power of Ram's name, which is given
    to the dying person by Shiv, the lord of Kashi.

17. Ganesh is the god of wisdom and the remover of obstacles; he is therefore
    propitiated at the start of any enterprise. The Puranas relate how one day
    there was a dispute amongst the gods as to who should be worshipped
    first; they took their quarrel to Brahma, who suggested that they race
    around the universe, and the one who won the race would be rewarded
    with the right to be worshipped first. Ganesh, riding on his steed the rat,
    was lagging far behind the others on their fleeter mounts; fortunately for
    him, he ran into the sage Narad, who advised him to scratch the word
    'Ram' into the dust and walk around it, for the Name contained within it
    all creation. Ganesh did as Narad advised, and Brahma, appreciating his
    cleverness and acknowledging the Name of Ram, gave to him the right to
    be worshipped first. Since then Ganesh has always been the first god to be
    worshipped in any endeavour or undertaking.

18. Tradition maintains that before he became a sage and the author of the
    Ramayana, Valmiki was the dacoit Ratnakar, who would waylay travellers
    and rob and mercilessly kill them. One day, he ran into the sage Narad,
    who asked him why he did what he did. Ratnakar replied that it was for
    his family; Narad asked him whether his family appreciated the burden of
    sin that he was accumulating for their sake and whether they would share
    it. Ratnakar staunchly replied that they would, but when he asked his wife
    and children, they refused to accept the burden of his crimes. Ratnakar
    realized the folly of his ways and begged for forgiveness. Narad then gave
    him the mantra of Ram's name, but since this was a mantra that could not
    be given to thieves and murderers, Narad told him to recite it backwards.
    Ratnakar did so, and meditated on the name sitting so still and for so long
    that anthills grew around him. He continued his penance for many long
    years, till finally a divine voice declared him to be free of the guilt of his
    crimes, and renamed him Valmiki, or 'the one born of anthills'.

19. The Padma Purana relates how once, when Shiv asked his wife, Bhavani,
    to join him in a meal, she replied that she could not because she had not
    yet chanted the thousand names of Vishnu. Shiv then asked her to say the
    name of Ram, for saying his name once was equal to chanting a thousand
    other names of Vishnu.

20. This refers to Ardhanarishvara, 'the god who is half a woman', the androgynous form of Shiv. Ardhanarishvara is depicted as half-male and half-female. Usually the right half is Shiv, and the left half is Parvati. This form of Shiv shows the inseparability of masculine from feminine, of Shiv from his cosmic energy, Shakti.

21. At the churning of the ocean, along with nectar, a deadly poison was thrown up; so that it would be rendered harmless, Shiv swallowed the poison and held it forever in his throat, which gives his throat the blue colour, and him the epithet Nilkanth or 'the blue-throated one'.

22. The fifth and sixth months of the Hindu calendar; these are the months of heaviest rainfall during the rainy season.

23. Uttered separately, the two letters 'ra' and 'ma' are pronounced differently, bear different meanings as seed-letters, and so their utterance yields different results for the devotee.

24. Nar and Narayan were two ancient sages; the strength of their penance alarmed even the gods. They were the twin sons of Dharma (Brahma's son) and his wife Ahimsa (daughter of Daksh). The brothers are considered by some to be the fourth avatar of Vishnu. Conceptually, Nar represents the human soul, which is the eternal and inseparable companion of the divine Narayan.

25. According to Hindu mythology, the world rests upon the tortoise Akupara and is supported by the serpent Shesh. The Puranas also tells the story of Vishnu's second incarnation, when he assumes the form of a tortoise—the gods and Asurs rest Mount Mandar on his back as they churn the ocean.

26. This refers to Vishnu in his avatar as Krishna, with Krishna's elder brother Balram, who is also called Haldhar ('he who bears a plough'); the brothers were brought up by Jasomati, Krishna's foster mother. She is also called Yashomati or Yashoda.

27. The letters 'r' and 'm' have half/conjoint forms written above the horizontal line under which Devanagari letters are written: the r is written as a curved line, called a 'ref', and the m as a dot, called an 'anusvara', above the line. Tulsi has compared the former to a royal umbrella, the latter to a jewel in the crown; both are symbols of royalty.

28. Taraka was the daughter of the Yaksha, Suketu; turned into a Rakshasi by the sage Agastya, she lived in the forest at the confluence of the Ganga and the Sarju and ravaged the surrounding land and terrorized the rishis in the forest. She was killed by Ram upon the request of the sage, Vishvamitra (Balkand 209).

29. Ram lived in this forest for a part of his exile.

30. It is believed that the Ramayana was composed by Brahma himself; it
    consisted of a 100 crore (1 crore = ten million) verses and was delivered
    to Shiv through Narad. The three worlds—of gods, men and demons—
    each demanded the Ramayana. So Shiv divided the 100 crore verses into
    three sets of 33 crores and gave one set to each of the three worlds. The
    remaining one crore he again divided into three sets of 33 lakhs (1 lakh =
    100,000), the remaining one lakh into three sets of 33,000, the remaining
    one thousand into three sets of three hundred each, the remaining hundred
    into three sets of thirty-three each, distributing them equally between the
    three worlds. Finally one verse remained, of thirty-two letters, which he
    divided into three sets of ten letters each, giving one set to each of the
    worlds. The two letters that remained, 'ra' and 'ma', made up the name of
    Ram; these two letters Shiv kept for Himself.

31. Shiv is portrayed with matted locks and covered in ashes; he wears a
    garland of human skulls and snakes and serpents are twined around his
    neck; his garments are of tiger skin or deerskin, or made from the hide of
    an elephant.

32. The story of Ajamil is related in the sixth skand of the Bhagavat Purana:
    Ajamil was a Brahman who led a thoroughly dissolute and disreputable
    life. He married a prostitute and had ten sons by her. As he lay upon his
    deathbed, he called his youngest son to his side. By a happy coincidence,
    this son was called Narayan; hearing his name being invoked, the Lord
    himself answered Ajamil's call and granted him liberation from the cycle
    of birth and death.

    The story of the elephant is related in the eighth skand of the Bhagavat
    Purana: An elephant went down to the river to bathe; there his foot was
    seized by a crocodile, and though he struggled for two thousand years, he
    could not free himself. At last, in despair, he called the name of the Lord.
    Vishnu answered the elephant's call and cutting off the crocodile's head
    with his divine discus, the Sudarshan Chakra, freed him from its clutches.

    The story of the prostitute is given in the Bhagavat Purana: Pingala
    was a prostitute in Videha. One evening, as she is soliciting for business, it
    dawns on her that sensual and material gratification is temporary and will
    fade away, and that true pleasure lies only in the Lord. From then on, she
    immersed herself in devotion to Vishnu.

33. Bhang is the hemp plant from the leaves of which is made an intoxicating
    drink, also called bhang; this is especially popular amongst worshippers
    of Shiv. This is being contrasted with the tulsi shrub, said to have been
    produced from the hair of the goddess Tulsi, and held in great veneration

by all Hindus; the tulsi plant is also valued for its medicinal properties. And of course, Tulsi does not pass up this chance for a play on his own name.

34. These are: north, south, east, west, northeast, southeast, southwest, northwest, up and down.

35. Ram killed Baali for the sin of taking his brother, Sugriv's, wife as his own. Sugriv, too, took his brother's wife, Tara, as his own after Baali's death and Vibhishan took Mandodari, his brother Ravan's wife, as his own after Ravan's death. The difference between Baali's action, and that of Sugriv and Vibhishan's, is that Sugriv and Vibhishan married their brothers' wives only after the death of their brothers, with the full consent of the women, and in keeping with the customs of their people. Baali, on the other hand, used force and his power as king. Thus, Baali's fault is a crime, that of the others a misdemeanour.

36. The River Jamuna or Yamuna, and Jam or Yama, the god of Death, are the twin children of the sun god Surya, and his wife Saranyu. While Jam is Death, Jamuna is Life, and bathing in her waters absolves one of sin. Perhaps Tulsi is referring to these opposite characteristics of the twins when he says that Jamuna (as life) has the power to 'blacken the faces' of Jam's messengers (of death), i.e., to dismiss them and send them away in shame.

37. According to tradition, Hulsi is supposed to be the name of Tulsidas's mother. The word also means happiness or joy.

38. Vikrami Samvat, or era of King Vikramaditya, is about 56.7 years ahead; so Samvat 1631 corresponds to 1574 CE.

39. The three kinds of sin are those relating to thought, word and deed; the three kinds of sorrow are of birth, old age and death; the three kinds of poverty are poverty of body, poverty of means and poverty in men.

40. The chaupai, chhand, sortha and doha and are the poetic metres used by Tulsidas in the *Ramcharitmanas*.

41. The three kinds of listeners are liberated souls, those who are seeking liberation, and those who are caught in sensual pleasures.

42. Ravan was a devotee of Brahma. Once, he did intense penance for several years and Brahma, pleased, appeared before him and offered him a boon for his devotion. Ravan asked for immortality. When Brahma refused him that, Ravan asked that no god, demon, Gandharva, Kinnara or Naga may kill him. Brahma willingly granted him that boon. Ravan now believed himself to be invincible, not realizing that he had not included men in his list. He was now safe from death, except at the hands of a man.

43. Literally (sat+chit+anand)—'existence (or entity), thought (or knowledge) and happiness'; an epithet of the Supreme Spirit.

44. Virbhadra was an emanation of Shiv, created from his mouth. According to the Vayu Purana, '. . . he had a thousand heads, a thousand eyes, a thousand feet; wielded a thousand clubs, a thousand spears; he held the shell, the discus, the mace, and bore a blazing bow and a battleaxe; he was fierce and terrific, shining with a dreadful splendour, and decorated with the crescent moon; clothed in a tiger's skin, dripping with blood, with a huge mouth and formidable tusks . . .' He was created for the specific purpose of stopping Daksh's sacrifice, and to scare away the gods and others gathered there.

45. In Hindu philosophy, dissolution/destruction is associated with reproduction or regeneration. So Shiv as Shankar is the reproductive power continually restoring what has been destroyed.

46. The woodapple tree; it is sacred to Shiv and its leaves are used as an offering to him.

47. The Haryashva were the five thousand sons of Daksh, begotten by him for the purpose of peopling the earth. Narad dissuaded them from having children, and they scattered themselves across the earth, never to return. Daksh then had another thousand sons, whom Narad similarly dissuaded. For this, Daksh cursed Narad that he too would always be a homeless wanderer.

48. King Chitraketu, the powerful king of Shurasena, was childless though he had ten million wives. One day he was visited by the Rishi Angira. The king made the rishi welcome and treated him the reverence that was his due. The rishi understood that despite his great wealth and power, his youth and good looks, the king was not happy. Chitraketu explained his problem—that despite his ten million beautiful young wives, he did not have a child. The rishi understood the king's sadness and performed a sacrifice as a result of which the king's chosen queen, Kritadyuti, became pregnant. 'A son will be born to you. He will be the cause of great joy ('harsha') and great sorrow ('shok')—therefore, name him Harshashok,' said the rishi and departed. In due course, Queen Kritadyuti gave birth to a beautiful baby boy, whom they named Harshashok, as the rishi had advised. As time went on, Chitraketu showered all his love and affection upon Kritadyuti, so much so that his other wives became wildly jealous and poisoned his little son. The king and his queen were plunged into grief. Chitraketu lost his mind with sorrow and came close to death himself. Learning of the king's great sorrow, Rishi Angira came once more to visit

him, this time accompanied by Narad. Narad had the power to bring the dead back to life, and to assuage the king's grief (as well as to show him the true nature of existence and the soul), he brought his dead son back to life. The child sat up and began to speak. He spoke of the nature of the soul and the impermanence of relationships. 'In one life,' said he, 'these were my parents, in another, I was their father, their enemy, their friend. These relationships are because of your body, which is mortal; when you die you leave your body and these relationships behind. Ultimately the soul is alone.' And when his discourse was over, the child lay down again and died. At this, Chitraketu's grief for his son abated. He had understood the temporary nature of affection and the illusion of existence; he was now able to perform the last rites for his son. Narad then instructed him in the way to true knowledge and departed. Chitraketu followed Narad's instructions and losing all desire to have a son, he gave up his throne and devoted himself to penance and the pursuit of knowledge.

49. The Daitya king, Kanakakasipu, performed severe penance in order to gain immortality. While he was engaged in these austerities, the other gods attacked his home, but Narad intervened to protect Kanakakasipu's pregnant wife, Kayadhu, and took her into his care. While she was with him, he discoursed to her on the glory of Vishnu, and her unborn son, Prahlad, heard his words and was so influenced by them even in the womb that when he was born he became an ardent devotee of Vishnu. Meanwhile, Kanakakasipu had obtained from Shiv sovereignty over the three worlds and the boon that he may not be killed either by man or beast. This had so emboldened him that he had declared that his subjects give up the worship of Vishnu to worship him instead. Prahlad refused, and his steadfast devotion to Vishnu led ultimately to the death of Kanakakasipu, who was killed by Vishnu in his form of Narsingh, half-man, half-lion.

50. Kamdev would be reborn as Pradyumna, Krishna's son by Rukmini.

51. The god of Death, Jam or Yama, is represented as green in colour and clothed in red; he is armed with a huge mace and a noose, and rides upon a buffalo.

52. Good-natured teasing and bawdy songs (known as 'gari', literally 'abuse'), mocking the bridegroom's family, were traditionally sung by the women of the bride's family as part of the wedding festivities.

53. Bhakti: devotion
Gyan: sacred or religious knowledge (such as is derived from meditation on the higher truths of religion and philosophy, and which teaches man his own nature, and how he may be reunited to the supreme spirit)

Vigyan: worldly knowledge of any kind (including all subjects except that understanding of the true nature of God or Brahma which is acquirable only by abstract meditation and the study of the Vedas)

Vairagya: detachment

54. Jalandhar was born from the sea as a manifestation of the radiance of Shiv's third eye. As a newborn child, his crying so distressed the gods that they pleaded with Brahma to search for the source of the cry. Brahma did so, and when he went down to the seashore, the sea put the baby in his arms. The child pulled at Brahma's beard so hard that it brought tears to Brahma's eyes. For that reason, Brahma named the child 'Jalandhar'. He took the baby back with him to his palace, and brought him up with love and care. When Jalandhar grew up he married Vrinda, the beautiful daughter of the demon, Kalnemi. Vrinda was a devotee of Vishnu, and because of her intense devotion to him, she was endowed with enormous yogic powers. She was also a chaste and faithful wife, and deeply devoted to her husband, and her prayers to Vishnu for his well-being strengthened the already strong Jalandhar. Ultimately, Jalandhar became so strong that he was crowned king of the Asurs. Very soon, Jalandhar had defeated every king on earth. Now, with the whole earth under his sway, he set about conquering the gods and defeated them easily. In despair they turned to Brahma, who advised them to ask for Shiv's help since Jalandhar was born of his third eye. Shiv tried to reason with Jalandhar, but Jalandhar was now so powerful that he was rude and dismissive even to Shiv. Controlling his anger with a huge effort, Shiv decided to lead the gods in battle against the Asur king. But Jalandhar, reinforced by his wife's prayers, trapped Shiv and the gods in a web of illusion. Jalandhar then took on the form of Shiv himself and approached the goddess Parvati. Parvati, however, was not fooled and recognizing him, challenged him to a battle. Jalandhar knew he could not take on the goddess and retreated. Parvati related Jalandhar's insolence to Vishnu, and asked for his help. So, as Vrinda prayed for her husband's success on the battlefield against Shiv, Vishnu appeared before her in the guise of her husband. Vrinda was completely taken in by Vishnu, and taking him to be her husband, was overjoyed at seeing him safe and sound. She stopped praying and embraced Vishnu, as a result of which her power was broken, and consequently, her husband's. At that very instant, Shiv, released from Jalandhar's trap, killed the Asur king. Vrinda felt that something was wrong, and Vishnu, abandoning his disguise, appeared before her as himself. Angry and grief-stricken, Vrinda cursed Vishnu to

be separated from his wife. It is for this reason that he had to take form as Ram, and suffer separation from Sita.

55. Vishvamohini, 'world-enchanting', was also the female form take by Vishnu at the churning of the ocean to distract the demons.

56. By placing a garland around a suitor's neck, the unmarried girl indicates her choice of husband.

57. 'Hari' is an epithet for Vishnu, and 'hari' means ape—so Shiv's attendants were punning on the dual meaning of 'Hari' and 'hari'.

58. In the hands of Vishvamohini, the object of his infatuation, as well as, more profoundly, in the hands of Vishnu's maya—which is actually and literally one and the same thing in this case.

59. The first Manu, Svayambhuva (born of Swayambhu, the self-existent Brahma) and his wife Satarupa. According to one account of creation, Brahma divided himself into two, male and female. The male half was identical with himself—he is known as Svayambhuva Manu; the female half was Satarupa, whom Manu took as his wife. From them sprang the entire human race.

60. The Sankhya Shastra or treatise expounding the Sankhya doctrine or system of philosophy, one of the six schools of Hindu philosophy, founded by the sage Kapil; based on systematic enumeration and rational examination, it takes its name from the Sanskrit word 'sankhya' which means to count, enumerate, or reason by numerical enumeration.

61. Vaasudev, 'son of Vasudev,' is a name for Krishna, i.e., Vishnu. The mantra referred to here is 'Om Namo Bhagavate Vaasudevaya'—which requires twelve letters to be written in Devanagari; the mantra means 'Om, I bow to Lord Vaasudev'.

62. The Shrivatsa is a particular mark, or white curl of hair, on the right side of Vishnu's chest; it is a sign of Supreme Godhead. It is also interpreted to be Shri's mark, the place where she rests on the Lord's chest.

63. The Suryavansh or solar lineage was the dynasty of Kshatriyas who sprang from Ikshvaku, grandson of the Sun. Ram was of this lineage.

64. Sarangpani, 'the one who bears the bow called Sarang'—a name for Vishnu (Sarang is the name of Vishnu's bow).

65. These are the conch, the discus, the club and the lotus.

66. These are signs of divinity that Vishnu bears on the soles of his feet.

67. Once, the sages could not decide who amongst the three gods, Brahma, Vishnu and Shiv, was the greatest. In order to come to a decision, Brahma's son, the sage Bhrigu, was sent to visit the three gods one by one. The sage first went to his father, but did not greet him as a dutiful son.

Bhrigu's lack of courtesy angered Brahma greatly, though he somehow managed to calm his rage with reason. Bhrigu then visited Shiv upon Kailash. Shiv rose to meet him, and held out his arms in an embrace. But Bhrigu refused to allow Shiv to touch him, saying that he had broken social conventions by reaching out to him. At this, Shiv lost his temper and picked up his trishul to strike the sage. But Parvati intervened, and calmed him down. Bhrigu then went to visit Vishnu, and found him asleep with his head on Lakshmi's lap. Angered by this discourtesy, the sage kicked Vishnu on the chest to awaken him. Vishnu started awake, and seeing the sage, apologized for his rudeness in not greeting him, and then gently rubbed the sage's foot with his hands, expressing concern that it might have been hurt by striking his hard chest. Bhrigu declared Vishnu to be the greatest of the three gods, and since then Vishnu bears the imprint of the sage's foot upon his chest, as a mark of his unparalleled courtesy and forbearance.

68. The Puranas say that the heavenly stream of the Ganga emerges from the toe of Vishnu. The river was brought down to earth by the prayers of the sage Bhagirath (by which she is called Bhagirathi) to purify the ashes of the sixty-thousand sons of King Sagar, who had been destroyed by the angry glance of the sage Kapil. The gods feared that the force of the Ganga's descent to earth would be too strong for the earth to bear, so Shiv agreed to receive the river upon his head and checked its furious rush in his matted locks (this is why Shiv is called Gangadhar—the one who holds the Ganga). The river descended from Shiv's brow in seven streams, thus forming the Sapta-sindhava (the seven rivers); the Ganga proper is one of these streams.

69. 'Videh' is Janak, king of the kingdom of Videha; 'videh' also means 'without a body' or 'bodiless'. Tulsi puns on this dual meaning, implying that King Janak lost all awareness of his own body upon beholding Ram.

70. Here, Tulsi is probably referring to an earlier incident (not explained in the *Manas*) in Sita's life when Narad had visited Janak's family and predicted that Sita would meet her future husband in a garden.

71. Nimi was the son of Ikshvaku, and the founder of the dynasty of Mithila. According to the Vishnu Purana, he was cursed by the sage Vasishtha to lose his corporeal form, and in response, he pronounced the same curse upon the sage. Both then abandoned their bodily forms. Though Vasishtha took birth again, Nimi's corpse was embalmed and preserved in death as he had been in life. The gods offered to restore him back to life, but Nimi refused, saying that the separation of the soul from the body was

so painful that he did not want to have to experience it again. The gods respected his wishes, and instead, placed him in the eyes of every living creature, because of which their eyelids are always blinking. (A blink of the eye is called 'nimish'.)

72. In Hindu belief, the twitching or fluttering of various parts of the body are omens of good or bad fortune. For a man, the twitching of the right side of his body foretells good fortune; for a woman it is the left side that is auspicious.

73. The moon, along with poison, was amongst the fourteen treasures received at the churning of the ocean.

74. Some commentators say that the story that Janak told is how the bow was given by Shiv to his ancestor Devarata. After Sati killed herself at Daksh's fire-sacrifice, and Virbhadra laid waste the ceremonies, Shiv himself appeared, with his formidable bow, Pinaki, in his hand, and determined to destroy the gods who had stood by as Sati died. But the gods managed to calm him down, and Shiv handed his bow to Devarata, who was amongst the kings invited to the fire-sacrifice. Shiv asked Devarata to look after his bow, so that it could not be used for any further violence. Devarata was Janak's ancestor—he was the son of Nimi, who was the son of Ishkvaku, founder of the dynasty of Mithila. The bow remained with the kings of Mithila, handed down through successive kings. And this is how it came into Janak's possession. Other commentators say that Janak related an incident from Sita's childhood, when she had effortlessly picked up Shiv's bow, upon which Shiv had instructed Janak to give her hand in marriage only to one who could break the bow.

75. Gira (Sarasvati) is the goddess of speech, and hence too talkative; the other half of Bhavani's body is that of Shiv (this refers to the Ardhanarishwar form of Shiv), so Bhavani has only half a body; Rati's husband is Kamdev, reduced to ashes by Shiv and condemned to live in bodiless form, so she is ever-sorrowing for him; and Ramaa (Lakshmi) emerged from the churning of the ocean—since posion and liquor also emerged at the same time from the ocean, they are her 'brothers'.

76. These are the eight mythical elephants that support the earth at each of the eight quarters of the compass. (See also glossary: 'guardians of the eight quarters')

77. Kamdev's banner carries the sign of the fish; the shape of a woman's eye is also compared to a fish; such a shape is a sign of beauty.

78. The lotus closes at night, imprisoning the bee. Her modesty (the night) caused her mouth (the lotus) to close and imprison her voice (the trapped bee).

79. These are all the celestial creatures that support the earth and hold it
    steady: the eight elephants that support the earth upon their backs at the
    eight points of the compass; the tortoise or kurma, the second incarnation
    of Vishnu, which carries the earth upon its back; the snake or serpent king,
    Sheshnag, the couch and support of Vishnu, and who holds the earth
    steady in its coils; the boar or Varaha, the third avatar of Vishnu, which
    supports the earth upon its tusks.

80. Parashuram is the first Ram and the sixth avatar of Vishnu; though he
    appeared in this world before Ram, the seventh avatar, they were both
    living in this world at the same time. In early life, Parashuram was under
    the protection of Shiv, who taught him the use of arms and gave him his
    weapon, the parashu, or axe. A follower of Shiv, he was much aggrieved
    that Ram had broken Shiv's bow, and challenged him to a trial of strength,
    which he lost. In some ways this led to him being excluded from the
    celestial world.

81. The tripund or tripundra, three curved horizontal lines made across
    the forehead with the ashes of burnt cow-dung and sandalwood, by the
    followers of Shiv; the mark is indispensable in the worship of Shiv.

82. In Hindu belief, every person is in debt to three people: his father,
    his mother and his guru. Parashuram is said to have paid his debt to his
    parents in rather dramatic fashion: Once, his father, Jamadagni, asked his
    sons one by one to kill his wife, their mother Renuka, whom he suspected
    of having impure thoughts. The sons all refused, except Parashuram, who
    did as his father asked. Jamadagni was so pleased with his obedience that
    he told Parashuram to ask him for a boon. Parashuram asked that his
    mother be restored to life. Jamadagni granted his request, and his mother
    was brought back to life immediately, with no memory of her son's cruel
    act. Another time, Sahasrabahu (Kartavirya) paid a visit to Jamadagni's
    hermitage. Though the sage was not present, he was received with great
    hospitality by his wife. In return, Sahasrabahu carried off a sacrificial calf
    belonging to Jamadagni. This so angered Parashuram that he followed
    him and cut off all his thousand arms and killed him. In retaliation,
    Sahasrabahu's sons killed Jamadagni. Parashuram vowed to avenge his
    father and swore vengeance against them and the entire Kshatriya race.
    He is said to have cleared the earth of Kshatriyas twenty-one times.

83. Tulsi plays on the word 'gun' here, which means 'bowstring' as well as
    'virtue'. The nine cardinal virtues are equanimity, self-restraint, penance,
    purity, forgiveness, straightfrowardness, spiritual knowledge, knowledge
    of worldly things and faith in the Supreme Being.

84. A complete army is made up of four divisions; these are elephants, chariots, cavalry and infantry.

85. The messengers, since they are from Janak, regard Sita as their own daughter; and by Hindu tradition, a girl's family cannot accept gifts from her (in this case, future) in-laws.

86. A rare and valuable breed, these horses had black ears and were as white as milk all over; they were considered especially suitable for performing the horse-sacrifice.

87. Purandar is Indra, king of the gods, and Brihsapati, the guru of the gods.

88. This is the Indian roller, known as 'nil-kanth', literally 'blue-throat', which is also a name for Shiv. It has a blue crown and blue wings and tail (though not a blue throat). Its breast is pale brown. It can be easily seen in India, and is believed by many to be sacred to Vishnu. It is associated with festivals such as Dussehra.

89. These were the eight siddhis, mystical or magical powers often attained through yogic practice and penance.

90. Shankar is often portrayed with five faces, each face with three eyes, hence fifteen eyes; Brahma has four faces, each with two eyes, hence eight eyes; Skand has six faces, each face with two eyes, hence twelve eyes, or one a half times as many as Brahma. But Indra, has a thousand eyes, the result of a curse pronounced upon him by the sage Gautam for seducing his wife, Ahalya. This curse Indra now finds a blessing, for he has a thousand eyes with which to look upon the wedding of Ram and Sita.

91. The five kinds of musical instruments that are played on auspicious occasions, the sounds of which are considered to bring good fortune are tantri or stringed instruments such as the vina, tal or an instrument that sets the beat (this could even be the clapping of hands), jhanjh or cymbals, nagara or the kettledrum, and turhi or a wind instrument such as the trumpet or the shehnai. The five kinds of auspicious sounds are veda-dhvani or the chanting of the Vedas by the brahmins, vandi-dhvani or the eulogies and songs of praise sung by the family bards, jaya-dhvani or the hails of glory, shankh-dhvani or the sound of the conch, and hulu-dhvani or ululation.

92. Tulsi mentions one in particular—madhuparka. This is a mixture of honey and milk, or honey, ghee and curd offered to gods or to Brahmins during sacrifices and ritual worship.

93. As Agni, the fire-god or fire embodied.

94. This the stream of the River Ganga, which flows from Ram's feet, and which Shiv carries upon his head, entwined in his matted hair.

95. Once again, Tulsi plays on the double meaning of 'videh' here (see stanza 215)—the literal meaning of 'videh' is 'without body or incorporeal'; this is also the title held by the kings of Videha, in this case, Janak. So Tulsi says that beholding Ram's form, Janak lost all sense of his own corporeal existence.

96. The gods know that the marriage of Sita to Ram is required for the killing of Ravan and rejoice that their end, the death of Ravan, is one step closer to being achieved.

97. Sindur, or vermilion, applied on the head of a woman indicates that she is married; it is applied to the head of the bride for the first time by the bridegroom upon the completion of the wedding rites.

98. The four states of being are jagrat or waking, svapna or sleeping, sushupti or deep repose, and turiya or the state in which the soul has become one with the Supreme Spirit. These four feminine states are each paired a male consort; these are vishva or the creation, tejas or power, pragya or wisdom, and brahm, the universal Absolute.

99. The four ends of life are dharma, arth, kama, and moksh—these are masculine, and are paired with the feminine actions or deeds (kriya) that are the means to their realization, which are variously enumerated, for instance as shraddha or piety, yagya or the performance of sacrifices, tapasya or meditation, and gyan or sacred or religious knowledge such as is derived from meditation.

100. All the queens regarded Ram as their own son—there was no distinction in the love they gave him.

101. Kangans are sacred threads tied ceremoniously around the wrists of the brides and bridegrooms; they are untied after the wedding (the bride unties the bridegroom's kangan, and he unties hers) amidst much revelry and rejoicing. This is a happy occasion, and often an ice-breaker between the married couple if they do not know each other well. The accompanying games and teasing give the bride and the bridegroom a chance to interact in a light-hearted atmosphere.